The *Centinel*

Warnings of a Revolution

UNIVERSITY OF DELAWARE BICENTENNIAL BOOKS:

The Stamp Act Congress
The Loyalists of Revolutionary Delaware
History of Delaware

The Centinel

Warnings of a Revolution

Edited with an Introduction by
Elizabeth I. Nybakken

A University of Delaware Bicentennial Book

Newark
University of Delaware Press

London and Toronto: Associated University Presses

Associated University Presses, Inc.
Cranbury, New Jersey 08512

Associated University Presses
Magdalen House
136–148 Tooley Street
London SE1 2TT, England

Associated University Presses
Toronto M5E 1A7, Canada

Library of Congress Cataloging in Publication Data
Main entry under title:

The Centinel, warnings of a revolution.

"A University of Delaware Bicentennial book."
Essays originally published as the "Centinel," the "Anti-Centinel," and "Remonstrant."
Bibliography: p.
Includes index.
1. Church of England in America—Doctrinal and controversial works—Presbyterian authors—Addresses, essays, lectures. 2. Episcopacy—Controversial literature—Addresses, essays, lectures. 3. United States—Church history—Colonial period, ca. 1600—1775—Sources. 4. United States—History—Colonial period, ca. 1600-1775—Sources. I. Nybakken, Elizabeth I.
BX5881.C46 283′.73 77-92570
ISBN 0-87413-141-3

Printed in the United States of America

Francis Alison, George Bryan, and John Dickinson, authors of the "Centinel," were men of great influence on the revolutionary generation of Delaware. It is therefore fitting for the University of Delaware to honor its founder, Alison, and the third chief executive of the state, Dickinson, by republishing these essays which contributed to their effectiveness. The Bicentennial Committee of the University of Delaware also hopes to increase an understanding of the whole generation by presenting this series of articles, which both reflected their concerns and encouraged them to begin thinking of themselves less as Englishmen and more as Americans.

Note to the Reader:

The "Centinel," "Anti-Centinel," and "Remonstrant" have been printed exactly as they appeared to the public. Neither modernization in spelling nor capitalization has been imposed nor have substitutions been attempted for words which the contemporary newspaper editors omitted. The only exception is the substitution of alphabetical for numerical indications of internal notes. The internal notes, labeled as such, appear at the end of the respective chapters just above the editor's own notes. "Centinel" numbers XX and XXI, which appeared in the *Pennsylvania Journal and Weekly Advertiser* on November 24 and December 8, 1768, have not been included. Their tone, quality, and repetitious arguments set them apart from the other essays and suggest that they are not the work of the principal authors.

. . . [W]ho will believe that the apprehension of Episcopacy contributed fifty years ago, as much as any other cause, to arouse the attention, not only of the inquiring mind, but of the common people, and urge them to close thinking on the constitutional authority of Parliament over the colonies? This, nevertheless, was a fact as certain as any in the history of North America. The objection was not merely to the office of a Bishop, though even that was dreaded, but to the authority of Parliament, on which it must be founded. . . . All denominations in America became interested in it [the controversy] and began to think of the secret latent principle upon which all encroachments upon us must be founded, the power of Parliament. The nature and extent of the authority of Parliament over the colonies was discussed everywhere, till it was discovered that it had none at all.

—John Adams to Dr Jedidiah Morse
December 2, 1815

Contents

Acknowledgments

Any historical research depends on the expertise of too many manuscripts librarians to be cited with convenience. Yet I should like to express my gratitude for the particular aid provided by the staffs at the Historical Society of Pennsylvania, the American Philosophical Society, Beinecke Library, the Library of Congress, Presbyterian Historical Society, and Lambeth Palace Library. Consultants at the Library Company of Philadelphia were assiduous in helping me to ferret out particular citations from specific books available to the authors of the "Centinel." I extend the deepest appreciation to the Bicentennial Commission of the University of Delaware for its moral and financial support in the preparation of this manuscript.

E.I.N.

Introduction

On March 24, 1768, the first installment of the "Centinel" appeared in the *Pennsylvania Journal and Weekly Advertiser.* The piece was written by Francis Alison, John Dickinson, and George Bryan to alert Pennsylvanians of the movement to introduce an Anglican bishopric into the colonies and to warn them of the pernicious effects of such an innovation. As the series continued, the authors found themselves ranging through a wide variety of religious and secular sources to construct an integrated argument against a colonial bishopric. Although focusing on the religious events of 1768, they reviewed the matter of earlier controversies, alluded to current dissatisfactions, and suggested future problems. In the process they brought themselves and their readers to the beginning of an understanding of themselves as Americans, distinct from Englishmen.

The Peace of Paris, signed in 1763, had ended the war between England and France, brought peace to the North American continent, and elicited extravagant and sincere professions of loyalty from the American colonists. They were delighted with their position. That their western borders were now free from the threats of the French and their Indian allies was just one more accretion to their increasingly comfortable existence. As provincials, they enjoyed the most extensive civil and religious rights in a country that was prospering within a benevolent empire and under the British constitution which their enlightened age had judged to be the best in the world. They were proud to be Englishmen.

Twelve years later these same colonists were fighting to be free of British rule. In that short time the most enlightened empire in the world had become, to American eyes, an oppressive tyranny willfully attempting to enslave its free subjects—or so polemicists would later argue. But the public statements of the mid-1760s were not so definite. Their authors considered themselves to be loyal subjects within an empire that was flexible enough to accommodate an American emphasis to their British citizenship. They did not welcome developments which suggested that this assumption was a misapprehension: that England would tolerate no significant variation within its empire. Neither were they pleased to accept the implication that since a divided loyalty was unacceptable, a choice had to be made. Those who opted for a primarily American identification eventually accepted the polemicists' characterization of the British empire.

Men ever since have attempted to understand the cause of this profound change in the American colonial mind. Increasingly, historians find themselves drifting back to the view of the eighteenth-century participants: that this reversal in loyalties came when Americans began to define their rights within the empire, vis-à-vis Parliament and the king. With their articulation of the boundaries to parliamentary authority over them came the simultaneous realization that they had evolved into a society more distinct from England than they had ever understood. They sought to defend what was peculiarly American and still retain their British identification by an appeal to their rights as Englishmen. When Parliament rejected the Americans' definition of their rightful position within the empire, the resultant confrontation became revolution.

The question then becomes, What prompted colonists to engage in the onerous business of defining rights? What confluence of events possibly could have motivated a remarkably disparate group of men to pour over learned texts, read and write the complicated essays that appeared in newspapers, or sit in taverns and chat casually about the most intricate of constitutional questions?

The reassertion of parliamentary authority over colonial economic and political affairs inconvenienced many. Since Parliament had not exercised effective or consistent control over internal provincial matters before 1763, local officials had filled this gap by developing practices which answered their needs. In the process a version of the English constitution evolved that was different from what had developed in the mother country during this period of "salutary neglect" even though the basic outlines and guaranteed rights remained the same. When the king's ministers attempted to supplant these indigenous usages with British forms, Americans were forced to articulate and defend what they previously had simply done.

Revenue-producing measures—the Stamp Act of 1765 was the most blatant example—incited them to reject the legitimacy of Parliament's taxation of them. "No taxation without representation" became their cry, for this was a right guaranteed to all

Englishmen.[1] By claiming this, however, the Americans did nothing to set themselves apart from England. Theoretically, Parliament could have accepted colonial representatives, thereby legitimizing all legislative innovation. Something more radical was necessary, such as a denial of parliamentary authority over almost all areas of provincial life, including taxation. This position was established but the impetus did not arise primarily from economic or political concerns.

The majority of eighteenth-century Americans were Protestants to whom religious faith and institutions retained considerable importance. Many of these provincials were still endeavoring to implement the goals of the Reformation by living only according to the pure theology and within the primitive church structure set out in the New Testament. They considered these to be God's instructions for individual salvation. Although desirous of separating church from state and giving each its due, they assumed that their secular society must also encourage men to act in the virtuous manner prescribed by God. Even those with no formal church affiliation joined religious leaders in their desire to create a virtuous society far from the corruptions of Europe. Thus, anything that the ministry or Parliament might do to thwart this endeavor would threaten their undefined but acute sense of America's special destiny.

When the ministry contemplated the settlement of a colonial Anglican bishop in 1768, many Americans reacted violently against what they perceived to be a threat to their individual souls and collective virtue. The Church of England retained too many Roman Catholic additions to the pure scriptural church and continued to introduce others. More damning, as an established church, it used the power of the state to force obedience to this human construct and denied many civil and religious rights to those who dissented.

American dissenters did not wish to live under such an oppressive religious regime and viewed a colonial bishopric as the first step toward its establishment.[2] In their search for legitimate grounds on which to oppose such an innovation they were driven to define more than just their religious liberties. A state church would affect their political and economic lives as well. Their considerations led them to the conclusion that only they had the right to determine local practices. Parliament could claim no legislative authority over the internal workings of the colonies. Provincial charters granted by the king were designated as constitutions which established assemblies to work with governors who served as royal agents in ruling the inhabitants: just as the king in Parliament made laws for

England. The direction of the empire as a whole was to be a matter of accommodation among the various segments. By this formula Americans awarded themselves a constellation of rights and a position within the empire which Parliament could not accept.

The men who led the alteration in American thought and loyalty necessary for such a definition of rights had set out only to awaken public opinion to the dangers of a bishop and to stimulate active opposition against one. The fight was centered in the middle colonies of New York and Pennsylvania, directed against Thomas Bradbury Chandler, and carried on mainly by Presbyterians.[3] These combatants rejected the New England tactic of issuing only pamphlets, taking to the newspapers as well. There they published weekly columns that reached a broad-based audience and sustained a high level of popular discussion by offering new material periodically.

Of the opposition literature, none was more learned and persuasive than the "Centinel" articles planned and written by Francis Alison with the aid of John Dickinson, George Bryan, and, possibly, other aroused Pennsylvanians. The series appeared regularly in William Bradford's paper, *The Pennsylvania Journal and Weekly Advertiser,* from March 24 through July 28, 1768. Seeking to convince, these perceptive essays were so insidiously moderate that they offered little for the Anglicans to attack. William Smith, provost of the College of Philadelphia and self-styled leader of the Pennsylvanian Anglicans, finally contributed his "mite" in September 1768.[4] His "Anatomist" vowed to cut up the arguments of the sleeping "Centinel." It did entertain but did not speak to the basic points raised by the "Centinel," an oversight which Alison delightedly pointed out in his subsequent "Remonstrant," Number III.

> What have all these trifles to do with the present dispute? They solve none of our objections; they are only designed to draw our attention from a gathering storm, ready to burst on us and destroy us.[5]

Alison wrote four installments of the "Remonstrant" to review and summarize the main points of the arguments raised against an Episcopate "in the Most striking point of view." He deliberately timed them to appear in October and November, when they would "come under publick notice" and reach the English "about the time of their next parliamentary meeting."[6]

Neither the "Centinel" nor the "Remonstrant" was aimed primarily at the British nor toward the inhabitants of other colonies. The authors mainly spoke to Pennsylvanians in their peculiar vernacular, using a knowledge of provincial issues and prejudices to couch their arguments in a manner most persuasive to their chosen audience. Discussions ranged through religion, history, politics, economics, imperial structure, law, social psychology, and natural, British, and colonial rights. To read these essays is to gain insight into the interconnections of all these human concerns in colonial Pennsylvanians who rapidly were recognizing how different they were from England.

The "Centinel," perhaps unconsciously, goaded its readers along this revolutionary path. By early 1769 it had fixed a definition of colonial rights in the minds of a significant number of Pennsylvanians and ceased publication. The authors realized that the colonists now had to unite and force England to agree to these rights. American dissenters must join with American Anglicans against the British Parliament, which threatened them all. Alison patiently explained to an ally in Connecticut in the summer of 1769 that "our Contests with the Commons of England made Harmony in all the Colonies necessary." It was now "more important to drop the debate" with the Anglicans and "mind the main chance" of uniting in preparation for the "gathering storm."[7] This storm became the American Revolution.

1
The Authors

None of the twenty-one installments of the "Centinel" was signed. This was not unusual, for anonymity was a common eighteenth-century precaution against personal retribution for exercising freedom of speech. Usually, interested parties eventually discovered the identity of reticent authors, but they always found it difficult to pinpoint the specific writer of particular essays appearing in a series. Contemporary historians still cannot match with absolute certainty the creators of the "Centinel" to their particular contributions. However, evidence supports the report of perhaps the most "interested party," Thomas Bradbury Chandler, that "the Authors of it are supposed to be Dr. Alliston, Vice-Provost of the College of Philadelphia, assisted by a Number of his Presbyterian Brethren, and Mr. D———n, the very popular Author of the 'Farmer's Letters.' "[1] Andrew Eliot, a Congregational minister in Boston, unequivocally placed "one Mr. Bryant" at the top of the list of these brethren, with Dickinson assisting.[2]

Francis Alison was the supervisor, coordinator, and main author for the series.[3] Initially, he had planned one long rejoinder to Chandler but realized that a single letter presumed too much knowledge on the part of the reader and could only touch on issues whose major importance demanded deeper exploration. Before him was the example of "Letters from a Pennsylvania Farmer," which John Dickinson had just published in the *Pennsylvania Chronicle.* The effectiveness of this approach proved that sequential essays printed in a newspaper reached more of the people whom Alison wanted to arouse. His original manuscript did provide the substance for numbers I and II and the outline for subsequent articles dealing with religion.[4]

Dickinson confined his attention to the more secular aspects of the controversy, which he explored in numbers VI, VII, VIII, and XVI.[5] George Bryan's contribution is more difficult to assess. Quite likely he was responsible for number XI and probably collaborated with Alison on other pieces. The integration of material and consistent arguments suggest that all three men worked closely together on the manuscripts.

Numbers XX and XXI bear the mark of none of these men. Their tone and timing suggest that sympathizers sent them in unsolicited. They appeared after Alison's "Remonstrant" had already begun to sum up the major arguments and answer potentially dangerous points raised by the Anglican "Anatomist."[6] The satirical "Anti-Centinel" remains totally anonymous, its wit well within the abilities of any of these three men and a host of literate supporters.

At first glance, the Reverend Dr. Francis Alison appears ill-cast as the general behind the "Centinel."[7] He was a pious Presbyterian minister and learned scholar who had devoted his life to education, away from the limelight. At sixty-three his well-deserved reputation for learning had spread throughout the British empire. Friend Ezra Stiles, president of Yale, pronounced him to be "the greatest classical scholar in America": enemy Benjamin Franklin introduced him as a "Person of great Ingenuity & Learning," and extolled his knowledge of "agriculture, philosophy, your own catholic divinity, and various other parts of learning equally useful & engaging." Colleague Matthew Wilson placed him "beyond the common race of learned men," a "living" library of "all the liberal arts and sciences evinced."[8] Student plaudits were too numerous to mention.

Yale awarded Alison an honorary masters degree in 1755 for "his extraordinary erudition and conspicuous virtue." More impressive still, the University of Glasgow granted a Doctor of Divinity a year later to this man for "the promoting of solid Piety and useful learning." It had bestowed this honor on only one other colonist, and did, in the words of a contemporary, "seldom confer it but on some distinguished favorite."[9]

The learned doctor hated writing controversies. He complained that he could find "little regard to truth, honesty and candor" in them.[10] It was this very commitment to "truth" and "honesty," however, that forced him to draw his pen. A lifetime of study provided the ammunition and a youth spent in northern Ireland supplied the charge.

Growing up in Ireland was a painful experience for a young Presbyterian. The Church of England was the established church and, until 1719, forbad dissenters to practice their religion. Marriages celebrated by Presbyterian clergymen remained illegal, the amorous criminals hauled before ecclesiastical courts. The Sacramental Test Act barred them from educational, military, or civil offices. Political power was confined mainly to the Anglo-Irish members of the established church, who alone could sit in the Irish parliament. This same group owned almost all of the land, sharply increasing the rents after 1720, when the original leases expired and driving out tenants who could not pay. Even nature conspired against Irish dissenters, sending droughts, frosts, and diseases to wipe out crops that might pay rents. Famine and oppression drove men to death—or to America.[11]

Alison arrived in 1735, a licensed Presbyterian minister with one of the finest educations that Europe could provide. Born in 1705 in the parish of Leck, County Donegal, he could trace his ancestry back to the original Scottish planters who were settled in Ireland during the reign of James I. It is a mystery how his father, a weaver, could afford to educate the lad beyond the primary schooling offered at the nearby free school in the Diocese of Raphoe, but Alison went off to Scotland, accepting a master's degree from the University of Edinburgh in 1732.[12] Quite likely he completed his four years of divinity studies, required of ministers by the Irish Presbyterian Church, under someone at the University of Glasgow.

The universities of Edinburgh and Glasgow enjoyed high repute in the eighteenth century as the most vital and progressive centers of higher education in the British Isles and probably even Europe. They had undergone a renaissance early in the century, completely reorganizing their structures, methods, and curriculum to introduce the latest advances in learning. Professors of the highest genius flocked to their halls, there to instruct those able young dissenters who were barred from taking degrees in English and Irish universities. The classics were not ignored but exciting supplements in science, medicine, and social sciences were added, all using the empirical methodology that formed the core of the Scottish Enlightenment.[13]

The "new learning," as it was commonly referred to, called for a pragmatic approach to knowledge. Thinkers such as Isaac Newton and John Locke suggested that, instead of intuiting laws or deducing them from first principles, men should study what actually happens in the world and plot the recurrent patterns of cause and effect, which were the laws of nature. Their exhortation was to learn by observation, experiment, and experience. The pious Scots, seeking ways to perfect man in all Christian virtues, eagerly seized on laws of human nature and actions which they could use to construct a society that would foster such virtues in its members. This led them to question the reasons behind almost all human behavior and institutions and to propose some highly practical alternatives. In the process they developed what we now call the social sciences.[14]

Thus enlightened, Alison returned to Ireland in June of 1735.[15] There was no parish for him in that depressed land. He did have powerful friends among the ruling class who offered him "the rich emoluments of an establishment," but he rejected them rather than join the Anglican Church. Instead, he sailed as "a poor man to the wilds of America" that summer and embarked on his crusade to promote the cause of learning in his adopted land.[16]

The roles of teacher and minister were mutually compatible in an age that believed that all knowledge revealed more of God's world. Alison began an informal tutelage of neighborhood boys soon after he was settled in 1737 as minister in New London, a frontier community in southwestern Chester county. Two years later the Presbyterians agreed to make the school their official seminary, but the Great Awakening interjected itself, absorbed all of their energies, and eventually split the synod. This revivalist movement was well advanced among the Presbyterians when the Anglican evangelist George Whitefield arrived in 1739 from England to spread its fever and publicize its effects.

Alison continued to teach even as he battled the New Side in a futile effort to maintain unity. To his mind the revivalists were preaching an unscriptural theology, turning Christians against each other by harsh and unwarranted accusations and demanding that uneducated men be admitted into the ministry. They opposed almost everything that Alison's study of Scriptures and human nature had showed would render Americans and their society virtuous in the sight of God and man.

When the synod separated in 1741 into the New Side Synod of New York and the Old Side Synod of Philadelphia, the latter adopted the New London Academy as its official school. There Alison taught the progressive curriculum of his university experience, the first to introduce the Scottish Enlightenment into American education. When it became clear that poor Presbyterian frontiersmen simply could not support a first-class college, Alison left the academy to assistants whom he had trained and accepted the position of rector of the Academy of Philadelphia and master of the Latin School. Inspired by Alison's success, Benjamin Franklin had founded the school, initially orienting it toward the more practical studies that would not offend the sensibilities of Quaker legislators and future benefactors. Alison, however, saw the potential for a fully endowed university where scholars of all denominations could study and he welcomed the aid of William Smith, who assumed the duties of rector in 1754.

"Soft, polite, insinuating, adulating, sensible, learned, industrious, indefatigable," were John Adams' adjectives for this Anglican educator who became Alison's professional friend, religious enemy, and sometime political ally.[17] The product of a Scottish education himself, Smith shared Alison's desire to transform this school into the best college in the colonies by replicating the curriculum and approach that Alison had initiated at New London. Together they convinced the trustees to graft a college onto the academy in 1755. Smith became provost and busied himself with politics; Alison became vice-provost and taught almost all of the courses dealing with philosophy and human actions until his death in 1779.

Amidst this heavy academic schedule, Alison somehow found time to serve as half-time minister in the First Presbyterian Church of Philadelphia, operate an insurance plan for ministers, serve as director of the Library Company, contribute papers to the American Philosophical Society, and supervise his old academy, which, by 1763, had moved to New Ark in the Lower Counties and was expanding rapidly into a college. Meanwhile he and his wife, the former Hannah Armitage of New Castle, raised and educated four children and managed a farm in New London.

As leader of the Old Side, Alison was instrumental in effecting a reunification of the synods in 1758. The two groups continued to squabble but at least they cooperated on matters of mutual concern. They joined to defend against Indian attacks, pressure the Pennsylvania Assembly for troops, thwart Franklin's efforts to turn Pennsylvania into a royal colony, effect an intercolonial organization of Calvinist denominations, and, finally, oppose the establishment of an Anglican bishopric. Alison led the combined forces in all of these endeavors—an old and venerable statesman but by no means a visible politician.

John Dickinson came easily to mind when men were assigned blame or credit for the "Centinel."[18] He was a young, aggressive, and politically active lawyer with a good record of publications that eventually earned him the title "Penman of the Revolution."[19] Born in 1732 into the English Quaker household of Samuel Dickinson of Talbot County, Maryland, and his second wife, Mary Cadwalader of Philadelphia, John moved with the family in 1740 to an estate near Dover in Kent County, Delaware. There he was tutored and, at age eighteen, decided to follow his father's example by training for the law. From 1750 until 1753 he read law in the Philadelphia offices of John Moland and then sailed for England to complete his legal education at the Middle Temple, as was customary for a law student of means. He returned in 1757 to practice in Philadelphia and to prepare himself for political life.

These bare facts suggest that Dickinson was a narrowly trained practitioner. In fact, his early tutoring gave him a thorough grounding in the liberal arts and an appetite for historical and political studies which he pursued throughout his long career in politics.

Public life began in 1760 with election to the Assembly of the Lower Counties, where he assumed the Speaker's chair. Dickinson retained his interest in what later became Delaware even after his election to the Pennsylvania assembly in 1762 thrust him into that colony's politics. Originally predisposed to ally with the Quaker party, he moved into opposition when its leaders began a crusade to revoke the Pennsylvania charter and place the colony under royal government. He announced his switch in a dramatic speech delivered on May 24, 1764. Assembly party leader Joseph Galloway rose to the challenge, tempers flared, and the two men engaged in a fistfight while leaving the session.[20] Thereafter Dickinson was the darling of the Proprietary party, which he still refused to join even though he acted as its spokesman in the assembly.[21] He may have disliked many actions of the proprietary government, but he valued the charter liberties it guaranteed and feared their loss under a royal government.

These fears intensified when the British Parliament persisted in passing legislation that he considered an abrogation of colonial rights. The animosity that Dickinson bore for the Assembly party now expanded to take in England as well.[22] The Stamp Act of 1765 aroused his ire and he joined with George Bryan and John Morton in a Pennsylvania delegation to the intercolonial Stamp Act Congress. There he absorbed the limelight by drafting its statement of protest to Parliament.

Dickinson returned to find that he had lost his assembly seat. Franklin's party had determined to keep one of its most volatile and literate opponents from public office. They succeeded, for the man was not reelected until 1771. They did not, however, defuse him. In November Dickinson publicly addressed his "Friends and Countrymen on the Stamp Act" and in December spelled out the dangers of the act more extensively in the popular pamphlet

"The Late Regulations respecting the British Colonies on the Continent of America considered."[23]

His newly acquired leisure allowed Dickinson to immerse himself in a concentrated study of colonial rights and to cement his ties to a party that was forming to defend them. The Presbyterian party welcomed his talents and, as it evolved into the Whig party, thrust him into a position of leadership. He first took the literary lead by publishing the celebrated "Letters from a Pennsylvania Farmer" in opposition to the Townshend Acts of 1767. These ran in the *Pennsylvania Chronicle* from December 2, 1767, until February 18, 1768, and vaulted their author into an empire-wide fame. Colonial newspapers from Boston to Savannah carried the series and Benjamin Franklin published them in England as the "*general sentiments*" of Americans.[24]

Simultaneously, "The Farmer" joined other leaders of the party in haranguing Philadelphia merchants on the necessity of joining with other colonies in a refusal to import British goods.[25] Meanwhile he added his political warnings to the "Centinel." Although religious, Dickinson refused to affiliate with any particular denomination. He joined the Presbyterian crusade against a bishopric only because he perceived it to be dangerous to provincial freedoms.

Judge George Bryan saw the same danger but for him, as for Alison, the perception was sharpened by his early years in Ireland.[26] Bryan was born in 1731, the middle of five children of Samuel and Elizabeth Dennis Bryan. His father was a well-known Presbyterian merchant in Dublin. The young man entered the business by forming a partnership with a Philadelphia merchant, James Wallace, who had established trade connections in Dublin. Bryan arrived in Philadelphia in 1752 just before his twenty-first birthday.

The firm of Wallace and Bryan prospered and, after the dissolution of the partnership in 1755, Bryan continued the business alone. He joined the Second Presbyterian Church, which was under the ministry of the revivalist Gilbert Tennent, and in 1757 married Elizabeth, the daughter of trustee Samuel Smith. A successful merchant with a growing family and active in his church, Bryan became a pillar of the merchant community and entered politics.

In view of his later role, Bryan's first involvement may seem odd. He began in 1755 as a polemicist, joining Joseph Galloway and William Franklin in composing a scurrilous defense of Benjamin Franklin. "Tit for Tat, or the Score wip'd off" by "Humphrey Scourge," directed its venom at William Smith.[27] The provost had attacked the proposed voluntary militia as a personally ambitious scheme which Franklin had devised to trick men into joining his new Assembly party, which he was using against the proprietors.[28]

Actually, Bryan's position made sense for a Presbyterian at this time. His western countrymen lay defenseless before Indian attacks and he blamed the proprietors for refusing to allow their lands to be taxed to finance defense efforts. The militia bill that Franklin had managed to get passed promised the only relief in sight.

Assembly actions after 1756 inexorably alienated Bryan, but he confined his reactions to a diary. Franklin's party seemed less interested in defending the frontier than in contending for "power and influence" by "lying, misrepresentation and false reports," he recorded.[29] Even the legislative trial of William Smith angered him by its arrogant illegality. By 1758 he was in open opposition to his former party, counting on the newly reunited Presbyterians to provide the force necessary to defeat it.

When Franklin embarked on his campaign for a royal government in 1763 instead of defending western settlers against Pontiac's Rebellion, Bryan was incensed. He organized opposition to the royal petitions and, for the first time, ran for a legislative seat from the city. He won, defeating Franklin, and allied with the other anti-royal newcomers who joined the Assembly after 1764. Proprietor Thomas Penn immediately appointed him as judge of Common Pleas and Orphans Court, a post he held throughout most of this revolutionary period.

Judge Bryan joined Dickinson at the Stamp Act Congress and, like him, lost his assembly seat while away. He returned to insure that the hated act was not executed in Pennsylvania and to pressure other merchants into joining him in nonimportation agreements. Stamp distributor John Hughes fumed against such unjudicial behavior, stamping him as a "Red hot Presbyterian."[30]

As the Presbyterian party formed, Bryan gained repute as one of its best political organizers. His advocacy of colonial boycotts hurt him financially. Even so, he fought again for nonimportation in response to the Townshend Acts of 1767. His business failed and the sheriff sold his land in 1771.

Educator-minister, lawyer, and merchant-judge: what drew them together was the threat of British oppression which either they or their ancestors had experienced. Their alliance formed when they feared that their province would pass under direct royal rule and lose its liberties; it was cemented when they responded to what seemed to be a conspiracy by Parliament to violate all colonial rights. An established church was viewed as just one facet of a comprehensive plot. The "Anatomist" was focusing on the "Centinel's" integration of the scheme for a bishopric with the other manifestations of the plan when he pointedly remarked,

> Our Centinel skips from Bishops to Stamp Acts, and from Stamp-Acts to judges of the admiralty and from judges of the admiralty back again to ecclesiastical courts, and canons, and Bute, and Grenville, . . . and tests.[31]

As they studied, wrote, and acted, these men led Pennsylvania into a revolt against the English Parliament. This was not their intention. They did not see themselves as revolutionaries seeking something new. Dickinson, for example, could not bring himself to sign the Declaration of Independence. These men were conservatives, defending their lives from British innovations.

Alison died before the conflict was resolved but his students joined the leaders of the Whig party in building the young republic that emerged. Bryan continued as a judge and a political force in Pennsylvania until his death in 1791. He was instrumental in creating the state constitution of 1776 and led the state, first as vice-president and then as president from 1777 until 1779. He used his high offices to oppose the Federal Constitution in 1788.

Dickinson employed his pen for the first and second continental congresses but retired to his farm in Dover after refusing to agree to independence. He soon reemerged to fight in the war and by 1779 was back in political office, first as a congressman from Delaware, then as governor of the state while simultaneously serving as governor of Pennsylvania. Meanwhile he joined with other prominent men to establish a college in Carlisle, Pennsylvania, which later took his name. Delaware sent him to preside over the Annapolis Convention in 1786 and then to the Philadelphia Convention. He returned to pen the "Fabius" letters urging ratification of the Constitution in opposition to his old colleague, Bryan. Dickinson remained a states' rights man, becoming a close friend and adviser to Thomas Jefferson. He died in Wilmington, Delaware, in 1808.

2
A History of Conflict

American resistance to Anglican efforts for a colonial bishopric could boast of a long and vicious history by the time the Pennsylvanians took the lead in 1768.[1] Their opposition, based on the fear that a bishop would evolve into an established church, was suspect in an age that did not distinguish religious duties from civil obligation and thus assumed that one national church was necessary to instill in a people the requisite loyalty and obediance to the state. "No bishop, no king" was the accepted cry of men who supposed that, without the moral weight of a state church behind them, the laws of king in Parliament would be ignored. High Anglican officals in England echoed this refrain whenever they wished to defend or extend their power.

Until the eighteenth century, the Church of England displayed little interest in extending its jurisdiction over much of America. Most colonies were defined as wilderness areas, settled by unruly "dissenters" whom the church was glad to be rid of. In 1702, however, the Reverend Thomas Bray founded the Society for the Propagation of the Gospel in Foreign Parts, which sent Anglican missionaries into the plantations to convert Indians and Negro slaves and to minister to random Anglicans there. The archbishop of Canterbury served as the president of the society, commonly called the S.P.G., and worked with the bishop of London who had jurisdiction over colonial Episcopalians. These church-supported missionaries soon launched a seventy-year battle for an American bishopric.

Victory seemed certain under Queen Anne (1702–1714) for she favored the high Churchmen. She died before the bill creating a colonial bishopric could be submitted to Parliament for ratification, however. Her death ended the Stuart line of monarchs and the throne passed to distant cousins from the German state of Hanover.

With the accession of the Hanoverians in 1714, the Church had a more difficult time. The supporters of George I, II, and III looked upon English dissenters as a mainstay of the new dynasty as well as a political force to be reckoned with. In the chaos of the multi-factional political scene that obtained throughout the rest of the eighteenth century, the ministry was more concerned with keeping a working coalition in Parliament than with alienating the dissenters by establishing a bishopric in the colonies.

In this more favorable royal atmosphere, the English Presbyterians, Independents, and Baptists gained confidence, settled their differences, and formed a unified front to protect dissenting interests and push for an easing of restrictions against them in England. They created a political arm called the Protestant Dissenting Deputies specifically to lobby in Parliament for their cause. It was to this agency that provincial dissenters turned whenever zealous Anglican officials took up the plea from their colonial missionaries to establish bishops in America.

These pleas became more numerous and insistent as the number of missionaries and their adherents increased in the new world. They emanated mainly from New England, where Anglicans suffered the disabilities of "dissenters" under the established Congregational churches and fought back under the effective leadership of Samuel Johnson. This man had been the center of controversy since 1722, when he and a few of his fellow tutors at Yale had followed their rector, Timothy Cutler, into the Anglican fold. From his church in Stratford, Connecticut, he directed a vigorous campaign for a bishop. The Dissenting Deputies counterattacked by calling for colonial petitions opposing an episcopate which they used in a judicious application of political pressure on the king's ministers. They also convinced Massachusetts and Connecticut to ease legal restrictions against nonchurch members and thereby assume a more defensible position against the next Anglican assault.

Johnson rejoiced when Thomas Sherlock became bishop of London in 1748. Now Thomas Secker, then bishop of Oxford, would have an ally in his battles against the Dissenting Deputies. The two bishops launched a sustained campaign for an American bishopric that was foiled only by the constant changes of ministries in England, each seeking to smooth over religious disputes which might shatter their precarious coalitions. Churchmen anticipated success in 1750 with a rather moderate plan drawn up by Joseph Butler, bishop of Durham.[2] Horatio Walpole, speaking for the ministry, squashed these hopes by citing the "heats and animositys" that would arise from dissenters whose support the government needed for other programs.[3] Bishop Sherlock informed Johnson in 1752 that he had "but little hopes of succeeding at present" but promised that he would continue his delicate political maneuvers.[4] Meanwhile the colonial Churchmen would have to content themselves with whatever gains they could effect quietly on their own.

When the conflict entered this new state in the 1750s, the battlefield shifted to the middle colonies, where Thomas Bradbury Chandler resided. Chandler was from an eminent Congregational family and the top student at Yale when Samuel Johnson discovered him. After graduating in 1745, he studied theology under Johnson and settled at St. John's church in Elizabeth, New Jersey, where he devoted himself to furthering the cause of Anglicanism in general and a colonial episcopate in particular. The two men remained in close contact. When Johnson moved to New York in 1754 to assume the presidency of the newly founded King's College, they formed an able team of Anglican generals in the middle colonies. William Smith became provost of the College of Philadelphia in 1753 and completed the triumvirate.

The maneuvers of these Anglicans did not go unresisted. Another triumvirate arose in New York to lead the Presbyterian forces. William Livingston, a wealthy farmer, lawyer, and essayist from a prominent New York family enlisted the aid of two other lawyers, William Smith, Jr., and John Morin Scott, in composing a series of essays designed to reform the "public abuses" perpetrated by the Churchmen.[5] The *Independent Reflector* appeared in the *New York Gazette* from November 30, 1752, until November 22, 1753, when Episcopal pressures forced the editor to reject further contributions. The "public abuse" that received the most attention was the Anglicans' endeavors to ease the contemplated New York college under their control. They eventually won a royal charter, a majority on the board of trustees and the presidency of King's College but in the process aroused other denominations to such a state of wrath that they were united and prepared to explode instantly against yet another ill-timed move for a colonial bishop.

When William Smith returned to England to seek ordination and await his appointment as provost of the College of Philadelphia, he carried with him a manuscript copy of Samuel Johnson's book *Elementa Philosophica*, to be published in London. Unfortunately, he appended a letter to the work in which he described the "lamentable" and "distressed" state of the Episcopal church in the colonies and advanced a plan for a bishop as her only salvation.[6]

Johnson was horrified and disclaimed any "notion" of Smith's intention.[7] Thomas Secker, newly elevated to the office of archbishop of Canterbury, was even more aghast at such an "unseasonable step" which set back his delicate negotiations for years.[8] England was preparing for yet another war with France and the ministry wanted no unnecessary internal divisions. He cautioned his zealous American followers to maintain a low profile and leave the politics to him.

Secker's advice was ignored temporarily during the storm that arose when Smith's letter was publicized in the colonies. Further installments of the *Independent Reflector* appeared, now joined by the new "Watch Tower," composed by essentially the same men, and the Anglicans castigated both. This virulent public controversy subsided only when the Churchmen abandoned the fray in the face of a *History of the Province of New York*, written by William Smith, Jr., and published in 1757. They simply threw up their hands at the prospect of "fencing against a foil" and disputing a whole book, point by point.[9] Instead, they followed Secker's lead and abandoned the public arena in favor of collecting information, organizing themselves into regional conventions to meet yearly, and relaying to England possible plans for an establishment that might be implemented when peace came, rendering the ministry more receptive to their pleas.[10]

The colonial opposition was fully aware of the Anglican strategy and fearful that peace might bring a bishop. They too began to gather data to prove that American souls were under competent care and bishops were neither needed nor desired. This information was relayed to the Dissenting Deputies in London, along with intelligence on the various plans that the Anglicans were suggesting. Some brave souls even sent out signals to test potential receptivity for an intercolonial union of all dissenters. The two "sides" of the Presbyterians had reunited formally in 1758 and it was hoped that other denominations might heal those old wounds inflicted by the Great Awakening and present a united front against the expected Anglican onslaught.

The Peace of Paris was signed in February 1763. Within a month the Anglicans moved, this time with the blessings of archbishop Secker. After years of watchful waiting, he finally judged the political scene to be ripe. In the peace settlement, England had taken from France all of Canada plus the land from the Appalachian mountains to the Mississippi River. Now the government had to devise a plan to organize and rule this vast new territory. It seemed logical to merge it with the existing American colonies and transform the present unwieldy empire into an integrated political organism. A bishop easily could be incorporated into this new order that was projected.

The British empire had evolved in a random manner and tidy men shuddered when they viewed the resultant chaos. Furthermore those English officials who had come to the North American continent to direct the war against the French angrily reported the effects of this neglect. Each province was a little country unto itself, refusing to work with each other much less with England during the war. There was a bewildering array of governments, religions, and economies. What the colonists did share was a wholesale flaunting of imperial trade regulations, aggrandizement of royal power to their local assemblies, evasion of British laws, and a fixed determination to do exactly as they pleased. An English observer would be hard pressed to accept their self-characterization as loyal British subjects.

Powerful men who led Parliament and occupied influential positions in the empire began to heed those who had been arguing the need to integrate the American colonies more closely into existing British law, politics, economics, and foreign policy. Undersecretaries busied themselves drawing up plans to restructure the provinces so that all would have identical governmental structures, enforce revised trade regulations, collect requisite duties, and obey similar laws that did not conflict with those of England. What better time to institute a national religion to support the state and instill obedience in its subjects? It would be simple to graft a bishopric onto whatever settlement was made. If colonial charters were revoked, such provisions could be included when the new ones were issued. Otherwise, prelates with limited power might suffice, supported by income derived from the lands taken from the Catholic church in Canada.[11] Secker laid his plan before the king's ministers that very summer and the sweet scent of victory drifted across the ocean to raise Anglican spirits over here.

American dissenters did not have detailed evidence of Episcopal movements but they did expect some activity and responded quickly to the alarming rumors that began to circulate. Individual essays appeared in the newspapers even before their authors had anything concrete to attack. Jonathan Mayhew, Congregational pastor of the West Church in Boston, focused on the S.P.G., assailing it in a series of pamphlets that began in April of 1763. These were in answer to the publications of the Reverend East Apthorp, a neighboring society missionary, who had attempted to explain and defend the work of the S.P.G.. Mayhew raised such telling indictments that Henry Caner, rector of King's Chapel in Boston, felt constrained to respond. Mayhew had the final colonial word in November, by which time the pamphlets had reached England and were adversely affecting the proposals for colonial bishops now before the ministry.[12] Secker ordered Johnson to drop the emphasis on the S.P.G. lest the plan for bishops become a public issue. The archbishop himself planned to answer the American dissenter in the calm and dispassionate prose that would please the government.[13]

Secker was having some trouble with the ministry. It was not his fault entirely. No sooner had he convinced one set of ministers of the desirability of his plan than a crucial man would die, forcing the archbishop to wait until the replacement entrenched himself in power before reopening the case.[14] A major setback occurred in the summer of 1763, when George Grenville replaced the unpopular Lord Bute as prime minister. Grenville's main concern was the British economy. To his mind, political reorganization and religious innovation were matters that could wait.

The French and Indian War had saddled England with such an enormous debt that the current rate of taxation would not cover even the interest. Moreover, the newly acquired land demanded additional revenues to support a government and an army to prevent French repossession of the territory in some future war. Englishmen already bore a heavy burden of taxation and many members of Parliament were adamant in their refusal to increase it. The colonies, in contrast, had never been taxed for the imperial services which they enjoyed. Grenville determined to make custom duties reasonable, devise efficient machinery for collection, and apply the proceeds to help defray the costs of the British troops who were protecting the colonies. He brought the necessary legislation, the Sugar Acts, before Parliament in the spring of 1764.[15]

Once this economic program was passed, the Anglicans sighed with relief and resumed their campaign. In spite of the delay, they remained sanguine that the impetus remained and they would soon have a colonial bishopric. Thomas Chandler rejoiced that Secker had enlisted the support of the archbishop of York and the bishop of London in "bringing to perfection that good work." Samuel Johnson expected that "our first news in the spring will be that it is done" since "it should seem scarce possible that it should miscarry," and provost William Smith confidently predicted that the "affair could be completed before another year." Joyfully they entertained each other by discussing the merits of the possible choices for the post of the first American bishop.[16]

Even the dissenters prepared themselves for the worst. Samuel Chandler, head of the Dissenting Deputies, contented himself with assurances from Secker that the bishops would have limited powers and would not be sent without first informing the deputies.[17] Chandler gloomily reported these developments to his anxious American correspondents. Even so, he held out a ray of hope which underlined his belief that "*I believe they will not yet be* [sent]."[18]

Chandler was correct. Grenville chose to introduce the remainder of his revenue program in the spring session and governmental energies were directed at getting the Stamp Act through Parliament. America had been warned the previous year that such a measure was contemplated and men from each colony had been nominated as agents to distribute the paper. Later in the session came the Quartering Act. In the lull that followed passage of this legislative package the Anglicans resumed their campaign for a colonial bishopric. Once again they were interrupted, this time by events in America.

The colonists did not simply refuse to obey the Stamp Act, they did so in a spectacular manner. Mobs roamed through the major cities, threatening the stamp distributors, destroying their property, and forcing them to resign their commissions. The Sons of Liberty formed, directed the mobs, effectively coopted provincial governments, and set up a network of intercolonial intelligence. Most newspapers, judges, and customs officials carried on their normal business without the stamped paper. Northern merchants boycotted English goods in an attempt to bring economic pressure on Parliament. Provincial assemblies applied political pressure by passing resolutions of protest and sending delegates to an intercolonial Stamp Act Congress which also sent a set of resolves to the British Parliament. Royal governors threw up their hands in futility and watched their colonies teeter on the brink of rebellion.

This violent disobedience was provoked by the colonial fear that this new imperial policy was designed to take away their rights as Englishmen. British citizens could only be taxed by their elected representatives. The Sugar Act, under the guise of a trade regulation, was designed to raise revenue; the Quartering Act forced them to pay for the army; and the Stamp Act was an undisguised direct tax. The colonists sent no representatives to the Parliament that passed these laws. Likewise, Englishmen were entitled to a trial by jury. Yet suspected violators of the Sugar and Stamp Acts went before vice-admiralty courts where the burden of proof was on the defendant and no juries were present. A standing army, forbidden in peacetime since the Bill of Rights of 1689, was stationed in the colonies and maintained by the Quartering

Act. Was this to be used to force the provincials into a second-class citizenship?

Then there was that highly ominous section of the Stamp Act that levied taxes on documents in courts "exercising ecclesiastical jurisdiction." There were no ecclesiastical courts in the colonies for there were no Anglican bishops to preside over them—yet. Possibly England was contemplating an established church as the next step to inculcate Americans with a sense of submission and predispose them to accede to these denials of their rights.

These fears were heightened by the implications inherent in other movements afoot in the colonies. Governor Francis Bernard of Massachusetts was circulating a proposal to create a colonial aristocracy and gaining favorable responses from those who expected to be included in the class. This plan dovetailed with plots that were gaining strength in Rhode Island, Connecticut, and Pennsylvania to recall the charters of those provinces and place them under royal rule. Everything seemed to point to the existence of a deliberate and well-coordinated conspiracy to deny the colonists their basic rights as Englishmen and force them into unqualified submission to the king in Parliament, using an aristocracy, an established church, and a standing army to enforce this will.

Lord Rockingham, the successor to Grenville, who had been dismissed over unrelated matters, managed to convince Parliament to repeal the Stamp Act only by emphasizing the deleterious effects of the colonists' boycott on the English economy and smoothing over their denials of parliamentary authority to tax them. To proclaim its power, Parliament passed a Declaratory Act, which announced its right to pass "laws and statutes" binding on the colonies but which neglected to specify whether these would include taxation. The Americans did not press for clarification. They wanted to believe that Parliament's repeal of the Stamp Act signified an agreement not to tax the colonists without their consent. Thus, they paused in their celebrations only to address messages of thanksgiving and loyalty to England. The crisis had passed and in the euphoria that followed, the Anglicans once more gathered their forces to press for a bishopric.

"Now that all America are over-flowing with joy for the repeal of the Stamp Act," Samuel Johnson proclaimed that the time for the episcopate had come. Anglicans had expected no action during the "tumults" of 1765 but were enraged at Parliament's timing that had caused the riots and set back the cause of bishops.[19] "Had it been done last spring (when the dissenters themselves expected nothing else) and the Stamp Act postponed til the next, it would have been a nine day wonder," raged Johnson to the bishop of London, the secretary of the S.P.G., and the archbishop of Canterbury.[20]

Secker meekly agreed, defending himself quietly by reviewing his near success at the end of Grenville's ministry and citing his renewed efforts with the weak ministry that followed. "Yesterday the ministry was changed again," he sighed and resigned himself to yet another start. He sounded very tired.[21]

American Anglicans were not tired: they were exasperated. "What else can be expected from such an unsettled state of the ministry" in all its "perpetual and violent justling about in and out?" Johnson demanded of his son. They can do no good for us.[22] News that Parliament had adjourned after repealing the Stamp Act, thereby postponing the matter of bishops for yet another year, set Thomas Chandler into a near fit. "The Parliament was rising and would do nothing!" he shrieked. Who asked them to do anything?

> What reasons can there be for consulting the Parliament? How in the name of goodness does it concern them, whether such a bishop as we have requested be sent us any more than whether an astronomer or a poet should come over to America. . . . All that we desire is that they will not oppose us.[23]

Ignore Parliament, the ministers, and the dissenters, they advised each other. If, as was reported, the king, the ministers, the S.P.G., and the Church hierarchy all supported the plan, then why not simply implement it? It could always be maintained that the Church was established in the colonies already, for there was some legal precedent. If not, one could simply cite the supremacy of the king.[24]

This latter tactic would have evoked instant antagonisms in England but the missionaries were beyond caring. They began to doubt whether the archbishop's "quiet, private, and conciliating method" was the best approach. "What has the Church ever gained and what have its enemies not gained by that thing which the courtesy of England calls prudent?" they wailed. Their conclusion was that the "irresolution & pusilanimity of its friends" was hurting more than the dissenters and they began to wonder whether someone like William Laud might be a more desirable leader at this point in time.[25] It was time to change their methods and embark on a new strategy. The colonial Anglicans took the lead and aroused themselves to a frenzy of activity designed to force the issue in England.[26]

S.P.G. missionaries already had opened this new phase of the struggle. In October of 1765 the clergy of New York and New Jersey had held a convention at Perth Amboy, New Jersey, and composed strong petitions which they shipped off to the king, high Church officials, and universities. Since these were framed in the midst of the Stamp Act riots, one of their most effective arguments was that England had brought this crisis on herself by not establishing the Church of England, which would have instructed the colonists in obedience. They maintained that the Congregationalists and Presbyterians were as much opposed to monarchy as to episcopacy and by allowing them to dominate, England was losing the loyalty of North America. This refrain had been a constant echo in missionary arguments, but American reaction to the Grenville program now lent it more credibility. The letters were timed to arrive in England just as the *Annual Register*, an influential British periodical, republished Butler's 1750 plan for American bishoprics.[27] Before they adjourned, the delegates agreed to hold annual voluntary conventions to better design and implement a coordinated battle plan.[28]

The next year the clergy assembled at Shrewsbury, New Jersey, agreed on their course of action, and set to work. They rejected a compromise measure involving commissaries or agents which William Smith of Philadelphia had proposed. Nothing short of a bishop would do. First they must allay dissenters' fears for their religious liberty, convince the reluctant southern Anglicans to join their crusade, and present England with a concrete proposal. Thomas Bradbury Chandler was appointed to compose an acceptable plan that could be defended in England, supported by the South and offer an impervious front to any effective dissenter assault.

When the delegates reassembled at Elizabethtown that fall of 1767, a mood of buoyancy prevailed. Apparently their efforts were having positive effects in England. John Ewer, bishop of Llandaff, delivered an anniversary sermon before the S.P.G. that was an unequivocal argument for an American bishopric. Within a few months, William Warburton, bishop of Gloucester, expressed similar support before the same audience.[29] The convention unanimously endorsed Chandler's tract "An Appeal to the Public in Behalf of the Church of England in America." It was published immediately and sent off to England.

Copies of the "Appeal" moved more slowly southward. It was not until the early months of 1768 that dissenter responses appeared. In the interim the Anglicans congratulated themselves on the success of their efforts. They were convinced that their energetic offensive had been received so favorably at home that the dissenters were cowed and the Chandler plan would be implemented.

The Anglicans were only partially right. Ever since the spring of 1765 the dissenters had been expecting a Butler-Chandler type bishop to be sent "when we least expect it."[30] Their response in no way suggests that they were cowed. Naturally, they continued to rely on their English allies who had proved so successful in the past and collected information for the Dissenting Deputies to use in countering Anglican petitions. Gradually, however, the colonists enlarged their sphere, opening correspondence with other dissenters in the British Isles with an eye to consolidating all non-Anglican objections into a single roar of protest. First they had to unite themselves.

Francis Alison and the Pennsylvanian Presbyterians led the effort. Their success in submerging their own differences in the provincial elections of 1764 in order to oppose Franklin's scheme for a royal government made them sanguine about the prospects of an intercolonial alliance. To cement this tentative unity, Presbyterians throughout the middle colonies began negotiations to combine their educational forces by enlarging the College of New Jersey, which had been founded by the New Side in 1746, adding some Old Side professors then teaching at the College of Philadelphia, and sending all their sons to one seminary financed by the entire denomination. The plan eventually failed, but the support it received illustrated the strong impetus for unity that existed.

Even as the Presbyterians were struggling to erase their differences, they initiated an even larger scheme to join with northern dissenters in a religious confederation. "If we succeed in Uniting our Strength in the Jersey College, & the intended Union with our Friends in N. England," a Philadelphia leader mused, this will "Render us a formidable Barrier against both Civil & Religious Encroachers."[31]

The Pennsylvanians engaged the services of Ezra Stiles, a moderate clergyman in Rhode Island, to help them convince the receptive Congregationalists in Connecticut and the reluctant clergy in Massachusetts, New Hampshire, and Rhode Island of the desirability of such a union.[32] They were not entirely successful for many of the northern churches feared a loss of independence under the "Plan of Union" hammered out by Alison and Stiles in 1766. Further, they wanted to avoid alarming England with an intercolonial assembly until a clear and present danger of bishops appeared.[33]

Nevertheless a meeting at New Haven in 1767 marked the birth of the General Convention of the Presbyterian and most of the Connecticut churches. They established communications with the other societies, which were free to join whenever the Dissenting Deputies sent word that an American bishop was imminent. At its first regular meeting in Elizabethtown, New Jersey, in October of 1768, the convention drafted a letter to the Dissenting Deputies in England, informing them of its existence and purpose:

> To give information of the public state of our united interests; to join our counsels and endeavors together for spreading and preserving the religious liberties of our Churches; . . . to keep up a correspondence through this united body and with our friends abroad.

The rest of the statement centered on the subject of an American bishopric, which made the prime purpose for the convention's existence obvious. The General Convention met annually and followed these purposes until the fall of 1775.[34]

The formal channels of colonial and imperial correspondence that the dissenters had now opened allowed them to plan and coordinate their defense. Historical and current intelligence that was useful for their fight against a colonial bishop crisscrossed the Atlantic and provincial boundaries, giving imperial dissenters the advantage of the most current information.[35] Americans wanted to be kept constantly informed on the mercurial temper of Parliament so that they could maintain their opposition within safe bounds. Their strategy was to protest with enough vigor to illustrate their "disposition of uneasiness," but in a style that would not provoke the establishment of bishops through pique or pride. Presbyterians and Congregationalists had to be particularly tactful since England blamed them for inciting the Stamp Act riots.[36] Yet they felt constrained to respond to the British Churchmen.

At the first meeting of the General Convention in November of 1766, the delegates agreed to publish answers to the Butler plan republished in late 1765 and to correspond with pastors of the absent churches for advice and aid.[37] They had begun their research when news arrived that the archbishop had abandoned hope for a bishopric for that year. Ewer and Warburton still had to be answered so Charles Chauncy and William Livingston lifted their intrepid pens once again. Not yet aware of Chandler's pamphlet, the dissenters judged the situation to be under control in the fall of 1767.[38]

3
The Crisis of 1768

The Anglicans had expected some answer to Chandler's "Appeal," probably emanating from New York, where the triumvirate of the 1750s was still intact, and possibly from New England, whose clergy were well practiced in the art of pamphleteering. They were amazed when Pennsylvania joined New York and even more astonished at the sustained and virulent explosion that rocked these middle colonies. William Livingston reassembled his group and began publishing "The American Whig" in March. At the same time, Francis Alison formed a "Sort of Society" to compose "Centinel" articles.[1] Together, they precipitated a crisis.

The "Appeal" was designed specifically to raise no alarm. It explained the difficulties that the Anglicans faced in ordinating and disciplining their clergy in the colonies. The Episcopal church believed in uninterrupted succession—Jesus had given the holy power to accept men into God's priesthood only to the apostles. They, in turn, passed it on to bishops, in whom it had reposed ever since. Therefore, all provincial candidates for the Anglican ministry had to travel to England to be ordained by a bishop there. It was an expensive and hazardous journey that could be avoided only if there were a resident prelate in America.

Such an official could also discipline the clergy, who now were free to live and minister pretty much as they pleased. He could perform these functions, Chandler insisted, without exercising the civil power that a bishop enjoyed in England. In the colonies his authority would be of a purely ecclesiastical and spiritual nature and would not extend to the laity or to other denominations. There would be no ecclesiastical courts, new laws, or tithes collected for his support. A bishop would exist on the same grounds and with the same rights as the officials of the other voluntary churches. In short, all the evils of establishment would be avoided.

By stressing the point that bishops would have no authority over the laity, Chandler hoped to soothe the Southerners. They were perfectly happy with Anglicanism as established in their colonies because vestrymen conducted church affairs and selected their ministers. They had little desire to share this power with an outsider, even if he was their official spiritual leader.

If the Southerners joined with the northern missionaries in pleading for a bishop with limited powers, how could Parliament deny them? For that matter, how could the dissenters object to such a reasonable request for religious equality? Chandler did contradict himself and allowed some unguarded statements to pass which suggested that his final goal was a little less "reasonable," but on the surface the plan was insidiously moderate.

Opposition was difficult, doubly so because few colonists objected to the limited office that Chandler said he was proposing.[2] Their fears were for the future. Once introduced, what could prevent a colonial bishop from gradually claiming an authority equal to that exercised by his fellow bishops in England? Chandler's plan looked suspiciously like the first act in a play for the establishment of the Church of England in America. "Our peculiar Objections are much founded in the Anticipation of Futurity," Stiles noted, and how can one mount an effective attack based on suspicion?[3]

Initially, the dissenters hesitated, awaiting information on the impact of the "Appeal" in England and advice from their allies there on an effective countermeasure. When that intelligence came, leaders from the middle colonies took the initiative, urging dissenters to act in coordination so that pamphlets and newspaper articles would appear simultaneously in every colony. Their efforts were in vain. Only Charles Chauncy of Boston responded with "The Appeal to the Public Answered in Behalf of the Non-Episcopal Churches in America," which he admitted was inadequate. Despite frenzied pleas, the Congregationalists remained silent and left the entire burden of defense to the middle colonies.[4] Obviously, the Northerners were not particularly apprehensive.

The Presbyterians of New York and New Jersey were alarmed, for they stood in the eye of this new storm for a bishop. New Englanders were ignorant of the vigorous activities by Johnson, Chandler, and Smith. Since the northern missionaries remained relatively quiet, dissenters there underestimated the strength of the renewed campaign. Alison despaired that the "northern Govermts . . . could hardly be persuaded that the Episcopal Clergy with us . . . were writing petitions, & using all endeavors with the zealous part of the Church of Emgland to get an Episcopacy established among us."[5] New England, after all, had not even seen fit to join under the Plan of Union that the Presbyterians were pushing as a defensive measure. William Smith, one of the more active Anglicans, kept Francis Alison informed on the imperial efforts and progress, possibly to convince the man of the inevitability of a bishop and the futility of further resistance.[6] He did not need to tell Alison of informal exertions to enlarge the Episcopal influence for these were easily observable.

Unlike Massachusetts and Connecticut, Pennsylvania had no established church. Indeed, the Charter of Liberties issued by Proprietor William Penn in 1701 guaranteed equal rights and liberties to all religious denominations. These groups bickered, jockeyed for converts and power, and yet survived in tolerable harmony. The Anglicans defended proprietary interests against the Quaker-dominated assembly and received some high provincial officers in return. However, they were willing to join the assembly after 1766 in ousting the Penns in return for its assistance in obtaining a colonial bishopric which promised even greater rewards.[7] As in New York, they were ever restless to ease the nonsectarian provincial college under their control. Smith boasted of his progress in the College of Philadelphia, using "soft and easy means." By the fall of 1766 Alison almost acceded to Anglican domination by considering resigning because "the College is artfully got into the hands of Episcopal Trustees."[8]

The Anglicans were never completely successful in their quest for power for no religious interest could ever become dominant in Pennsylvania so long as rival groups were free to counter it. The Presbyterians were as frightened of the Quakers as of the Anglicans. If either denomination had the force of government behind it, they would suffer. It was not just the establishment of the Church of England that they opposed: it was any established church.

The Pennsylvania Presbyterians were perhaps more sensitive to the evils of an established church because so many of them had come from northern Ireland. There they had suffered civil and religious oppression under the established Anglican church and since the 1720s increasing numbers of them had fled to Pennsylvania because of its charter. Their memories were vivid and bitter. Alison himself had "groand under an Establishment" and tried to relay to his friend, Stiles, a sense of the hardships his people had experienced. "These things are serious evils to us," he explained, "but are words of no force with you." Native "Americans have no notion" of what it meant to be a dissenter under an established Church of England.[9] Furthermore, they seemed oblivious to the real possibility that they might learn very soon. Alison knew and became a sentinel to warn others of their danger.

The prospect of bishops was seen as more imminent in 1768 than ever before. What first alerted the Pennsylvanians was the fact that Chandler's was an American plan. Before this time, missionaries may have penned appeals and addresses, but all concrete proposals had come from England. Their network of intelligence informed dissenters that English Churchmen had been warning missionaries constantly to stay in the background and do nothing overt. Yet here was an American plan brazenly published in London as well as in New York. This marked a qualitative change and, coupled with the recent hyperactivity of the domestic Anglicans, might well indicate that the opinion in Parliament was so favorable that this final push was all the Anglicans needed for their long-sought victory. "Straws and feathers are light things, yet when they float on the water, they serve to shew how the wind blows," Alison warned.[10]

Parliament's actions since 1763 raised the colonists' suspicions that they could expect only an ill wind from that quarter. The recent laws affecting the colonies were only consistent insofar as they displayed an amazing ignorance of American conditions, preferences and liberties. Parliament as a whole might well agree to a colonial bishopric in a fit of indifference. A more frightening interpretation was that certain members of that body were engaged in a conscious plot to deprive Americans of all their rights and liberties and the bishop was but one facet of their master plan. This view was much too awful for loyal Englishmen to contemplate seriously. Rather, they preferred to characterize the Sugar, Currency, Quartering, and Stamp Acts as unwise regulations passed by men who were unaware of the violence they were doing to the natural and civil rights of Americans. The most glaring violation, the Stamp Act, had been repealed, presumedly because Parliament agreed that it could not tax unrepresented Englishmen. Many provincials did not even want to scrutinize this action too closely. They joined Alison in his determination to "be thankful without examining or deciding whether the repeal was a matter of Right or of Favor."[11] Defining rights is a ticklish business and unnecessary unless someone is conspiring to deny them. Most colonists were not yet willing to believe that this was the British intent.

What lent some credibility to the conspiracy theory were the Townshend Acts, passed in the summer of 1767 and implemented in the fall. The full force of this legislation was being felt at the same time the colonists were searching for ways to dissuade or prevent Parliament from introducing a colonial bishop.

Charles Townshend, Chancellor of the Exchequer, convinced Parliament that his program would extract money from the colonists in a painless way. If Americans made the silly distinction between accepting external duties on trade and rejecting internal or direct taxation, which in Parliament's misunderstanding they did, then why not tax items that, by law, could only be imported from England? To this end, new duties were laid on glass, lead, paper, paint, and tea. This was clearly a tax, designed to raise revenue, and not a trade regulation, which imposed duties as a way to discourage certain imports. The colonists raged that Parliament had reneged on its promise, implicit in the repeal of the Stamp Act, not to tax them without their consent. It simply had waited until the furor over that act subsided and then done exactly the same thing again. The action smacked of a determination to deprive Americans of this basic natural and British right.

A second act in Townshend's program offered further evidence for this view. The Quartering Act of 1764, still in operation, required colonists to tax themselves to support British troops in their midst. Unless they agreed, this too was taxation without consent. Therefore the assemblies had taken care to limit their compliance by offering a free gift for the military as a matter of principle. New York was the most conspicuous example for it seldom gave enough to supply the large number of troops within its borders. To force submission, the royal governor of New York was instructed to veto all legislation until the assembly provided full support. This, in effect, took away the colony's self-government and alerted all the provinces to the fact that Parliament was willing to violate their charters in order to get its illegal way. Were all of their rights to self-government to be wrested from them, they wondered? That would make them slaves.

The Americans saw themselves as free Englishmen with more virtue than those who were trying to enslave them. They certainly did not want the rapacious officeholders who had so corrupted the mother country to spread their poison to the colonies. Yet this is exactly what the final section of the Townshend Acts threatened to do. A separate Board of Customs Commissioners, who had bought their positions with the expectation of gain, was now to be stationed in Boston. They were to supervise the collection of the new duties and be paid from the proceeds. As before, officials would prosecute suspected violators in local vice admiralty courts, but now they could appeal unfavorable decisions before newly created district courts. The arbitrary lumping together of separate colonies into districts with no regard to their charters gave added weight to the conspiracy theory.

A Parliament that could accede cheerfully to the Townshend Acts was quite capable of imposing a bishop on recalcitrant dissenters for fun, for revenge, or, more darkly, to instill an obedient disposition among the colonists. In the previous controversies the dissenters could count on Parliament to ignore Anglican efforts for a bishop. In 1768 they feared they could not. Furthermore, the type of prelate that Butler and Chandler proposed was unknown in English common law. Parliament would have to pass a law to create a truncated official and insure that he would not lay claim to the authority he would have exercised in England. Americans might have accepted this kind of warranty before; they would not in 1768. They doubted that Parliament would compose such a law and even if it did, they had no guarantees that a repeal would not follow in a later session. In sum, Americans no longer trusted the British Parliament.

The colonists began to search for ways and reasons to prevent Parliament from altering their religious life. To do so, they were forced to draw up a blueprint of the empire and define the rights of the colonists within it. During this consideration, it became increasingly obvious to them that they and the way of life they had evolved were different from the English. Somehow, they had become Americans. This search for an acceptable imperial structure, accompanied as it was by a reluctant nationalism, is what the "Centinel" illustrates so well.

To warn Americans effectively of their "Common Danger," and to incite them to a proper state of alarm, the "Centinel" had to dip into a pool of common knowledge and prejudice. Their experience in convincing juries, congregations, and students had taught the authors the value of playing on familiar arguments. Therefore, much of the series reviewed the major ecclesiastical and theological arguments of the earlier religious controversies and alluded to the contemporary political crisis of 1768.

There was little need to paint the Anglican church as a theologically and ecclesiastically unscriptural edifice erected by misguided and arrogant humans to the everlasting pain of the Savior. No dissenter questioned that and it would have been foolish to alienate native Episcopalians by dwelling on the point. Besides, this line would have subverted the image of sweet reasonableness and Christian charity that the authors wished to project. Rather, the overall statement was designed to read something like this: if the Anglican church wishes to compete on an equal footing with all other colonial religions and abandon her partnership with the state, it is welcome. Given its past actions and present spirit, we doubt that it will do this and, in our present situation, we can find no way to prevent it from foisting the evils of establishment upon us.

Chandler's plan provided the focal point so that all of the arguments raised in earlier controversies were reorganized and presented in the form of an answer to his proposal. First, the authors had to tear away the moderate facade, to "unmask him, & follow him thro all his doublings, & dark shelters."[12] They did this by exposing his arrogant use of terms and unguarded statements, which suggested that an established church was his ultimate goal.[13] The earlier indictments against the S.P.G. and some recollection of the unfair and unchristian activity of the Anglicans in the past alerted the readers to the fact that such an establishment would not take the tolerant and easy form that Americans were accustomed to.[14] A persecuting spirit still existed among the English and colonial Churchmen that would not rest until it had saddled free Christians with the oppressive yoke that choked the English and Irish dissenters.[15]

A quick review of established churches "contains little else than the follies, absurdities, frauds, rapine, pride, domination, rage, & cruelty of spiritual tyrants," according to "Centinel" number III. Leaders who grasp for civil power seem unaware that they destroy their institutions in the process of persecuting others. Edifices of form and ceremony slowly replace the vital spirit of religion. Lucrative offices attract power-hungry men seeking "the fleece not the well-being of their flock," so that the laity starves for spiritual guidance as it blindly reveres the outward trappings of an empty religion.[16] Discipline disappears when a church must admit profligate sinners simply because they are seeking civil or military offices and later pardon all of their horrid transgressions. Periodic reforms necessary to wipe off the encrustations of time are nearly impossible where civil and religious bureaucracies are planted together in contented indolence. Nothing short of a state convulsion can effect the slightest alteration in a national church, Alison concluded.

This total disregard for biblical instructions on erecting a church probably is necessary if the Anglicans are to persecute other Christians for freedom of conscience, the essays continue. If the Act of Uniformity demands punishment for any who disparages something contained in the Book of Common Prayer, then the whole document must be considered sacred and no thinking Churchman is allowed to expunge those sections which are irrelevant or irreverent. Likewise, if the Test and Corporation Act denies the natural right to hold office to any Christian who cannot ascribe to the Thirty-nine Articles of the Church of England, then logic demands that the church must admit to its communion any man who says he does. These acts would bear heavily on Americans seeking salvation in ways and institutions prescribed by the Bible. Under them, the majority of the colonists would be unable to hold political office, lead in the defense of their land in the military, obtain university degrees, or teach in most schools. Further, they would have to pay taxes to support the luxurious trappings of this persecuting church and submit to the jurisdiction of its courts. An established church, then, would wipe out most of the religious and civil liberties that Americans now enjoy.[17]

Chandler, however, maintained that he was not asking for an established church, merely for a bishop with limited powers. The problem as the "Centinel" saw it was that there was no lawful way to prevent such a bishop from later grasping the authority of an established church. The British common law recognized a bishop as an office with particular powers. This was the same law that governed the colonies. Alison searched through volumes of ecclesiastical law while Dickinson and Bryan reviewed common and statutory laws.[18] All emerged with the same dismal conclusion which they shared with their readers. If an American bishop appealed to the law, it would have to allow him to exercise the powers attached to that office in England. Obviously, the British common law, which was basically good, had evolved some peculiarities that fit conditions on the island of England very well but were irrelevant to the American situation. Veneration for this enlightened body of laws had blinded Americans to this unsettling observation before. The "Centinel" shrank from the implications of such a discovery and searched for other ways to avoid an establishment.

There was a possible escape. The Episcopal church might create a new office with the power to ordain and discipline the clergy but without the title or trappings of a bishop. "Centinel" XV and XIX pummeled readers with citations from the Bible and Anglican divines to prove that the exalted office of bishop and the concept of uninterrupted succession were Catholic inventions inherited by the Church of England. In fact, the Bible gave many names and equal powers to those who were to oversee the church. Therefore, it was scripturally legitimate for the Church to design an office specifically to fill their members' needs within an American environment. The point was academic and raised to appeal to Americans by showing that this option was always open to the Church of England. Few thought it would be chosen. In their view, high Church officials were too greedy for power to relinquish a potential source of it voluntarily. It was highly unlikely that such men would choose to follow the example of all other religions operating in America even though colonial Episcopalians were agreeable.

Where else might America look to for protection against an established church? To the British Parliament, which claimed to represent the colonies virtually? To their credit, the authors did not play on the root word, "virtue," but only appealed to colonial common sense to show that since "virtual representation" had proven to be a farce in protecting other American interests, it would be of little help here.[19] A mere allusion to the Grenville and Townshend programs and some technical explanations of the operation of the vice admiralty courts in England and America was all that was needed to drive home this telling observation, "Can any Thing more fully manifest the Difference between a *virtual* Representation and a *real* one?" Parliament knows little and cares less about the colonies, the authors continued, other than as they affect its pride or its pocketbook.[20]

Even if Parliament were to pass a statute limiting the powers of a colonial bishop, the law probably would emerge as a monument to this ignorance. In view of the current imperial crisis, it was much more likely that English legislators would deliberately impose a traditional Episcopate to force the colonists into submission. A constant theme throughout the "Centinel" series was that religious innovations were always considered whenever England was attempting to subvert other colonial liberties. Oppressions seemed to run in packs and bay of conspiracies. Better, then, not to seek parliamentary action at a time when the colonists were trying to prevent that body from meddling in American affairs.[21]

The "Centinel's" conclusion was that there were no traditional channels open to prevent a moderate Episcopacy from evolving into an oppressive establishment. To add to this horror, it was also clear that "The Church of England in America" would be more tyrannical than it was in England. The mother country had the protection of countervailing forces which were absent from the colonies. No aristocracy existed here, supported by large estates and ever watchful lest the Church usurp any of its prerogatives.[22] Colonial common-law courts lacked the traditional power and jurisdiction to keep ecclesiastical courts within bounds. Without an intercolonial assembly, there was no legislative body with sufficient strength to prevent church aggrandizement of an increasing number of civil powers. Perhaps more to the point, few colonists wanted these institutions anyway and the "Centinel" knew it.[23]

The more that all American denominations, including the Anglican, viewed the changes that an established church would force onto their lifestyles, the more aware they became of their distinctiveness. Somehow a society had evolved that fit the conditions in the new world and the temper of its inhabitants. Some colonists even suspected that it was better than what existed in Europe.

Eighteenth-century British thought heralded free competition in all things as the source of truth, virtue, wealth, and happiness. An age that produced Adam Smith, believed John Locke's "Letter on Religious Toleration," and read at least the political essays of David Hume, concluded that competing men, organizations, and political factions would balance one another and naturally produce the best economy, religion, and government. According to this rather mechanistic view, America's religious environment was designed perfectly to produce good Christians and a virtuous nation. Each denomination competed for adherents solely on the truth of its doctrine and the purity of its conduct. They watched each other carefully for signs of error, immorality, or encroachment on the religious and civil liberties of others. The nation benefited from the resultant environment of determined truth and virtue. If any one religious group enjoyed the added force of the state, these beneficial efforts would cease. Already, the "Centinel" was advocating a new theory of complete separaton of church and state which the Old World was not ready to accept until America eventually adopted it.[24]

Just as the colonists were reluctant to unbalance their nature by allotting undue power to one religious interest, so were they unwilling to introduce impediments to free competition in related areas of their lives. They did not want an aristocracy to monopolize political power and economic gain. Offices and fortunes now ebbed, flowed, and distributed themselves in a frustrating but equitable fashion in most colonies. Legislators were voted into office to pass laws and out of office to live under them. Assemblies exercised just enough influence over judges to keep them responsive but not dependent. Naturally, political controversies and power plays occurred but always within the province and among local factions. No one felt the need for an all-colonial council to dictate from without. Fewer still wanted the British Parliament to meddle. Even if this environment changed and necessitated the formation of new institutions, they should be indigenous, honoring each colony's integrity, reflecting an American society, and composed of native sons. They would not be English.

One significant leitmotif running through the "Centinel" score is the supposition that the colonies are distinct from each other and all are decidedly different from the English.[25] The overwhelming majority of colonial Anglicans are quite happy with the various arrangements they enjoy in each province. As Americans, they "detest Spiritual Domination as much as others, and . . . are as tenacious of their Civil and Religious Liberties, as the Members of any other Church, and therefore . . . alarmed at this dangerous Innovation." They desire no "new Masters" and fear the "Yoke" of the Church of England.[26]

It is the British Churchmen, the authors insist, who demand a bishop in unison with a few ambitious missionaries to the north. Only they are willing to violate freely the charters in order to establish one man over all of the disparate provinces. They wish to enlarge their wealth and power by forcing the colonists under their dominion and replacing America's religious arrangements with the British system. The lordly prelate will no doubt be an Englishman or one of his hirelings who has no interest or allegiance to our nation, the authors darkly warned. We will have no choice in his election or control over his actions.[27] They called for Americans of all denominations to join in a common defense of those civil and religious liberties which protected their society. It was this sense of a unique identity which later evolved into nationalism. To keep it intact, Americans were forced to define a structure of the empire that kept Parliament out of their internal affairs.

The rallying cry of the Stamp Act crisis had been "no taxation without representation." Parliament could not tax the colonists. By 1768 the "Centinel" had expanded that slogan to "no interference in any internal matters." Parliament could legislate only for the island and possibly for intra-imperial relations but not for the colonies. Furthermore, the series offered a detailed blueprint of how the empire ought to operate. It was remarkably close to the commonwealth solution that England eventually adopted.

The plan is spelled out primarily in numbers VI, VII, and VIII, but it is an assumption that underlies all of the articles in the series. It builds on John Locke's interpretation of the nature and formulation of governments, as did much of British political theory at that time. In this view, men derive their liberties and natural rights from God. For convenience and protection they join together and then form a government to serve as an agent in executing their common will. They find it necessary to give up certain of their rights to facilitate matters but can never devolve themselves of the inalienable rights of life, liberty, and property.

Since the purpose of government is to promote their happiness and defense and since only the people themselves know how best to effect this, the British constitution provided for a king to work with representatives of the people in passing beneficial laws. When the colonists left England for a new land, they kept the structure of this constitution and their British liberties but left behind the island's legislature and laws that would not reflect their new conditions accurately. In its stead, each colony organized its own respresentative assembly to work with the king and his agents to pass laws suitable to their peculiar environment. A charter spelled out their rights and privileges in relation to the authority and prerogatives of the monarch.

The British empire, then, "consists of several Provinces united in Allegiance to one Prince. The Legislative power of and for each Province consists of the King or his Representative, with the Deputies of the People in that Province."[28] Very simple: Parliament and the king legislate for England; the Pennsylvania assembly and the proprietor as royal agent rule Pennsylvania; and everyone is bound by allegiance to the king and under the protection of British rights. Who rules the empire as a whole is not clear, but the "Centinel" suggested that right-thinking men could work that out for the mutual benefit of all. What was unequivocal was the fact that Parliament had absolutely no say in the internal affairs of any colony. Popular consent for acts governing such internal matters as religion, taxation, local commerce, and law enforcement could only be obtained through colonial assemblies.

Most of the legislation passed by Parliament after 1764 was therefore unconstitutional. Certainly an attempt to subvert all colonial charters by lumping all the provinces together under an imposed and undesired religion was a blatant violation of all natural and British rights. Merely by appealing to England's Parliament instead of the colonial legislatures, the S.P.G. missionaries had committed a gross constitutional outrage. Religion was an internal matter, as were the taxes, courts, prerequisites for office, and educational institutions that an established church would try to control. This was the "Centinel's" definition of colonial rights vis-à-vis Parliament and the king. It retired from print and waited to see if Parliament would accept this American view of the British constitution.

4
An Appeal to the Colony

The "Centinel" was aimed at three audiences: the British Parliament, the southern Anglicans, and the inhabitants of Pennsylvania. It provided information and logical arguments to the Dissenting Deputies in the restrained tone that would allow them to present whole sections to members of Parliament without alienating them; it attempted to convince Southern Anglicans that a bishopric would bring more oppression than spiritual guidance; and, finally, it endeavored to alarm Pennsylvanians of their common danger and incite them to join together in resistance. The latter goal was by far the most important for the authors and the most difficult to attain.

Naturally, the authors spoke to those suppositions and fears that were common among all the colonists. But, to be effective in Pennsylvania, they had to couch this general appeal within particular emphases and allude to the unique concerns of these inhabitants. To understand the ticklish local situation which confronted Alison, Bryan, and Dickinson and their written response to it is to gain a heightened respect for their political acumen, powers of persuasion, and literary skill. A brief survey of how these peculiar circumstances evolved also explains why large numbers of fearful Scotch-Irish were so late in joining the colonial resistance to a bishopric.

In the latter part of the eighteenth century, Pennsylvania was a morass of religious and political factions which were rearranging their priorities and alliances.[1] Quakers had been dominant since William Penn founded the colony in 1681. They lived in the southeastern sections and monopolized most of the provincial wealth and political power. The Quaker oligarchy maintained its control of the unicameral assembly by wooing German support, accepting Scotch-Irish votes and denying equal representation to western inhabitants. It directed much of its legislative energy toward wresting power away from the proprietor and his governors.

This became even more the case after 1755, when Benjamin

Franklin brought other groups into alliance with moderate Quakers to forge the Assembly party, whose professed aim was to create a voluntary militia to fight the Indians but whose long-range goal was to attain complete legislative control over internal provincial government. The immediate issue in the resultant power struggle was to what extent and in what manner proprietary lands within the colony were to be taxed for defense against recurrent Indian attacks. By the mid-1750s the assembly and the proprietor had reached a stalemate which continued until the mid-1760s and left the western inhabitants essentially unprotected. Resentment against the assembly grew among these German and Scotch-Irish settlers, slowly but inexorably.

The proprietor had his supporters, but they did not really conform to any particular ethnic or religious category. Anglican William Smith became their most vociferous spokesman but Presbyterians, Germans, and even some Quakers could be counted within the Proprietary party. Increasingly it wooed dissatisfied Germans and Presbyterians to support a proprietor who exhibited more concern for them than did the assembly. Eventually it was subsumed within the Presbyterian party once the bickering and apolitical Scotch-Irish closed ranks behind men who could lead them into political effectiveness.

The Presbyterian party took a long time forming. As long as the Scotch Irish were left alone and reasonably secure to build their communities, practice their religion, and advance their economic fortunes, they seemed willing to leave the government to the Quakers and the proprietors. These immigrants were grateful enough for those civil and religious liberties which had been denied to them in northern Ireland. Further, they remained divided throughout most of the period by the religious conflicts that stemmed from the Great Awakening. The moderate Old Side and the revivalistic New Side continued their vicious battles even after their two synods had reunited formally in 1758. The wounds were still festering when the Revolutionary War broke out.

These religious factions would interrupt their bickering and join with each other, the Anglicans, and the Germans only when defending their settlements against Indian attacks or rebuilding their communities later. The worst outbreaks of violence were from 1755 until 1757 and again in 1763 to 1764, when all of the backcountry was aflame and refugees poured eastward begging the assembly for protection. When their pleas were ignored, some westerners tried threats. A Lancaster tavern owner led a predominately German group of from 600 to 800 men into Philadelphia on November 24, 1755, and "demanded Protection in such a manner as threatened outrage if it was denied."[2] Money for troops was then appropriated. This threat, a proprietary gift for defense and Franklin's success in forming an Assembly party that had no religious scruples about defending the frontier or allowing a voluntary militia to be formed can all be credited for this sudden assembly responsiveness. In gratitude, many westerners began casting their votes for the Assembly party.

Moderate Quakers who dominated this party were delighted with the divisiveness of the Presbyterians, whose immigration threatened to render the Scotch-Irish a majority which might some day wrest power from the Quakers. According to their political analysis of 1755, the Germans would continue their old loyalty, the Anglican laity would be forced to support the Quakers because they "dred the Presbyterians and Germans more," and the "Presbyterians are divided into several sects—mostly Disliking, if not hating one another." In such a situation "it seems Absolutely Necessary to keep the Quakers as a Ballance here."[3]

In these circumstances and with so astute a political manipulator as Franklin at its head, aided by his loyal lieutenant Joseph Galloway, it is not surprising that the Assembly party faced no real threat to its dominance from 1756 until 1764. Its actions and inactions during this period, however, awakened opposition and alienated men capable of uniting and leading the Presbyterians.

Francis Alison was called "my particular friend," by Franklin in the fall of 1755. By 1764 he had earned the dubious distinction of being Franklin's "old enemy."[4] The reason for this change in Franklin's perception can be found in another significant yet nasty characterization of Alison by the Assembly party as "the Presbyterian Pope."[5] Events had forced this pious educator into the uncomfortable role of opposition leader.

Many of Alison's countrymen lived on the frontier, underrepresented and easy prey for the Indians. He, like them, initially welcomed the Assembly party for the defense it promised and later grew disgusted when it used this issue as a mere tool in its power play with the proprietors. He turned first to informal ways to aid the westerners by establishing the Presbyterian Ministers Fund in 1758, a life insurance company for frontier clergy who wished to guarantee support for their families in the event of their death. After 1763 the corporation collected contributions, some of which were used to help the victims of Indian attacks to rebuild their communities and ransom the captives. The Assembly party had not only refused to do this but even lost the money that the fund gave it for these purposes.[6]

The Presbyterian Ministers Fund was simply an institutional manifestation of Alison's ceaseless efforts to unite the two Presbyterian factions in matters of common concern. In one sense, the Indians helped by convincing the frontiersmen that they would receive no help from the legislature until they banded together and used their political strength to elect responsive officials and demand redress of their grievances. This grass-roots reconciliation was a long and tedious business, but by 1763 the Presbyterians had reached the rationally schizophrenic posture of uniting to protect their lives and rights so that they might wage their theological wars undisturbed.[7]

The assembly's actions after 1756 suggested that it would not grant these rights easily. It refused even to discuss reapportionment. Then it brought William Smith, its most vocal opponent, to trial on a charge of libel. The case was weak, the pretext was dubious, the trial was before the assembly without a jury, and the verdict was guilty. This was blatant political revenge against a man it felt was a "Tool to narrow Presbyterian Politics."[8] What might lay in store for other opposition leaders?

The Assembly party also used its attack on Smith as a means to hurt the College of Philadelphia, which Franklin had helped to found in 1749. Quakers had been opposed to the school from its inception because "there is too many of the presbyterian Clergy concerned" who might turn the students into "Educated prispeterians so that in time they have the rule and governing [of] the province."[9] As vice-provost, Alison was committed to education in general and the college in particular as a means of enlightening the colonial wilderness. Furthermore, Presbyterians demanded educated ministers, many of whom studied here. To destroy the institution for petty political reasons was, to him, an unconscionable display of shortsighted vindictiveness. Yet that is exactly what the assembly tried to do by banning public lotteries, by which the school raised a large portion of its revenue, and then chortling when Smith left for England to appeal his conviction, thus deserting "poor Philadelphia & by removing his Candlestick leave the Academy in the Dark."[10]

These minor objectives of Franklin's party annoyed Alison. Its major goal was to wrest the colony from the proprietors and place it under the control of the crown. This threw the man into a highly controlled panic. He and his people had left Ireland for Pennsylvania largely because the Charter of Liberties guaranteed them civil and religious rights. The revocation of that charter opened up dismal prospects. Either unconcerned royal placemen would dominate and probably establish the Anglican church to harass them further or the Quaker-controlled assembly would be free from proprietary constraint and thus able to deny them political equality more easily. Alison wanted to retain a proprietor who had defended the best interests of the colony as a whole against both king and assembly.

Actually, Franklin had been in England as an assembly agent from 1757 until 1762 arguing for a royal government. In that period Alison had done nothing overt for he expected the mission to fail anyway and realized that the Presbyterians were too weak and divided to offer any effective resistance. When the campaign revived in 1763, it coincided with a major Indian attack that unified the Presbyterians and with the first of England's new imperial regulations, which suggested frightening prospects of life under royal rule.

Pontiac's Rebellion broke out in May of 1763 and by June terrified westerners were again pouring from their burning settlements to beg the assembly for protection. It did nothing, hoping that the crisis would force the proprietor to relinquish his stand and allow passage of a defense measure paid for by a tax bill on assembly terms. When he did not, it simply adjourned. A small group of frontiersmen, assumed to be from around the town of Paxton, reacted by murdering some Indians under government protection at Lancaster. By February their numbers had swelled to 250 and these infuriated settlers marched to the city limits to threaten those Indians residing in Philadelphia, to present their grievances, and to demand protection. The arrival of the Paxton Boys brought the legislature to life. It quickly passed a supply bill for the defense of the city against these inhabitants on terms which the proprietor could accept.

The crisis of 1764 also fanned the smoldering antagonisms between the Quakers and the Presbyterians into a blazing confrontation. The assemblymen accused the Presbyterians of being inveterate rebels, vowed never to give them equal representation, and characterized them as hirelings of a proprietary plot to "attempt a revolution" and destroy provincial government.[11] Alison, charged with being among "either the Principals or Abettors of all the riots," was both saddened and infuriated that these two religious groups would rail at each other at a time they should be uniting against Franklin's scheme for a royal colony. "I fear the consequences of these Squabbles," he confided to his friend Ezra Stiles. "[T]he mice & Frogs may fight, till the Kite devours both."[12]

Alison was correct. Franklin was preparing to fly a new kite to test parliamentary winds on the revocation of the charter. This time his tactic was to amass such an enormous number of signatures on petitions for a royal government that the British ministers would have to take notice. The energy, organization, and singlemindedness of his campaign, waged while assemblymen were pledging political obliteration of Presbyterians and reneging on solemn promises made to the Paxton Boys, galvanized the Presbyterian leaders into active opposition. They alerted the westerners of the threat to their religious and civil liberties which a change in government would pose "and let no man perswade you to the contrary."[13]

By rallying the opposition, the Presbyterians kept the number of signatures obtained down to thirty-three percent of Philadelphians and three percent of the rest of the population.[14] Nevertheless, when the assembly reconvened in May of 1764 it elected Franklin as Speaker, followed his leadership in approving a petition for royal government, sent him off to London to present it, and prepared for the October elections, which it assumed would be a mandate in support of its actions. This was an incredibly stupid assumption.

"Some madness has taken possession of the assembly of this Province," Alison exploded to Stiles.[15] A royal charter—now? The Sugar, Quartering, and Currency Acts were already in oppressive operation, reports of an impending Stamp Act were flowing, and the British Churchmen were pressing for an established church. It hardly seemed an auspicious time to place the colony at the mercy of the king and Parliament. Presbyterian leaders promptly set up religious committees of correspondence which organized districts into a tight political network that covered the province and awakened opposition. They joined with Germans, some Anglicans, and even some Quakers, forming an enlarged Proprietary party to defend their charter.[16] Their arguments, numerous, logical and persuasive, were most succinctly stated by spokesman Hugh Williamson in "The Plain Dealer. Number I."

> But the change of a Governor is not the only thing we are to expect; if we must have a change, we shall have a thorough one. For if we get a new government, the Parliament must alter our Charter first, and then we shall have new privileges and new laws. . . . We know what we have, and we can hardly get better, but we may get worse, when it is too late to repent. It is very

probable that we shall soon have stamp-offices, customs excises and duties enough to pay, we don't want to pay tythes into the bargin.[17]

The election of 1764 brought a stunning defeat for the Assembly party, which barely retained a working majority. Franklin, Galloway, and many of their staunchest supporters lost their seats. The decisive issue was a change in provincial government. By pressing perhaps the only point on which Presbyterians, moderate Quakers, Germans, and the Proprietary party could suppress their minor antagonisms and vote as a bloc, the assembly leaders insured their own defeat.[18]

They also alienated influential members of their own party. George Bryan conducted Presbyterian leaders over to the proprietary side of the assembly room. Quaker Issac Norris dramatically resigned his Speakership and made overtures to the Proprietary party. John Dickinson joined prescient Quakers in protesting the royal petition and the appointment of Franklin as agent.[19]

The Quaker oligarchy was breaking up, its members floundering on the horns of a dilemma. On one hand, they wanted to maintain their dominance over the hated Presbyterians by wresting more power from the proprietor, whose governors had both blocked the legislative quest for power and offered support to the westerners.[20] The crisis precipitated by the Lancaster murders and the arrival of the Paxton Boys had driven some Quakers to isolate Presbyterians as the major enemy of the province and one which only a royal governor could control. Yet they feared to dismiss the Penn family entirely and become a royal colony.

The Society of Friends, too, had been persecuted in Great Britain and suffered under an established church both there and in New England. Only in Pennsylvania did they escape the label "dissenter" and rise to political domination. Most Quakers were unwilling to trade their constitution for a royal government unless they could be assured of the continuation of those rights and privileges guaranteed by the Charter of Liberties. Initially, Franklin convinced them that this would be the case, but contradictory rumors from the ministry and the unwelcomed imperial legislation that continued to issue from Parliament undermined their confidence. Increasingly their leaders viewed it to be "a very critical time for such an application from the proofs which the ministry and parliament have given of their disposition towards the colonies."[21] At their yearly meeting, held after the elections in 1764, moderate Quakers from Philadelphia united with the country Friends to convince "all but a few" who had signed the assembly petition that the Society should "guard against such men and measures as would endanger the loss of our excellent constitution." This mental withdrawal from the Assembly party left them with no comfortable political nest. So aware were they of their drift that they dared not even answer some of the pamphlets published against them in the midst of the Paxton anatagonisms.[22]

The spectrum of Quaker solutions to the dilemma illuminates their divisions by three colorations of preferences. Some "warm Brethren" remained staunchly committed to a royal government as the ultimate weapon against the Presbyterians. Probably the largest group cagily planned to use the petition only to threaten the proprietor and force him to comply with assembly demands. A growing faction opposed both Franklin and the petition, fearful that a royal government "will bring such Burden on the Frds. of this Province as they have not been accustomed to, & will think hard to bear." The respective numbers adopting any of these stances fluctuated according to the actions and reactions of England, the Assembly party, the proprietary government, and the Presbyterians.[23]

The Presbyterians and their allies continued amassing signatures on antiroyal petitions and shipping them off to Thomas Penn for use as a counterweight against the assembly petition. Franklin's party retaliated by vindictive attacks on Presbyterians, and the matter became the main business and entertainment of the province until May of 1765, when fateful news diverted their attention. The Stamp Act had been passed and neither party knew how to respond to it.

Leaders of both groups wanted to avoid violence: the Assembly party to prove to the king that Pennsylvanians were loyal subjects who would be obedient to a royal governor; the Proprietary party to show that Penn could control his colony. Separately, they managed to approach their common goal by at least moderating the riots which they could not prevent. By demanding submission, they had to range themselves behind Parliament and royal prerogative. This became an increasingly unpopular stance among the people who were moving on their own initiative and would soon demand leaders to aid in their opposition to the recent British measures. A new political party was almost inevitable.

The Presbyterian party did not form until after the immediate crisis had passed even though John and Thomas Penn used the label as early as December of 1765.[24] First, it needed some reason to break with the old Proprietary party, an action it would take only if the threat of a royal government subsided. By November of 1765 that was the case, although it took some time before Pennsylvanians were convinced. The English Privy Council postponed any consideration of the assembly petition with the strong suggestion that it would not consider the matter again.[25] Franklin continued to press, but his provincial support melted away. Samuel Purviance, one of the most active Presbyterian politicos, boasted of the "Number of Quakers who had been strongly agst. us formerly, began to declaim with great violence agst. their own leaders & made Overtures to our people of joining them in a Ticket." Even those elected on the Assembly party ticket were more receptive to the Presbyterian persuasion "so that tho' we have not chang'd the Men, yet its plain we have changed their Principles." He was delighted to "meet the Q———rs half Way, shake Hands & be Friends, Rejoice at their Conversion." As a measure of their welcome in 1766, the Presbyterians even gave up George Bryan, "our own Hero," and allowed John Dickinson to run in his stead for a city seat in the Assembly.[26]

This volatile and historically unlikely alliance of Presbyterians with some Quakers materialized mainly in reaction to the threat of royal rule, which current English actions suggested might be less than gentle. It did, however, suggest that the Quakers, like the Old and New Side Presbyterians, were able to suppress their enmity long enough to unite against a common external danger. To the Scotch-Irish, the revitalized campaign for an Anglican bishopric posed just such a menace. It led them to sever their ties with the Anglican leaders of the old Proprietary party, hopeful that a large number of Quakers would join in their exodus.

William Smith had been treading a delicate, if not dishonest, path through all the confusions that had followed the French and Indian War. Ambitious as he was, he naturally wanted an established Anglican church, fancying that he might become its first bishop.[27] Yet he dared not push openly for it and antagonize the proprietor, who provided him with offices, favor and support. In the elections of 1766 he made his surreptitious move by suggesting to Franklin that, if he would stop his Quaker followers from opposing a bishop, then the Anglicans would acquiesce in a royal provincial government.[28] It would have been an irrelevant political deal anyway. At this stage, Franklin could no more control the Quakers than Smith could deliver the Anglican vote. It did serve to expose the man's duplicity and weaken the bonds which held the Presbyterians within the Proprietary party.

It was the Presbyterian party, then, that led the fight against the Townshend Acts of 1767, holding mass meetings, harassing reluctant merchants into joining the nonimportation agreements, directing the reawakened Sons of Liberty, and petitioning for the repeal of the acts. John Dickinson publicized its stance in "Letters from a Pennsylvania Farmer." Increasingly the party attracted a following which cut across class and religious lines, ate away support from the Assembly party, and evolved into the Whig party, which led the revolutionaries.

Until 1768, then, the Pennsylvanian Presbyterians were engrossed in the more immediate business of uniting themselves, protecting their people from Indians, and fighting against a revocation of their charter. Through these activities they gained the political experience and confidence which rendered them such formidable adversaries when they finally felt free to lead the battle against a colonial bishop. In this sense, Chandler could not have timed his "Appeal" better for the dissenters and worse for his cause. The authors of the "Centinel" exemplify nicely the main elements in the coalition hammered out in the previous local conflicts: Francis Alison, Old Side Presbyterian; George Bryan, New Side Presbyterian; and John Dickinson, formerly of the moderate Quakers.

This coalition was by no means stable. Groups had been splitting and shifting since 1763 and there was no indication that this flux would freeze suddenly into permanent parties. Furthermore, the Presbyterian party was still forming, not yet a majority or in control of the assembly. It needed to retain its present followers and attract others from the ranks of those men who were fearful of opposing any British laws, determined to remain unattached to any party, or repulsed at the prospect of joining former enemies.

Presbyterians continued to tear each other apart on theological issues which threatened to disrupt their tolerable accord on civil matters. Quakers were drifting fearfully in and out of the coalition. Many still considered the Northern Irish to be a "multitude devoid of humanity, ready to conspire on every trivial Occasion, blood thirsty and avaritious for rapine."[29] This hatred was deeply ingrained and could not be expected to dissipate magically in a euphoria of rational self-interest.

As the specter of a royal charter continued to fade after 1766, the ghost of Scotch-Irish domination reappeared. Many Quakers were convinced that these "Outcasts" from Ireland were determined to employ their increasing numbers to seize control of the assembly, oppress all other inhabitants, and possibly even establish the Presbyterian church in the colony. To their mind, the rashness and intemperance of this nationality were well illustrated by the Stamp Act riots, which were blamed on the Presbyterians. True, others in control had moderated this potential rebelliousness which threatened to draw parliamentary ire down on the colony, but in Quaker eyes the overreaction only reinforced what the Lancaster murders and the Paxton Boys' march had revealed about the Scotch-Irish character.

Pennsylvania Quakers had learned to live with the Anglican religion as long as it did not demand tithes or a monopoly of political offices. Some even mused that, if a resident bishop could select more moral and qualified candidates for the ministry and then discipline them, the church would attract adherents from the Presbyterians, decrease their numbers, and "relieve us from the unfavorable prospect of the evils to be feared from the increase of these people."[30] On the other hand, the Society had been oppressed in England and memories of martyrs were not buried too deeply in Quaker consciousness. Of more recent vintage were the political animosities generated by the Anglican alliance with the proprietor in his conflicts with the assembly. An ambitious bishop with his retinue who could call on external support might present an equally formidable challenge to Quaker political ascendency in the colony. These considerations made the Presbyterian party sanguine about the prospects of enlisting at least some of these people in its battle against a bishopric.

The Anglicans were even more of an unknown commodity, possibly because of their own divisions and problems with priorities. Their enmity toward Quakers was historical. Their dislike of Presbyterians was returned with vigor, and yet the two groups had maintained a tentative alliance in support of the proprietor against the Quaker assembly. Several Anglican leaders, including William Smith, owed their present positions to the proprietor. They knew his commitment to religious liberties and hesitated at any overt action lest they lose what they now possessed in an unsuccessful gamble on higher offices of an established church. Many of their young ministers came from the colony and felt the tug of divided loyalties during this imperial crisis. Their home was Pennsylvania; their church was England. Furthermore, they had been educated, for the most part, at the College of Philadelphia under Alison and alongside Presbyterian classmates. The ties remained.[31] Under the Charter of Liberties granted in 1701 the province provided an Anglican minister whenever twenty or more inhabitants asked for one. The laity was not at all certain that they wanted to be tithed for the full support of a minister who was now subsidized, simply to introduce a bishop to discipline them.

However determined, Pennsylvania Churchmen had been very cautious in their moves for a bishopric, possibly because of their ambiguous position. After 1762 Smith, aware of the furor that an outright plan for a bishopric would cause in the colonies in general and Pennsylvania in particular, pushed for a more moderate scheme as an interim measure. He proposed to divide the northern colonies into three districts and appoint a commissary or agent for each. This official, assisted by a "corresponding society," would report faithfully on church affairs to London, solicit larger subscriptions from the laity, aid in establishing schools and missions among the Indians, and, presumedly, serve as mediator and disciplinarian among the clergy.[32] Smith was piqued when the Episcopal convention of 1766 rejected his idea in favor of an immediate bishopric and downright angry when his rival, Chandler, issued the "Appeal."[33] The Presbyterians had good reason for thinking that, with careful handling, they might yet retain an alliance with at least some of the Anglican leaders and laity.

The dispersion of the Germans was so random that they canceled out each other politically. With the subsidence of the Indian and royal government threats, some drifted back into their traditional alliance with the Quaker Assembly party. Others returned consciously, having become alienated by the Proprietary party's efforts to Anglicize them through German Charity Schools. Perhaps an equal number joined the Presbyterian party to oppose an established church that would oppress their denominations. No doubt most were confused by the subtle disputations over the peculiar nature of the British constitution.

Given this perplexing and fluid situation, how was the "Centinel" to appeal to every faction of each group without alienating another and then rally them all into a unified opposition to an Anglican bishopric? Carefully, very carefully.

What first strikes the reader of these essays is their moderate tone. There is none of the character assassination, name calling, innuendo, or unfounded charges that permeate most of the eighteenth-century writing controversies. Even Chandler was forced to pay tribute to their tone of "politeness, meekness, candor and honesty."[34] When wit is used it is always within the context of sober argument rather than as a scurrilous ornament. Satire does become a bit pointed, however, as the "Anti-Centinel I" defends the "Appeal" and "Anti-

Centinel II" interprets the "Anatomist," deliberately damning them both in the process.

Throughout, the emphasis is on argument: logical, skillful, learned argument that bombards the audience's reason with facts and citations. The only general insult that opponents could concoct against the "Centinel" was, in fact, a backhanded compliment to its purpose—they called it dull.[35] The authors deliberately excluded froth in order to deny their adversaries any extraneous material which could be used to divert attention from the main issue. Words were chosen carefully so that no phrase could be lifted from context and twisted into an insult on any provincial faction.

The whole series was well considered and planned in advance. This was to insure a consistent argument and prevent the authors from being lured into angry rebuttals to inevitable attacks. They were contending for principles and ideals and were determined to present them in a constructive fashion. Each essay opens with a summary of the main points of the preceding piece and concludes with a brief mention of what will follow in the next. The order is interrupted somewhat by an interjection of numbers VI, VII and VIII, which comprise a miniseries, concentrating on civil rights and imperial structure. The points raised here are then tied into the matter at hand by placing the scheme for an established church within this context before continuing with a detailed investigation of the proposed establishment itself. The authors deliberately repeated words and ideas which they knew their readers were familiar with and thus would be more receptive to. At no point in the projected series did the sentry interrupt its warnings to answer the "nay-sayers." This was reserved for a subsequent "Remonstrant" designed to counter those objections which might prove harmful and for any later pieces sent in by supporters.[36]

The "Centinel" astutely hammered away at the specter that would alarm almost all Pennsylvanians—an established church whose persecuting spirit would be directed by English officials against all the provincials. Almost all denominations in the colony had fled from a state church, but it seems that the Quakers were the prime target for this emphasis. Their experience had been much earlier. Time and provincial accommodation had softened their fears of the Church of England, which needed to be sharpened. The horrors of what Friends had suffered at the hands of the Anglicans were both chronicled and described before the suggestion was offered that vestiges of this persecuting spirit remained, awaiting the attainment of the political means to reassert itself. The fact that the English Churchmen allied themselves so closely with recent parliamentary attempts to undercut provincial liberties showed that they were trying to gain that power.[37] The job of the "Centinel" was to convince the Quakers that under an established Church of England they stood to lose just as many rights and in just as thorough a manner as if their charter had been revoked. Many of the arguments reviewed below were designed to do just that.

Quakers, unfortunately, also had been persecuted by the Presbyterian church of Scotland and the Congregationalists in New England. Great pains, therefore, were taken to emphasize that any established church was an anathma to the authors—whether "Roman Catholic, Episcopal, Independent or Presbyterian."[38] They condemned all past persecutions, especially those committed by fellow Calvinists. More specifically, they vehemently denied that they had the remotest intention of ever establishing the Presbyterian church in Pennsylvania. The very notion was abhorrent to them.

By attacking the fact of establishment rather than the theology of the particular denomination, the "Centinel" hoped to avoid arousing Pennsylvania Anglicans to a visceral defense of their religion. In fact, its whole management of the Anglican faction is a study in orchestrated subtlety. All barbs passed over local Episcopalians to lodge in "them"—high English Churchmen, bigoted S.P.G. missionaries in New England, ambitious agents in New York and New Jersey—outsiders all. Our clergy, the authors pressed, "are Men of too much Understanding to complain without Reason, and too well acquainted with the Charter and Laws of the Province, not to know that they enjoy the same Liberty as any other religious Denomination. They claim no Superiority over their fellow Christians."[39] The laity is also content with equal privileges and freedoms. Chandler's "Appeal" does not speak for Pennsylvania's Episcopalians, who did not even attend the convention that pleaded for a bishop.

And to whom did these few zealous missionaries appeal, the line continued? Why, to British high Churchmen, whose principles seem supiciously close to their papist ancestors. Their obdurate opposition to reform and their persecuting spirit have tainted the whole Church of England throughout its history. Our readers know well who they are. They are the very bishops who voted against the repeal of the Stamp Act; ruthless, power-hungry men who would like nothing better than to reassert their domination over colonial Anglicans, who up until now escaped their grasp. They need new and lucrative offices for their sons and hirelings. Always, the suggestion was that native Americans would be excluded from any projected establishment.

Certainly, such gentle treatment of provincial Anglicans was designed to convince them that they were Americans who enjoyed a pure religion that had been corrupted in England. It also served another function—to assuage the irrational fears of Presbyterians against local Churchmen. The authors did not want a repeat of the 1764 elections, in which dissenting sects in Lancaster county so feared the threat of a colonial bishop that they rejected all Anglican candidates and voted for the Quakers of the old Assembly party.[40]

The message was that all right-thinking Pennsylvanians must band together against a dangerous external threat. Almost nowhere are local affairs even mentioned, lest any matter reawaken past animosities or highlight current conflicts. The emphasis is on the distinctiveness of the colony, even to the extent of suggesting that, if other Americans want a bishop, they should have one as long as Pennsylvania was left alone.

Men with a closer attachment to Pennsylvania than to England certainly could agree in theory with the "Centinel's" analysis of the imperial structure and the rights of Parliament. They seemed unanimous in viewing recent British legislation as ill conceived and unfortunate. The consensus broke down when the question of obedience was broached. A generation raised with the secular commandment to follow their sovereign and submit to lawful rule could justify protest but balked at any suggestion of outright resistance. The "Centinel" wisely steered to the mainstream by omitting mention of particular actions during the Stamp Act riots or predicting the dire consequences of the Townshend Acts. "The Pennsylvania Farmer" might have been admired for his arguments against these acts but few of his readers were willing to embrace the implications of civil disobedience contained in the "Letters."[41]

Raising such matters would offend public sensibilities for other reasons. The Presbyterians had acquired a reputation for being rebellious and disloyal subjects, one of the most opprobrious aspersions that could be cast in that day. They were very sensitive to the charge that they had led most of the British uprisings against the monarchy and all of the provincial riots since 1755. Quite likely they would dissociate themselves from any spokesman who even hinted at rebelliousness. Law-abiding Germans and peaceable Friends were just as assiduous in ferreting out a refractory tone.

It would only serve to confirm their suspicions and justify open opposition to any project involving such a restless breed as the Presbyterians.

A balanced, logical, and learned argument was very congenial to the temperaments of the teacher, the lawyer, and the judge who composed the "Centinel." It was also the only tone that would make the essays effective in Pennsylvania in 1768.

William Smith, the logical Anglican spokesman, did not know quite how to respond to the "Centinel". His inclination was to remain silent—which he did for six months. Some Presbyterians attributed his reticence to the fact that "he knows too well the abilities of those opposed to him to really do much."[42] That might have been so, but Smith had never before been shy about speaking out in superior company. A more likely explanation is that the "Centinel" had addressed itself so nicely to the provincial equilibrium that any Anglican spokesman would find it hard to attack without upsetting the balance. This Smith did not want.

Pennsylvania Anglicans had enough political troubles. They were infuriated at the "extraordinary warmth of the Jersey convention" and Chandler's "Appeal," which they knew would raise a "great Flame" in their colony.[43] Smith and Chandler were already enemies, the latter muttering about the provost's "gross ignorance" and low "degree of affection either for the Church or her clergy, or right principles," and attempting to discredit him with the Bishop of London.[44] Possibly Smith did care more about his personal position than the welfare of his colony. It is certain that he blamed "the unlucky war commenced against the Church on Account of Dr. Chandler's publication which I wish had been let alone."[45]

Consequently, local Churchmen pretended the conflict did not exist. No one, for instance, told Chandler of Matthew Wilson's pamphlet, "A Letter Concerning an American Bishop, &c. to Dr. Bradbury Chandler," which had been published in January of 1768.[46] Wilson was a former student, friend, and colleague of Alison's, and Smith probably did not want some zealous outsider to antagonize him with an answer. Quite likely Chandler was correct in his suspicion that the inert Pennsylvania clergy "would let me and my Appeal for the episcopate go to pergatory before they would move a fibre of their tongues or their fingers to prevent it."[47]

Chandler gave up on Pennsylvania. His letters suggest that he considered it to be another world, peopled by strange inhabitants with whom he had no intention of getting involved. Actually, he did not want to answer anyone and kept hoping that some provincial knight in mitred armor would attack the dissenting hydra. When none such myth appeared, he reluctantly undertook "the drudgery to which I am doomed". He fixed his sights first on Charles Chauncy, hoping that, by slaying the "Whig" he would also cause the "Centinel" to expire.[48] It is rather a shame that contemporary dissenters could not have read his letters. They would have gotten vindictive pleasure from knowing that their learned rejoinders had forced him to do his homework. It took him over a year and a half of study before he could issue "A Reply to Dr. Chandler's Appeal Defended" and during that time he complained constantly about the difficulty of the assignment and the lack of available sources.[49]

Smith finally recognized that "we are at last obliged in this province to bear our part in the unlucky war commenced against the Church."[50] That was, in fact, the tack that the "Anatomist" took in its seventeen essays, which ran in the *Pennsylvania Journal* from September 8 until December 28, 1768. Smith defended only the Church—not Chandler, not the ministry, not the British Parliament—only the Anglican religion. "The design of these papers," the first installment declared, "is not the defence of Dr. Chandler," who is not the Church, had no commission from the Church, and was not encouraged by his brethren, most of whom had never even seen his plan.[51]

The "Anatomist" attempted to identify the Anglican church with British liberties and devoted many pages to discussing the persecutions it, too, had suffered—generally in other colonies. Smith was reluctant to speak of Pennsylvanians also, or to castigate most of the local Presbyterians. It was only a "sour turbulent party" among them who gave offense, he maintained.[52] He directed much more of his attention to New York, now arguing against the "Independent Reflector" essays of 1752–1753, then attacking William Smith's *History of New York*, which appeared at the same time.[53] New England was also villified for the 1734–1735 controversy in New Hampshire over missionaries, for persecuting Quakers, and for stomaching the pamphlets which Jonathan Mayhew had written in 1763.[54]

The only substantive argument raised to counter the "Centinel's" main points was an attempt to prove that the power of an English bishop was a recent development and could not be replicated in the colonies either by common or statute law in opposition to existing provincial laws.[55] This line of argument, in effect, allied the "Anatomist" with the "Centinel" on a definition of colonial rights. England could not interfere with the colonists' regulation of internal affairs. In the latter part of 1768 Smith dared not say otherwise.

5
Conclusion

When John Adams mused on what it was that caused English colonists to become American nationals, he might have been using recollections of Pennsylvania as a basis for his analysis. The only factor he omitted, possibly because he assumed it, was the necessity for the confluence of a receptive provincial milieu brought on by local conditions with the apprehension of an established church which could incite the already aroused colonial mind to undertake a serious inquiry into the nature and extent of parliamentary authority.

Pennsylvania Presbyterians had to unite and gain confidence in their collective strength before they could take effective action against the importation of an Anglican bishopric. Otherwise they would have remained an inarticulate collection of individual immigrants feebly applauding the efforts of their dissenting brothers to the northeast. This had been the case prior to 1768.

Two decades of Indian attacks and resentment against assembly neglect set the process of unification in motion. It was the opposition to a royal charter, though, which solidified their ranks, gave them practical political experience, and incited them to think further about their provincial rights. It also brought them allies. Even though the coalition tended to drift apart after the immediate threat of charter revocation faded, the members retained the constitutional knowledge of provincial and imperial rights gained in that crisis. The fight over the charter, then, was crucial in awakening the Pennsylvanian mind and preparing it to consider questions whose answers were ultimately revolutionary.

Fear of the power that a Church of England might exert in a royal colony certainly underlay much of the Presbyterian resistance to the revocation of the charter. The prospect of an Anglican bishopric threatened not only the rights of Presbyterians in Pennsylvania but also the liberties of all the colonists. This placed the local resistance within a larger context. In their opposition the Presbyterian party was able to win support among the Quakers and the Anglicans by convincing them that this religious innovation was just one part of a comprehensive plot to force the Americans into total submission to parliamentary whim. The colonists would have no grounds for resistance until they knew exactly what their rights were.

The "Centinel" offered Pennsylvanians a constitutional blueprint of the empire which they could defend. Under it Parliament had power over England and possibly over clearly imperial matters. It could claim no authority over the internal affairs of the colonies. Similar conclusions were being reached in other provinces as well. The definition of colonial rights set down by the "Centinel" in 1768 was the legitimatizing basis of future American resistance to England's acts. It remained to be seen over the next seven years whether the British Parliament would heed the implicit warning in this stand.

Notes

INTRODUCTION

1. See Edmund S. and Helen M. Morgan, *The Stamp Act Crisis: Prologue to Revolution* (Charlottsville, N.C.: University of North Carolina Press for the Institute of Early American History and Culture, 1953).
2. Technically, a "dissenter" was anyone who refused to ascribe to the doctrine and practice of a state church, in this case, the Church of England. Even though Anglicanism was established by colonial law in only a few of the colonies, England persisted in calling other American denominations, "dissenters." Usually the title was reserved for members of the Congregational, Presbyterian and Dutch Reformed churches, which shared a Calvinist theology, differed in ecclesiastics, and often accepted this rather chauvinistic label.
3. Delaware was then a semi-autonomous part of Pennsylvania, ruled by the governor of that colony but with its own legislature of the Three Southern Counties.
4. William Smith to the Bishop of London, May 6, 1768, William Perry, ed., *Papers Relating to the History of the Church in Pennsylvania, 1680–1778* (Privately Printed, 1871), p. 429.
5. "Remonstrant," Number III, *Pennsylvania Journal and Weekly Advertiser*, October 20, 1768 (hereafter *Pa. Journal*).
6. Francis Alison to Ezra Stiles, June 4, 1768, Stiles Collection, Beinecke Library, Yale University (hereafter: Beinecke.)
7. Alison to Stiles, August 1, 1769, Stiles Collection, Beinecke.

1 THE AUTHORS

1. Thomas Chandler to Dr. Burton, June 24, 1768, Correspondence of the Society for the Propagation of the Gospel in Foreign Parts, Series B., Vol. 24, No. 95, transcripts in Library of Congress; T.B. Chandler to Samuel Johnson, July 7, 1768, Herbert and Carol Schneider, ed., *Samuel Johnson: His Career and Writings* (New York: Columbia University Press, 1929), 1: 444.
2. Andrew Eliot to Thomas Hollis, October 17, 1768. *Collections of the Massachusetts Historical Society*, 46th Series (Boston: Little, Brown & Co., 1858), 4: 433. See also "The Kick for the Whipper," *New York Gazette, or, the Weekly Post-Boy*, June 6, 1768.
3. Alison to Stiles, December 12, 1767, May 7, June 4, October 20, 1768, August 1, 1769, Stiles to Alison, April 23, 1768, Stiles Collection, Beinecke; Matthew Wilson, "Memorial to Dr. Alison," *Pa. Journal*, April 19, 1780; Alison to James Wilson, November, 1768, Simon Gratz Collection, "University and College Presidents," Box 11, Case 7, Historical Society of Pennsylvania (hereafter: HSP).
4. Alison, "Untitled Manuscript," Alison Papers, folder 7, Presbyterian Historical Society (hereafter: PHS).
5. Richard J. Hooker, "John Dickinson on Church and State," *American Literature*, 16: 82–98.
6. Alison to Stiles, June 4, October 20, 1768, Stiles Collection, Beinecke.
7. Elizabeth A. Ingersoll, "Francis Alison: American *Philosophe*," (Ph.D. diss. University of Delaware, 1974); Thomas C. Pears, "Francis Alison," *Journal of the Presbyterian Historical Society*, 29 (December 1951): 213–25; Thomas C. Pears, "Francis Alison: Colonial Educator," *Delaware Notes*, 17 (1944): 9–22; Thomas C. Pears, "Colonial Education Among the Presbyterians," *Journal of the Presbyterian Historical Society*, 30 (June 1952): 115–126, (September 1952): 165–74; George H. Ryden, "The Relation of the Newark Academy of Delaware to the Presbyterian Church and to Higher Education in the American Colonies," *Delaware Notes*, 9 (1935): 7–42.
8. Franklin B. Dexter, ed., *The Literary Diary of Ezra Stiles, D.D., L.L.D.* (2 vols., New

York: Charles Scribner's Sons, 1901), 2: 338; Benjamin Franklin to Joshua Babcock, September 1, 1755, Franklin to Jared Eliot, September 1, 1755, Leonard W. Labaree, *The Papers of Benjamin Franklin* (17 vols., New Haven: Yale University Press, 1960–1974), 4: 174–76; Wilson, "Memorial to Dr. Alison," *Pa. Journal*, April 19, 1780.

9. James Coutts, *A History of the University of Glasgow* (Glasgow: James Maclehose & Sons, 1909), p. 248. The degree is on file at PHS. William Wallace to John Wallace, May 27, 1765, Wallace Papers, 5: 46, HSP. "Minutes of the Faculty," 1732–1768, 33: 91, University of Glasgow Archives.

10. Alison to Stiles, December 12, 1767, Stiles Collection, Beinecke.

11. See James Seaton Reid, *History of the Presbyterian Church in Ireland* (3 vols., Belfast: William Mullan, 1867), 3: 220–26, 284–85. See also J. C. Beckett, *Protestant Dissent in Ireland, 1687–1780, Studies in Irish History*, ed. T. W. Moody, R. Dudley Edwards, David B. Quinn (London: Faber and Faber, Ltd., 1948).

12. Alison to Stiles, March 24, 1762, Stiles Collection, Beinecke; "Raphoe Wills, 1684–1858," Ulster-Scot Historical Foundation; "Hearthmoney-Rolls, 1665," The Presbyterian Historical Society of Ireland; "A Muster Rolle of the Province of Ulster in the Barony of Raphoe," HSP; Dr. M. Quane Oakden, "History of the Raphoe Royal School," *Donegal Annual* (1967), pp. 154–56.

13. Alexander Bower, *The History of the University of Edinburgh* (3 vols., Edinburgh: Alex Smellie, 1817), 2; Coutts, *History of the University of Glasgow*.

14. Gladys Bryson, *Man and Society: The Scottish Inquiry of the Eighteenth Century* (Princeton: Princeton University Press, 1945); Douglas Sloan, *The Scottish Enlightenment and the American College Ideal* (New York: Teachers College Press of Columbia University, 1971).

15. *Records of the General Synod of Ulster from 1691–1820* (Belfast: Presbyterian Church of Ireland, 1897), p. 203.

16. Wilson, "Memorial to Dr. Alison."

17. L. H. Butterfield, ed., *Diary and Autobiography of John Adams* (2 vols., Cambridge, Mass.: The Belknap Press, 1961), 2: 115. See also, Albert F. Gegenheimer, *William Smith: Educator and Churchman* (Philadelphia: University of Pennsylvania Press, 1943); Thomas Firth Jones, *A Pair of Lawn Sleeves: A Biography of William Smith (1727–1803)* (Philadelphia: Chilton Book Company, 1972); Horace W. Smith, *Life and Correspondence of Rev. William Smith, D.D.* (2 vols., Philadelphia: Ferguson Bros. and Co., 1880).

18. See David L. Jacobson, "John Dickinson and the Revolution in Pennsylvania, 1764–1776," *University of California Publications in History* (Berkeley: University of California Press, 1965), vol. 78.

19. Paul Leicester Ford, ed., "Preface," p. ix, *The Writings of John Dickinson* (2 vols., Philadelphia: The Historical Society of Pennsylvania, 1895), 2.

20. David Hall to William Strahan, June 12, 1767, David Hall Letterbook, American Philosophical Society. See also John Dickinson, "A Speech, Delivered in the House of Assembly of the Province of Pennsylvania, May 24, 1768," Evans, 9671; Joseph Galloway, "Speech in Answer to the Speech of John Dickinson, Esq.," Evans, 9671; John Dickinson, "A Reply to a Piece called the Speech of Joseph Galloway, Esq.," Evans, 9640; Joseph Galloway, "To the Public, September 29, 1764," Evans, 9674; John Dickinson, "A Recept to Make a Speech," Ford, *Dickinson*, 2: 141–46.

21. John Dickinson to Isaac Norris, October 23, 1764, John Dickinson Copybook, HSP.

22. John Dickinson, "A Protest Against the Appointment of Benjamin Franklin as Agent for the Colony of Pennsylvania, Oct. 26, 1764," and "Observations of Mr. Franklin's Remarks on the late Protest, Nov., 1764," Ford, *Dickinson*, 2: 147–68.

23. Ford, *Dickinson*, 2: 197–246.

24. Benjamin Franklin, "Preface" to the English edition, May 8, 1768; Ford, *Dickinson*, 2: 288. For a thorough study of the impact of this series, see Carl F. Kaestle, "The Public Reaction to John Dickinson's 'Farmer's Letters,'" *Proceedings of the American Antiquarian Society*, 78, Part 2, pp. 323–57.

25. John Dickinson, "An Address read at a Meeting of Merchants to Consider Non-Importation, April 25, 1768," "A Song for American Freedom, July, 1768," and "Letter to Philadelphia Merchants Concerning Non-Importation, July, 1768," Ford, *Dickinson*, 2: 407–46.

26. See Burton Alva Konkle, *George Bryan and the Constitution of Pennsylvania, 1731–1791* (Philadelphia: William J. Campbell, 1922).

27. Evans, 8256; Joseph Shippen to Edward Shippen Sr., December 5, 1755, Balch Collection, Shippen Papers, 1, HSP.

28. William Smith, "A Brief State of the Province of Pennsylvania," *Pa. Journal*, April 15, 1756.

29. George Bryan's Almanac Diary, MSS. Division of Library of Congress as cited in Konkle, *Bryan*, pp. 35–36.
30. Morgan, *Stamp Act Crisis*, p. 311.
31. "Anatomist" VIII, *Pa. Journal*, October 24, 1768.

2 A HISTORY OF CONFLICT

1. For a detailed and comprehensive general survey of Anglican attempts to establish a colonial bishopric, see Carl Bridenbaugh, *Mitre and Sceptre: Transatlantic Faiths, Ideas, Personalities, and Politics 1689–1775* (New York: Oxford University Press, 1962).
2. The plan, as revised by Bishop Sherlock, circulated privately and was first printed in America in the *Pennsylvania Gazette*, December 8, 1768.
3. Horatio Walpole to the Bishop of London, May 29, 1750, Arthur Lyon Cross, *The American Episcopate and the American Colonies* (New York: Longmans, Green & Co., 1902), p. 330.
4. Sherlock to S. Johnson, April 21, 1752, Schneider, *Johnson*, 3: 246.
5. "Independent Reflector" I, November 30, 1752, Milton M. Klein, ed., *The Independent Reflector or Weekly Essays on Sundry Important Subjects More Particularly Adapted to the Province of New-York* (Cambridge, Mass.: The Belknap Press of Harvard University Press, 1963).
6. Letter of July 13, 1753, appended to the London edition of Johnson's *Elementa Philosophica* as cited in Schneider, *Johnson*, 3: 248–53.
7. S. Johnson to Secker, October 25, 1754, Schneider, *Johnson*, 2: 333.
8. Secker to S. Johnson, September 27, 1768, Schneider, *Johnson*, 3: 259.
9. S. Johnson to Secker, March 1, 1759, Schneider, *Johnson*, 1:283.
10. Schneider, *Johnson*, 1: 282–87, 297–301, 319, 322, 3: 261, 263; Perry, *Penn.*, 2:295–96, 364, 404–405; Bridenbaugh, *Mitre and Sceptre*, pp. 179–80.
11. Secker to S. Johnson, September 28, 1763, Schneider, *Johnson*, 3: 277; Henry Caner to Thomas Secker, October 6, 1760, Kenneth Walter Cameron, ed., *Letter-Book of the Rev. Henry Caner* (Hartford, Conn.: Transcendental Books, 1972), pp. 112, 223.
12. See Jonathan Mayhew, "Observations on the Charter and Conduct of the Society for the Propagation of the Gospel in Foreign Parts" (Boston, 1763), Evans, 9441; Henry Caner, "A Candid Examination of Dr. Mayhew's Observations" (Boston, 1763), Evans, 9360; Jonathan Mayhew, "A Defense of the Observations on the Charter and Conduct of the Society" (Boston, 1763), Evans, 9442.
13. "An Answer to Dr. Mayhew's Observations on the Society for the Propagation of the Gospel in Foreign Parts" (London, 1763), Evans, 9832. Mayhew answered that same year with "Remarks on an Anonymous Tract Entitled 'An Answer to Dr. Mayhew's Observations on the Charter and Conduct of the Society for the Propagation of the Gospel in Foreign Parts' " (London, 1764), Evans, 9738.
14. Secker to S. Johnson, September 28, 1763, Schneider, *Johnson*, 3: 278.
15. The best account of the English political background of the passage and implementation of the Stamp Act is P.D.G. Thomas, *British Politics and the Stamp Act Crisis: The First Phase of the American Revolution 1763–1767* (New York: Oxford University Press, 1975). See also, Morgan, *Stamp Act Crisis*.
16. Chandler to S. Johnson, August 20, 1764, Johnson to Secker, September 20, 1764, Schneider, *Johnson*, 1: 343, 346.
17. Thomas Secker to Richard Peters, August 11, 1764, Kenneth Walter Cameron, ed., *Facsimiles of Episcopal Church Documents (1759–1789)* (Hartford, Conn.: Transcendental Books, 1970), a reprint edition of William Stevens Perry and Charles R. Hale, eds., *Facsimiles of Church Documents* (Privately Printed, 1874–1879), p. 8; Thomas Chandler to Francis Alison, April 12, 1764, Hawks Collection, Church Historical Society; Francis Alison to James Sprout, November 15, 1766, "Minutes of the General Convention for Religious Liberty, 1766–1775," pp. 20–21, *Records of the Presbyterian Church of America Embracing the Minutes of the General Presbytery and the General Synod, 1706–1788* (Philadelphia: Presbyterian Board of Publication and Sabbath-School Work, 1904).
18. Chandler to Alison, April 12, 1764, Hawks Collection, Church Historical Society.
19. S. Johnson to Secker, May 2, 1766, Caner to the Secretary of SPGA, January 15, 1766, Schneider, *Johnson*, 1: 358, 361; Caner to Secker, December 23, 1765, Cameron, *Caner*, p. 125, #315.
20. September 15, 1765, Schneider, *Johnson*, 1: 355.
21. Secker to S. Johnson, July 31, 1766, Schneider, *Johnson*, 3: 286–88. See also Thomas Secker to William Smith, August 12, 1766, Smith, *Smith*, 1: 396.

22. S. Johnson to W. S. Johnson, June 8, 1767, Schneider, *Johnson*, 1: 404. See also S. Johnson to Secker, November 10, 1766, Schneider, *Johnson*, 1: 378.

23. T. B. Chandler to S. Johnson, September 5, 1766, Schneider, *Johnson*, 1: 368.

24. Caner to Secker, August 12, 1763, Cameron, *Facsimiles*, p. 66; Johnson to W. S. Johnson, June 8, 1767, Schneider, *Johnson*, 1: 404.

25. Laud was archbishop of Canterbury under Charles I who helped to precipitate a civil war in the 1640s by his zealous prosecution of uniformity in the Anglican church.

26. Johnson to Secker, September 20, 1764, T.B. Chandler to S. Johnson, November 12, 1765, Samuel Auchmuty to Samuel Johnson, June 12, 1766, S. Johnson to Secker, November 10, 1766, Schneider, *Johnson*, 1: 346, 356–57, 362–63, 378; Caner to Secker, October 20, 1766, Cameron, *Caner*, p. 129, #354.

27. Caner to Secker, September 1, 1764, Cameron, *Caner*, p. 119, #275; Caner to Secker, September 20, 1764, Cameron, *Facsimiles*, p. 65; T. B. Chandler to S. Johnson, November 12, 1765, T. B. Chandler to Secretary of SPGA, January 15, 1766, Schneider, *Johnson*, 1: 356–59; Francis Alison to James Sprout, November 15, 1766, "Convention Minutes," p. 21; Alison to Stiles, May 29, August 7, September 4, 1766, John Ewing to Stiles, August 6, 1766, Stiles to Charles Chauncy, August 26, 1766, Stiles to Alison, March 11, 1767, Stiles Collection, Beinecke.

28. Caner to Bishop Terrick, September 10, 1765, February 3, 1766, in William W. Manross, ed., *The Fulham Papers in the Lambeth Palace Library: American Colonial Section Calendar and Indexes* (Oxford: The Clarendon Press, 1965), pp. 79–80, #54–57.

29. T. B. Chandler to S. Johnson, August 20, 1767, Schneider, *Johnson*, 1: 416–17; Caner to Terrick, July 28, 1767, Cameron, *Caner*, p. 133, #377.

30. Alison to Stiles, June 19, 1767, Stiles Collection, Beinecke.

31. Samuel Purviance to Ezra Stiles, November 1, 1766, Stiles Collection, Beinecke.

32. *Records of the Presbyterian Church in the United States of America, 1706–1788* (New York: Arno Press & The New York Times, 1969), reprint edition of *Records* (Philadelphia: Presbyterian Board of Publication and Sabbath-School Work, 1904), p. 364; "Convention Minutes," p. 11; Alison to Stiles, May 29, 1766, Stiles to John Devotion, June 27, 1766, Stiles Collection, Beinecke.

33. Alison to Stiles, August 7, August 20, October 30, December 4, 1766, June 19, December 12, 1767, Stiles to Alison, August 26, September 5, October 8, November 22, 1766, March 11, August 17, October 3, 1767, Chauncy to Stiles, Sept. 29, 1766, Patrick Alison to Stiles, July 30, 1766, John Devotion to Stiles, September 17, 1767, Stiles Collection, Beinecke; "Convention Minutes," pp. 17–24.

34. "Letter from the General Convention to the Dissenting Committee in England, Oct. 6, 1768," "Convention Minutes," pp. 25–26. See also pp. 26–41.

35. "Convention Minutes," pp. 25, 29; Stiles to Rev. Thomas Vance, August 26, 1766, Stiles to Alison, September 5, 1766, April 23, August 26, October 4, 1768, Alison to Stiles, August 20, 1766, Stiles Collection, Beinecke.

36. Alison to Stiles, June 19, 1767, Stiles to Alison, April 23, 1768, Stiles Collection, Beinecke.

37. Alison to Stiles, December 4, 1766, Stiles Collection, Beinecke.

38. Alison to Stiles, June 19, 1767, Stiles to Alison, April 23, 1768, Stiles Collection, Beinecke. See also Charles Chauncy, "A Letter to a Friend Containing Remarks on Certain Passages in a Sermon Preached by the Right Reverend Father in God, John Ewer, Bishop of Llandaff" (Boston, 1767), Evans, 10579, and William Livingston, "A Letter to the Right Reverend Father in God, John Lord Bishop of Llandaff occasioned by his Sermon" (New York, 1768), Evans, 10948.

3 THE CRISIS OF 1768

1. Alison to Stiles, March 29, 1768, Stiles Collection, Beinecke.

2. Alison to Stiles, December 12, 1767, August 1, 1769, Stiles Collection, Beinecke; Hugh Neill to Sec. of SPGA, May 19, 1766, Perry, *Penn.*, p. 405; John Rodgers to the Protestant Dissenting Deputies, September 14, 1769, Minutes of the Protestant Dissenting Deputies, copies at PHS.

3. Stiles to Chauncy, April 22, 1768, Stiles Collection, Beinecke.

4. Alison to Stiles, March 29, May 7, May 23, June 4, October 20, 1768, Stiles to Alison, April 23, August 26, 1768, Stiles Collection, Beinecke; John Ewing to Ezra Stiles, July 1, 1768, Force Collection, Ezra Stiles Papers, Box 40, 1763–1781, Library of Congress.

5. Alison to Stiles, December 12, 1767, Stiles Collection, Beinecke.

6. Alison to Stiles, August 7, 1766, Stiles to Chauncy, August 26, 1766, Ewing to Stiles, August 6, 1766, Stiles Collection, Beinecke.

7. Samuel Purviance to Ezra Stiles, November 1, 1766, Stiles Collection, Beinecke; William Allen to Thomas Penn, November 19, 1766, Penn Papers, Official Correspondence, 10: 70, HSP.

8. Alison to Stiles, October 30, November 22, 1766, Purviance to Stiles, November 1, December 13, 1766, Stiles Collection, Beinecke; William Smith to Dr. Bearcroft, November 1, 1756, William Smith Papers, 2: 143, HSP.

9. Alison to Stiles, March 29, 1768, August 7, 1766, Stiles Collection, Beinecke.

10. Alison to Stiles, December 12, 1767, Stiles Collection, Beinecke.

11. Alison to Stiles, May 29, 1766, Stiles Collection, Beinecke.

12. Alison to Stiles, March 29, 1768, Stiles Collection, Beinecke.

13. See "Centinel" I, II, XII, XVI, XVII, XVIII and Alison, "Untitled Manuscript," PHS.

14. "Centinel" V, IX.

15. "Centinel" I, II, III, IV, V, X.

16. "Centinel" III.

17. "Centinel" I, III, IV, V, IX, XVII.

18. Alison to Stiles, December 4, 1766, October 20, 1768, Stiles Collection, Beinecke; see especially "Centinel" XI but also IX, XII, XVIII.

19. "Centinel" VI.

20. "Centinel" XI, XII.

21. Especially "Centinel" XVI.

22. "Centinel" IV, IX.

23. "Centinel" X, XI, XII.

24. Especially "Centinel" VIII.

25. Especially "Centinel" XIV.

26. "Centinel" XVIII. See also XII, XVII.

27. "Centinel" XVI.

28. "Centinel" VIII.

4 AN APPEAL TO THE COLONY

1. Works that deal with Pennsylvania politics during this period include William S. Hanna, *Benjamin Franklin and Pennsylvanian Politics* (Stanford: Stanford University Press, 1964); James H. Hutson, *Pennsylvania Politics, 1746–1770* (Princeton, N.J.: Princeton University Press, 1972); Benjamin H. Newcomb, *Franklin and Galloway: A Political Partnership* (New Haven: Yale University Press, 1972); Theodore Thayer, *Pennsylvania Politics and the Growth of Democracy, 1740–1776* (Harrisburg: Pennsylvania Historical and Museum Commission, 1953).

2. Daniel Dulany, "Military and Political Affairs in the Middle Colonies in 1755," *Pennsylvania Magazine of History and Biography*, 3: (1879): 24.

3. Isaac Norris, Jr., to Charles Robert, April 28, 1755, Norris Papers, Isaac Norris, Jr., Letterbook, 1719–1756, HSP; James Pemberton to John Fothergill, March 7, 1764, Pemberton Papers, Copies, 1740–1780, pp. 236–43, HSP.

4. Benjamin Franklin to Jared Eliot, September 1, 1755, Labaree, *Franklin Papers*, 6: 176. See also Labaree, *Franklin Papers*, 16: 125, footnote.

5. [Isaac Hunt], "A Looking Glass for Presbyterians, Number II," John Dunbar, ed., *The Paxton Papers* (The Hague: Martinus Nijoff, 1957), p. 311.

6. "Minutes of the Corporation for the Relief of Poor Ministers . . . . ," vol. 1, July 14, 1762, December 16, 1767, PHS.

7. This was recognized by Quaker leaders. See James Pemberton to John Fothergill, March 7, 1764, Pemberton Papers, Copies, 1740–1780, pp. 236–43, HSP.

8. Isaac Norris, Jr., to Benjamin Franklin, February 21, 1758, Norris Papers, Isaac Norris, Jr., Letterbook, 1756–1766, HSP.

9. Richard Smith, Jr., to John Smith, September 23, 1748, Smith Papers, vol. 3, Library Company of Philadelphia.

10. Benjamin Franklin to Joseph Galloway, April 7, 1759, Benjamin Franklin to Ebenezer Kinnersley, July 28, 1759, Labaree, *Franklin Papers*, 7: 311, 8: 415; Melvin Buxbaum, "Benjamin Franklin and William Smith: Their School and Their Dispute," *Historical Magazine of the Protestant Episcopal Church*, 34 (Dec., 1970), 361–383.

11. James Pemberton to John Fothergill, March 7, 1764, James Pemberton to Samuel Fothergill, June 13, 1764, Pemberton Papers, Copies, 1740–1780, pp. 236–43, 230, HSP. For a good collection of the literature of the crisis of 1764–65, see Dunbar, *Paxton*.

12. Alison to Stiles, April 15, 1764, Stiles Collection, Beinecke.

13. "Copy of a Circular Letter from Gilbert Tennent, Francis Alison and John Ewing to Stephen Collins, March 30, 1764," "Documents Relating to the Province of Pennsylvania and to the American Revolution," p. 26, American Philosophical Society.

14. Hutson, *Politics*, pp. 156–57, 166–67.

15. Alison to Stiles, April 15, 1764, Stiles Collection, Beinecke.

16. "The Circular Letter and Articles of 'some Gentlemen of the Presbyterian Denomination' in the Province of Pennsylvania, March 24, 1764" as reprinted in *Pennsylvania Chronicle*, September 18, 1769; James Pemberton to John Fothergill, December 18, 1765, Pemberton Papers, Copies, 1740–1780, pp. 250–53, HSP.

17. Dunbar, *Paxton*, p. 350.

18. William Allen to Thomas Penn, October 21, 1764, Penn Papers, Official Correspondence, 9: 282, HSP. For a similar analysis, see Mr. Petit to Mr. Reed, November 3, 1764, William Read, *Life and Correspondence of President Reed* (2 vols., Philadelphia: Lindsay and Blakiston, 1847), 1: 36; Henry M. Muhlenberg, *The Journals of Henry Melchior Muhlenberg*, trans. Theodore G. Tappert and John W. Doberstein (3 vols, Philadelphia: The Muhlenberg Press, 1945), 2: 123.

19. Hutson, *Politics*, pp. 156–57, 166–67; Newcomb, *Partnership*, pp. 88–89; Isaac Norris, Jr., to Charles Robert, October 27, 1764, Norris Papers, Isaac Norris, Jr., Letterbook, 1756–1766, HSP.

20. James Pemberton to John Fothergill, March 7, November 6, 1764, December 18, 1765, Pemberton Papers, Copies, 1740–1780, pp. 236–43, 230, 250–53, HSP.

21. James Pemberton to Samuel Fothergill, June 13, 1764, Pemberton Papers, Copies, 1740–1780, p. 230, HSP.

22. James Pemberton to Samuel Fothergill, June 13, 1764, Pemberton Papers, Copies, 1740–1780, p. 230; Israel Pemberton to David Barclay, Sr., November 6, 1764, Pemberton Papers, Copies, 1752–1775, pp. 243–47, HSP.

23. John Reynell to Mildred and Robert, November 23, 1764, June 17, 1765, Coates-Reynell Collection, John Reynell Letterbook, 1762–1767, HSP. See also James Logan to John Smith, July 27, 1764, John Smith Papers, Library Company; Isaac Norris to Charles Robert, October 27, 1764, Norris Papers, Isaac Norris, Jr., Letterbook, 1756–1766; James Pemberton to John Fothergill, March 7, September 3, October 11, October 21, 1764, Pemberton Papers, Copies, 1740–1780, pp. 230, 236–43, 245–47, 278; James Pemberton to John Fothergill, March 1, 1766, Israel Pemberton to David Barclay, Sr., November 6, 1764, Pemberton Papers, Copies, 1752–1775, pp. 243–47, 259–62, HSP; Labaree, *Franklin Papers*, 11: 409; Hutson, *Politics*, p. 180.

24. Thomas Penn to John Penn, December 14, 1765, Penn Papers, Thomas Penn Letter Book, 8: 329–30, HSP.

25. Thomas Penn to John Penn, November 30, 1765, Penn Papers, Thomas Penn Letter Book, 8: 326, HSP.

26. Samuel Purviance to Ezra Stiles, November 1, 1766, Stiles Collection, Beinecke; James Pemberton to John Fothergll, October 11, 1766, Pemberton Papers, Copies, 1752–1775, pp. 280–83, HSP.

27. "Humphrey Scourge," *Pa. Journal*, March 25, 1756; John Read to Benjamin Franklin, June 17, 1766, Labaree, *Franklin Papers*, 13: 320; William Gordon to Charles Beatty, January 14, 1764, Charles Beatty Folder, PHS; Samuel Johnson to Thomas Secker, April 10, 1762, Schneider, *Johnson*, 1: 320–21; Thomas Penn to William Allen, May 19, 1767, Penn Papers, Thomas Penn Letter Book, 9: 114; William Allen to Thomas Penn, November 19, 1766. Penn Papers, Official Correspondence, 10: 70, HSP.

28. Samuel Purviance to Ezra Stiles, November 1, 1766, Stiles Collection, Beinecke; William Allen to Thomas Penn, November 19, 1766, Penn Papers, Official Correspondence, 10: 70, HSP; Thomas Wharton to Benjamin Franklin, November 17, 1767, Labaree, *Franklin Papers*, 14: 138.

29. William Logan to Samuel Coates, January 24, 1767, Coates-Reynell Collection, Samuel Coates Letterbook, 1763–1781, HSP.

30. James Pemberton to John Fothergill, October 11, 1766, Pemberton Papers, Copies, 1752–1775, pp. 280–83, HSP.

31. William White to James Wilson, November 27, 1768, Simon Gratz Collection, Episcopal Bishops of the United States, Box 35, Case 8, HSP; Thomas Coombe, Jr., to Thomas Coombe, Sr., December 6, 1769, Thomas Coombe Papers, Correspondence and Business, HSP.

32. William Smith to the Bishop of London, April 17, 1764, Smith, *Smith*, 1: 348; William Smith to Bishop Terrick, September 26, 1764, Manross, *Fulham Papers*, p. 114.

33. Hugh Neill to Sec. of SPG, October 18, 1764, Perry, *Penn.*, pp. 364–66; T. B. Chandler to S. Johnson, October 19, 1766, January 19, March 31, 1767, Schneider, *Johnson*, 1: 369–70, 391, 395; William Smith to the Bishop of London, November 13, 1766, May 6, 1768, William Smith to the Sec. of SPG, October 22, 1768, Perry, *Penn.*, 429, 434–35.

34. T. B. Chandler to S. Johnson, April 7, 1768, S. Johnson to Thomas Secker, May 10, 1768, Schneider, *Johnson*, 1: 437, 439. That Philadelphians were quite capable of such a literary style can be seen by perusing the collection of essays in Dunbar, *Paxton*, or by reviewing the *Pennsylvania Chronicle*, the *Pennsylvania Journal* or the *Pennsylvania Gazette* during this period.

35. *Pa. Chronicle*, April 4, 18, 1768; "Anatomist" I, *Pa. Journal*, September 8, 1768.

36. See "Centinel" XX, XXI.

37. "Centinel" IV, V; "Remonstrant" II, III. The fact that of all the barbs and arguments which the "Anatomist" aimed at the "Centinel," Alison selected those pertaining to Quakers for extensive rebuttal in his "Remonstrant" gives some indication of the importance which he attached to this segment of his audience.

38. "Remonstrant" II, III; "Centinel" VIII.

39. "Centinel" XIII.

40. Thomas Barton to Secretary Burton, November 16, 1764, "Society for the Propagation of the Gospel in Foreign Parts," notes, copies at HSP.

41. Francis Alison to James Wilson (?), Simon Gratz Collection, University and College Presidents, Box 11, Case 7; William White to James Wilson, November 27, 1768, Simon Gratz Collection, Episcopal Bishops of the United States, Box 35, Case 8, HSP.

42. Charles Chauncy reporting the opinion of Samuel Purviance to Ezra Stiles, August 15, 1768, Stiles Collection, Beinecke.

43. William Smith to Bishop of London, May 6, 1768, Hugh Neill to Secretary of SPG, October 18, 1764, Perry, *Penn.*, pp. 429, 364; William Smith to Bishop of London, November 13, 1766, Smith, *Smith*, 1: 401.

44. T. B. Chandler to S. Johnson, October 19, 1766, March 31, 1767, January 22, 1768, Schneider, *Johnson*, 1: 369–70, 395, 433.

45. William Smith to Sec. of SPG, October 22, 1768, Perry, *Penn.*, pp. 434–35.

46. T. B. Chandler to S. Johnson, April 7, 1768, Schneider, *Johnson*, 1: 437. See the letter in Evans, 10947.

47. T. B. Chandler to S. Johnson, April 7, 1768, Schneider, *Johnson*, 1: 437.

48. T. B. Chandler to S. Johnson, July 7, 1768, Schneider, *Johnson*, 1: 443. See also, T. B. Chandler to S. Johnson, April 7, September 9, 1768, Schneider, *Johnson* 1: 430, 447.

49. (New York, 1769), Evans, 11203; T. B. Chandler to Samuel Johnson, April 7, July 7, September 9, 1768, Schneider, *Johnson*, 1: 437–38, 443–44, 447.

50. W. Smith to Sec. of SPG, October 22, 1768, Perry, *Penn.*, p. 434.

51. "Anatomist" I, *Pa. Journal*, September 8, 1768. See also "Anatomist" VIII, *Pa. Journal*, October 24, 1768.

52. "Anatomist" I, II, III, IV, V, VIII, XVI, XVII in *Pa. Journal*, September 8, 15, 22, 29, October 6, 24, December 22, 28, 1768.

53. "Anatomist" V, XIII, *Pa. Journal*, October 6, December 1, 1768.

54. "Anatomist" II, VII, VIII, *Pa. Journal*, September 5, October 20, 24, 1768.

55. "Anatomist" IX, XI, XII, XIII, XV, *Pa Journal*, November 3, 17, 24, December 1, 15, 1768.

The *Centinel*:

Warnings of a Revolution

Centinel Number I

March 24, 1768

Humano capite cervicem pictor equinam Jungere si velit—ut turpitur atrum Desinat in piscem mulier formosa superne
—Risum teneatis. Hor. Ar. Poet.[1]

Dr. Chandler's *Appeal to the Public in behalf of the Church of England in America,* which from his own Account seems rather to be *the united Effort of all the CLERGY in New-York and New-Jersey,* perfected by the kind Assistance of the CLERGY *from the neighbouring Provinces,* may by this Time be supposed to have circulated pretty generally. And as the Season advances, when we presume the CLERGY are again to meet in voluntary Convention, this may be the proper Time to propose a few Questions for *their* or if the Dr. pleases for *his Consideration.* The Performance seems replete with bold extravagant Assertions of Facts, many of which have no Foundation in Truth; it is greatly deficient in Christian Charity, tho' not deficient in low Craft, and seems dangerous to the Civil and Religious Liberties of the Colonies in America. But I perceive that if any Objections be made to his Plan, our new Doctor from a Persuasion already formed, is prepared to ascribe them, rather to "*the Dexterity and ill Will of the Inventors than*" to "*the real Fears and Uneasiness of the Inhabitants.*" (P. 112) Nay he is so bold, as to assert that "every Opposition to such a Plan" as he has proposed, "has the Nature of Persecution and deserves the Name." (82) Again he says, "if no Objections shall be offered, it will be taken for granted that all Parties acquiesce and are satisfied." (2) Thus on the one Hand, Silence is to be construed into Assent and Approbation, and on the other Hand, if we object to, or oppose his Plan, we are to be stigmatized as Persecutors and the worse of Mankind. However as he seems to admit a Possibility, that some "Objections may continue, which may be thought to deserve Notice" and is pleased to erect an imaginary Tribunal, and to invite the Objectors "to propose them that they may be debated before that Tribunal," it seems hard to oblige those, who cannot altogether approve his Plan, to yield the cause untried, or to bear the names of "malicious," "intolerant," "Persecutors," "Enemies to all Religion" and the Church, "hot headed Writers," "pragmatical Enthusiasts," &c. even to have their Loyalty called in Question.

I must confess there are some Objections to his Plan that "continue" with me, and which, to as many as I have mentioned them, seem to "deserve Notice" but before I propose them to be debated before the "Tribunal of the Public," I should be glad if the Doctor would deign to explain some of his Terms, and give us farther Information on some Points, that I shall propose.

He begins with informing us "that application has been made to our SUPERIORS, by the Clergy of several of the Colonies, requesting one or more Bishops to be sent to America," he complains of "unprecedented Hardships," and "intollerable Grievances," suffered by the "Church," the "American Church," the "Church of England in America" for Want of "an American Episcopate" and upon this founds his Appeal to the Public.

We should be obliged to the Doctor if he would inform us in plain terms, who are these *Superiors*, to whom the *Clergy* have applied; by whom these Bishops are to be sent, by what Authority this American Episcopate is to be established, or who are the Authors of these *intolerable Grievances* and *unprecedented Hardships*, that we may the better judge, whether the Apprehensions on Account of our civil Liberties, which this avowed Application has raised in the minds of many people, be well or ill founded. As he has appealed to the Public, would it not be proper for him to inform us, against whom he appeals? Whether against the King, his Ministers and the British Parliament, for not redressing those Grievances of which he complains, and for not establishing Episcopacy in America, as he seems to think they ought to have done? Or whether the Appeal is more against those, who, thro' Fear of an Invasion and Infringement of their civil and religious Liberties, think it their Duty to oppose such an Establishment? If against the former, the Court must indeed be august and respectable, which he has constituted to take cognizance of our Sovereign and the British Parliament. If against the latter, as by the Rules of all well established Courts, both Plaintiffs and Defendants are excluded from judging in their own Cause, I fancy there will be few in America to sit in Judgement. For let the Doctor flatter as much as he pleases, if ever the Attempt be made, he will find that the

Prejudices and Objections of most of our Colonies are too deeply rooted and too well founded, for them ever to submit quietly to an American Episcopate, established over them even by Act of Parliament; this would be to destroy their Charters, Laws and their very Constitutions and it will be well if the Doctor and his Associates are not considered as abettors of Mr. Greenville and those Enemies of America, who are exerting their utmost Endeavours to strip us of our most sacred, invaluable and inherent Rights; to reduce us to the State of Slaves; and to tax us by Laws, to which we never have assented, nor can assent.

We would also ask the Doctor, why is the Application made for a Bishop at this particular Time when the Liberties of America are at Stake? Why are some insinuations against their Loyalty thrown out against his American Brethren? For what are the tendency of his political Reasons, but to inflame the jealousy of the people of Great-Britain? Can there be no Bishops without Establishments; no Ordination without Act of Parliament? Must this be a new and a primitive, or a part of the English Episcopate.

The Claims of the Doctor, without an Establishment, notwithstanding all his seeming Modesty and Candour, are too great, not to awaken jealousies in the minds of free born Americans, if none had been conceived there before.

The "Church," the "American Church," "the Church of England in America," are the names which he affects to distinguish that denomination of Christians, to which he belongs. I wish the Doctor would please to define his terms, and tell us what he means, by Church, and why that name should be applied to English Episcopalians only. Are not the Lutheran & Calvinist Churches; are not the Congregational, Consociated and Presbyterian Churches; are not the Baptist, the Quaker and all other Churches in America, of what Denomination soever they be, Members of Christ's Catholic Church, if they profess Faith in Christ and hold the great Essentials of Christianity? Or does he mean to lay such a Stress on the unbroken Succession, and on Episcopacy as by Law established in England, as to make these essential to the being of a Church. His Words indeed seem to import as much, where he says, "Men may ridicule the Notion of uninterrupted Succession as they please", but "if the Succession be once broken and the Powers of Ordination once lost, not all the Men on Earth, not all the Angels of Heaven, without an immediate Commission from Christ, can restore it. It is as great an Absurdity for a man to preach without being properly sent as it is to hear without a Preacher, or to believe in him of whom they have never heard." This may be the Doctor's private Opinion borrowed from the Non-jurors and other Disturbers of the Church and State during the Reigns of King William, Queen Ann and King George the first, but surely it is not the Doctrine of the Church of England: it has long since been disclaimed by some of its greatest Doctors and ablest Divines. However, I should be glad if the Doctor would explain himself further, and try to reconcile these high Notions with Christian Charity, and with the Validity of Ordination in the foreign protestant Churches, or of those who make no pretenses to an unbroken Succession. The Candor of his Sentiments and (if we may believe him) of the Doctrine and Belief of the Church of England, with regard to the Government of those Churches in America, which are not Episcopal is worthy of Notice. "If," says he, "according to the Doctrine and Belief of the Church of England, none have a Right to govern the Church but Bishops, then the American Church must be without Government." (27) But least we may have misunderstood him, we desire he may tell us, whether he means that the Episcopal Christians are the only Church in America, and consequently excludes all other Churches who want Bishops, from being Members of the American Church; or whether he would assert that all others are without Order and Government for want of Bishops and therefore undeserving the Name of Churches.

The "Church of England in America," which he often repeats, is a new Expression unwarranted by Scripture, not known in Law, and hardly intelligible in Language, and therefore wants Explanation. We read in Scripture of the Church of Antioch, of Corinth and of Rome; and of the Churches in Asia and Judea; but we nowhere read of the Church of Jerusalem in Rome, or of the Church of Judea in Europe or Asia; in like manner, we hear of the Church of England, the Church of Ireland, and the Church of Scotland; but the Church of England in America is a new Mode of Expression: Yet by this new fangled Term, the Doctor and other Missionaries affect to distinguish themselves and their Followers, while with an air of Arrogance and Superciliousness, they call other Denominations of Christians, Dissenters.

We apprehend this is not a meer Impropriety of Speech adopted by a Man who seems not to be one of the most correct Writers, but a Phrase artfully introduced with a sinister Design.

The Doctor cannot have read so little either of Civil or Ecclesiastical History, or be so very little acquainted with Mankind as not to know the Magic of Words, and the blind Devotion paid to Names and Sounds. The Words *Pope* and *Priest* carry great Reverence with them in some Countries and terrible Confusions and Animosities have been raised in other Countries by the Words *Church, Clergy, Divine Right, Uninterrupted Succession, Indelible Character* and such like undefined Nonsense; we hope the like Game will never be played in America.

The "National Religion" is another Phrase of the Doctor, wherewith he Graces the peculiar Tenets of his Church; with what View he uses it, we may easily guess from the Privileges he has annexed to it, and the Doctrine he teaches and confirms with an "indeed" concerning it. Those, says he, "who dissent from the *National Religion*, have, *indeed*, no Natural Right to any Degree of Civil or Military Power." (109) As the Doctor in another place declares, that "nothing has been asserted in the course of his Work, but what the Author believes, upon good Evidence, to be true," we hope he will produce his Evidence to prove this Doctrine, which sounds strange in an American Ear. In the mean time, we would ask him, why might not Christianity have been allowed the Honor of being called the National Religion? Or why is Episcopacy alone honored with that name? Is it because it is established by Law in England? Is not Presbyterianism also established by Law and was it not established in 1707 a more enlightened Age, surely than that in which Episcopacy was established at the Reformation?[2] If the one is a National Church, because established in England, why not the other, because established in Scotland? But what is this to us in America? Because these Forms are established in Great-Britain, must they also be established here? Many Thousands fled to the Wilds of America from Episcopal Tyranny and Persecution and to enjoy the free exercise of Religion in a way most agreeable to their Consciences, (and as they conceived) to Scripture and Reason; established Colonies, formed Governments, framed Laws and founded Churches; and must all these be termed Dissenters, because the Doctor and they differ? Or have they "no Natural Right to any degree of Civil and Military Power," because they are not of the National Religion, that is, if we believe the Doctor, the Religion which he and "the Clergy of the several Colonies (meaning the Missionaries) profess?"

It is not doubted but every Man who wishes to be Free will by all lawful ways in his Power oppose the Establishment of any one Denomination in America, the preventing of which is the only means of securing their Natural Rights to all those at least who may differ from that Denomination. The Doctor seems sensible that the Opposition to these Lordly Prelates will not wholly rest with those whom *he* terms Dissenters, that their Encroachments in civil Matters are disagreeable to very many who admit their Authority in the Church; he therefore solemnly assures us that "the Bishops" he desires, "shall not interfere with the Property or Privileges, whether Civil or Religious of *Churchmen* or *Dissenters*"—"that they shall only ordain and govern the Clergy and administer Confirmation to those who shall desire it." But when he comes to explain himself further, he cautiously intersperses the Words, at "Present," "Now" and such qualifying Expressions as leave the Bishops when once established a full Liberty to revive every Claim and Privilege they have ever made or enjoyed. Even with regard to Tithes (105) while he is obviating Objections that might be raised on account of them, he expresses himself with such cautious Ambiguity, as to leave it doubtful whether he does not mean that a Bishop established in America may claim and recover them by the Laws of England. Nay such Ideas of Grandeur and Magnificence has the Doctor united with the word *Bishop*, that while he is pleading for such as he calls Primitive Bishops, he hints at Lordly Revenues; he lets us know a Committee was extraordinarily appointed to find out Ways and Means for the Maintenance and Support of Bishops in America; (49) that "a Fund has been established for that particular purpose for more than half a Century past;" "that many Thousand Pounds have been contributed to increase the Fund." (108) But, "if this Stock is not sufficient for the support of a proper Episcopate in America," "should a general Tax be laid on the Country and thereby a Sum raised sufficient for the purpose" "this would be no mighty hardship on the Country" and he who would think much of paying it, "deserves not to be considered in the light of a good Subject." (107) That hereafter they may be invested with some degree of Civil Power worthy of their acceptance. (110) In short hints, that Legislative and Executive Powers may both be placed in their Hands. (ibidem) And with all these Princely Revenues, with all this accession of Power, what are they to do? Only to ordain and govern the Clergy? No: They are "TO DEFEND AND PROTECT both the Clergy and Laity." These things are so unlike the Appearance of a Primitive Bishop, that we must say that though "at present" we hear the Voice of Jacob, we see and may "hereafter" feel the rough and hairy Hands of Esau.

One thing more I would beg to know from the Doctor; what Assurances (besides his own, which are too weak to be relied on in so momentous an Affair) are we to have that Bishops will be sent over with such limited Powers? Attempts are made upon

American Liberty from a quarter, where it ought not to be expected. A temper is shewn by some leading Prelates even now in England, that will not suffer us to place a Confidence in them. One of them at the head of the Society for Propagating the Gospel was not ashamed to oppose a Plan for the Conversion of the Indians, because concerted by a Denomination of Christians who "followed not with him." Another of them lately attended the Board of Trade to prevent the Grant of a Charter to the Presbyterian Church in New-York.[3]

But suppose these Bishops are sent over with these limited Powers, is there any probability they will be content with them? Can we suppose that the Clergy of a Society, which thinks itself peculiarly entitled to National Favour, and asserts itself to be so essentially connected with the State, will, if once established ever give Ease or Peace to other Churches in America, whom they now treat as Dissenters until they have a plenary Possession of every Privilege enjoyed by the Church in England by Law established? With Bishops as their Head, will not the cry be as loud, if they have not Ecclesiastical Courts, for Discipline and to harrass their Neighbours? A Bishop without a Court, is as unparalleled as any hardship complained of? Again must not the *Clergy* have a Maintenance? The Society for Propagating the Gospel is not able to provide for all that may be ordained; the Episcopal Congregations cannot maintain them; must they then starve in America? Where in England they have a legal right to the Tithes? Will not the cry at last be, nay does not the Doctor almost make it already, that they alone have a right to all places of Power and Profit in the Colonies as well as in England and Ireland, because the most friendly to Monarchy?

We hope the Doctor will Explain himself fully, and resolve the Doubts and Queries we have here proposed. On some other occasion we may enter the Lists and examine his Divine Right of Diocesan Episcopacy; his unbroken Succession; the Connection between natural Rights, and a national Religion; his Doctrine of Tithes; the Numbers of his Denomination and their unparalleled Sufferings in America, &c. &c.—*N.*

NOTES: "CENTINEL" I

1. The whole excerpt reads: "If to a human head a painter should wish to join a horse's neck, and to the trunk join limbs of diverse creatures, and deck these limbs with variegated

plumes—so the woman fair at top terminates below in an ugly dark-skinned fish; when brought to gaze, O friends, could you suppress a laugh?

Horace *Ars Poetica*, 11. 1–3, 5.

2. The Anglican or Episcopal church was established in England in the Reformation legislation passed in 1534. The Act of Union, passed by the English and Scottish Parliaments in 1707, formalized the action of the Scottish Parliament in 1690 by providing that the "Act for securing the protestant religion and presbyterian church government with the establishment in the said Act contained" so to be a "fundamental condition of the union" and is "to continue in all time coming." G. N. Clark, *The Later Stuarts, 1660–1714* (Oxford: Clarendon Press, 1934), p. 279.

3. In 1763, after the end of the French and Indian War, the General Court of Massachusetts chartered "The Society for Propagating Christian Knowledge Among the Indians of North America" to offset perceived gains made by the Catholic Church among the Indians. When the charter went to England, Anglicans there successfully fought to prevent royal approval. Sir William Johnson, Commissary for Indian Affairs, opposed the Society because it was not under Anglican control. Johnson later became a member of the S.P.G., in 1766. Carl Bridenbaugh, *Mitre and Sceptre* (New York: Oxford University Press, 1962), pp. 209–211.

Presbyterians had formed a church in New York city in 1716 and applied repeatedly for a royal charter of incorporation. It was always denied. To secure some legal status, the institution finally had to vest title to its property in the Church of Scotland. Richard Webster, *History of the Presbyterian Church in America* (Philadelphia: J. M. Wilson, 1857), pp. 328–29.

Centinel Number II

March 31, 1768

Aude alliquid brevibus Gyaris & carcere dignum,
Si vis esse aliquis——— *Juvenal*[1]

In my last Paper I took Notice of some of the favorite cant Words in Dr. Chandler's Appeal, &c. which he has used to amuse and impose on the Public; the common Practice of designing Men, who want to raise Disturbances in Church or State. Such kind of Words they usually throw out to catch the unwary; the more undefined and the less understood, so much the better. *Great* is Diana of the Ephesians, was the Watch-Word given, when Demetrius and his Fellow-Craftsmen threw the whole City of Ephesus into an uproar. Demetrius honestly told his Fellow-Tradesmen, that by the Preaching of St. Paul their Craft, and consequently their Wealth, was in Danger.[2] Whatever weight this Argument might have with them, he knew it would not have the same with the Populace; therefore it was necessary to tell them that the Temple of the Great Goddess Diana and her Image, were in danger of being despised. This was sufficient to alarm the People; and to raise their Spirits and inflame their Passions, the Cry was put into their Mouths: Great is Diana of the Ephesians, High-Church forever. It requires but very little reading to know how often and how successfully the same Art has been practised since. The *Church*, the Church is in danger, was a notable Cry, at a never to be forgotten Period of the English History, when the very Persons who raised it and kept it up, were labouring to introduce Popery, the Pretender, and arbitrary Power; and had not God in Providence blasted their wicked Designs, and opened the Way for the Accession of the present Royal Family, before they had brought their schemes to bear, the Consequences might have been ruinous to the Nation.[3]

The People had been taught from their Infancy to revere the Church without knowing what it meant; they were told by their spiritual Guides that it was in danger, without being informed from whence the Danger arose. Thus their Fears were awakened, their Passions inflamed and directed against the Friends of Liberty, Religion, and their Country. In short such Men as Tillotson, Tenisson, Hoadly, Burnet, the shining Lights and greatest Ornaments of their own Church, were vilely misrepresented as Betrayers of the same.[4]

Let us now see in what Manner Dr. Chandler endeavours to raise a Clamour in America. Throughout his whole Appeal, he takes it for granted that the Episcopalians are the *American Church*, and that his Associates the Missionaries are the *Clergy;* all other Denominations of Christians he treats as Dissenters, Schismatics, and Sectaries; and to their Pastors and public Teachers he hardly deigns to allow the Name of Ministers; "*Their Ordination*, he says, is *at least irregular and defective*, but in his Judgment, null and void, and of Consequence they are no Ministers of Christ; for says he it is as great an absurdity to preach without being *properly* sent, as to believe in him of whom they have never heard.—The Cry is then raised the American Church is in Danger, its Sufferings are unparalleled, it is perishing for want of common Necessaries, (59) its Oppression is such as to deserve the Compassion of the whole Christian World, (114). it is ready to expire, and nothing but its Ruin is forseen, unless Bishops be sent speedily." (113)

The *Clergy*, a Word of deep import, and used to Purpose in sounding the Trumpet of Sedition; the Clergy of several Colonies have taken the Alarm, and applied to our "Superiors for Aid and Assistance in this dangerous Crisis!" Who these *Superiors* are, he does not tell us, but doubtless they are the same on whom he calls for the Establishment of Episcopacy, namely the *British Nation* (87) *and the Guardians of its Interests,* (114) *those who are intwined with the Interests of the Nation, &c* (113) in short, notwithstanding the Doctor's studied Ambiguity, his Application must be ultimately intended for the Parliament of Great-Britain: And to rouse the Passions of the British Nation, and inflame their Jealousy, already too much raised by the Enemies of America, he strongly insinuates, that the State is not safe unless Episcopacy be established in America; and attempts to raise Suspicions of Disloyalty against all other Denominations of Christians. "*No Trumpet of Sedition,*" says he, "was ever heard to sound from *our Pulpits*; no Seeds of Disaffection have been suffered more privately to be shown in *our* Houses."[a] "*Our* Religion is a Security to the Government for our honouring the King, and not mediating with them that are given to change (41),[b] it may be reasonably expected from those in Authority, that they will support and assist the Church in America, if from no other Reason, yet from a *Regard to the State*" (115); nay in another place (113) he asserts, that Monarchy cannot subsist without Episcopacy; so that in his next Appeal we may expect to hear the old Cry "no Bishop no King," revived. But, as if this was not sufficient to alarm the Fears of the Nation, the Doctor endeavours to persuade that his Church is the Church of England by Law established, that they are essentially the same; that both must subsist or perish by the same Means; and that therefore unless Episcopacy is established in America, the Church in the Mother Country will be ruined (113); and to confound the Ideas in the Minds of the Populace, the Term *Church of England in America* is used, just as the Favourers of Popery use the Phrase Church of Rome in England, in Ireland and in France, to give a Colour and lay a Foundation for the Claims and Usurpations of the Pope in those Countries.

Let us now enquire who are the Clergy of the several Colonies, who have made this application. I believe that no Man will suspect that the Ministers of either the Baptist, Congregational, Consociated, Calvinist, Lutheran, Presbyterian, or Quaker Congregations are concerned in such an Application; and if I am well informed (and I believe I am) not one of the Clergy of any Denomination to the Southward of Pennsylvania had any Hand in it. The Missionaries only therefore seem to be the Doctor's Clergy. Though their Knowledge of the civil Rights of Mankind, and profound Erudition may not be disputed, yet their Rank in Life at present is not very high; for this Reason probably the Doctor thought it Necessary, in order to give some weight and importance to the Application to dignify them with the Title of the "Clergy of the several Colonies." By Acts like these Men of low Origin have been exalted into high Stations and thereby enabled to distress persons more worthy than themselves; thus the Cardinals rose to the high Rank they now hold in the Church of Rome.

As these Missionaries assume of late an Air of Importance, I hope I may be indulged while I endeavour to explain their Rise and the Nature of their Mission.

Our Forefathers harrassed by spiritual Courts and the Power of the lordly Prelates (which in Opposition to the Doctor I will venture to assert, and if he pleases, will undertake to prove, has always been *strained too high*, when the times would admit) being likewise denied the Privilege of peaceably worshipping God in a Way the most agreeable to their Consciences, at least wearied out with Persecution, resolved to leave their Native Country, and seek

Shelter in the Wilds of America. The Power of the Church of England by Law established, they imagined was confined to England; and for this Opinion they had Reason, and the Authority of some of the greatest Lawyers; having therefore crossed the Atlantic, they thought themselves secure from the oppressive Tyranny of any proud Ecclasiasticks.

What Hardships they endured in forming their Settlements, are not to be described, hardly to be conceived! However amidst these Distresses their Spirits were supported with the Enjoyment of their civil and religious Liberties, and the Hopes of transmitting them to Posterity.

No sooner was the Country settled, Towns built and Prospects of Peace and Plenty opening to their view, than those Prelates from whose Power and Persecution they had fled, began to envy them their Liberty and to lay Plans and conceit Measures to bring them again under the Yoke of Bondage. To prepare the Way, a Society is formed under the specious Pretence of propagating Christianity in foreign Parts; a Fund is established for defraying the Expences, and pious well disposed Persons are desired to contribute to this Fund.

For every proposal, there may be assigned a specious Reason and a true Reason; the specious Reason here alledged was the Conversion of the Indians in America; this being cried up, captivated many and procured large Donations from People of all Denominations. The true but latent Reason, as it seems, was to prepare the Way for Episcopal Dominion; Hence it came to pass that tho' many Missionaries were sent to America, with Salaries paid them out of the Money subscribed for converting Heathens to Christianity, not more than two or three (just enough to take of and keep up the Pretence) were ever sent among the Indians, the rest were chiefly employed in New-England, New-York, New-Jersey and Pennsylvania, and settled in the Cities and larger Towns and Villages, in which the regular public Worship of God had been long before duly kept up and a Ministry maintained.[c] These Missionaries to magnify their Office and shew the Success of their Mission transmit regularity to the Society, Journals of their Proceedings stuffed with Accounts of the Conversion of Quakers, Baptists, Presbyterians, &c. not to *Christianity*, but to Episcopacy. This calls to my Mind the Bishop of St. Asaph's Sermon before the Society who, speaking of the Popish Missionaries, says, "Their Missions do not seem to be managed with an *Apostolical Simplicity*. They settle Themselves in Nations that are Christians already and have been so from the Beginning; and under the Pretence of converting the Infidels that are among them, their chief Business seems to be to pervert Christians from their *ancient Faith*; and to draw them over to a Subjection to the *Pope*; the Want of which Subjection, they think the greatest Error they find among them, and which they zealously endeavour to eradicate, whilst the Infidels are very sparingly (if ever) applied to by them"—How applicable is this to the Conduct of the Society. Mutato Nomine de te Fabula narratur.[6]

In the latter End of Queen Ann's Reign a violent Push was made to establish Episcopacy in America by Act of Parliament, and to get Bishops sent over whose Power and Authority might influence or overawe the People there and prepare them for what was meditating in England; these Bishops were to have Power "to protect and defend both Clergy and Laity." (50) The Demise of the Queen and the Accession of the Hanover Family blasted their Hopes, whereupon the American Episcopate was dropt; and the Colonies left to the Enjoyment of their civil and religious Privileges, till this Time of Danger and Distress, which these restless ambitious men have again seized as their most favorable Opportunity.— Notwithstanding this Disappointment the Missionaries have been kept up, and their Numbers enlarged to the utmost Ability of the Society; but of late they have considerably diminished their Salaries. Whether this arises from a Failure in their Funds, occasioned by some Attempts that have been made to explain the Manner in which the Society have perverted the Design of their Institution and misapplied the Monies committed to their Care or whether it arises from the exaggerated Accounts sent over by the Missionaries of the Numbers by them converted, (who if the Case had been so would undoubtedly have been able to have supported their Ministers as is done by the People of all other Denominations;) or from whatever Cause it proceeds, such is the disagreeable Situation of their Affairs; and this seems greatly to alarm the Missionaries and make them struggle hard for a Maintenance from other Societies. For notwithstanding (if the Doctor is to be believed) there are a Million of Souls belonging to their Church, yet he confesses "that they have no Prospect but must still depend in a great Measure upon the Charity of their Benefactors, until God shall either enable or dispose their Friends in this Country to do more for them." (107) With Bishops at their Head, their Forces will be better united and their Attempts to have this "*more*" done for them, will probably be attended with greater Success: then to be sure will be the Time to try for a general Tax for the Support of the Bishops and Clergy, which last "now depend on the Charity of their Benefactors at Home," and should they be able to carry their Point and "a general

Tax be laid on the Country, and thereby a sum raised sufficient for the Purpose" the Doctor peremptorily declares "that he that could think much to say it deserves not to be considered in the Light of a good Subject or Member of Society." (108) This he modestly demands only for the Bishops at present, but leaves Room to think he desires to have the Missionaries included, as he has the remarkable Expression, *for any Use*. I dare say if the Doctor should live to see that Time, he would have no Scruple to excommunicate such a Person, as his Predecessors in the *unbroken Line* have frequently done in like Cases.

The Doctor seems sensible that the present Crisis of public Affairs is favourable when a powerful Party at Home is formed against America, and therefore he presses the Establishment of an American Episcopate with all *possible Speed*; and no Doubt it is to encourage the Attempt that he exaggerates the Numbers of his Party and would persuade his Superiors in England, that it is desired by near a million in America, a Deception so barefaced, that if his Appeal had been designed only for the people of America, it would need no Refutation.—*N*.

INTERNAL NOTES: "CENTINEL" II

[a] For fear this should not be applied, the Doctor adds a curious Note in the following Words; "This Accusation is not intended to imply any Accusation of others; who are able, 'tis hoped, to make their own Defence, whenever the Occasion shall require it. His Majesty's American Subjects of all Denominations, belonging to the old Colonies, have always protested sentiments of Loyalty, and the Author believes they have generally been sincere in these Professions, &c."

[b] Notwithstanding the Doctor here insinuates, that passive Obedience and Non-Resistance are the reigning Principles of the American Church, yet to the Honour of the Episcopalians it may be allowed, that they are not of the Doctor's Stamp; But are zealous Friends to Liberty, and have always been, and no doubt are as ready to oppose any Attacks on their own Rights, and those of their Fellow-Subjects, as any Set of Men in America.

[c] The Candid Doctor Bray, the Bishop of London's Commissary in Maryland, just before the Incorporation of the Society (who our Doctor calls the Father of the Society) after having taken great Pains to inform himself, says "that from New-York Northward he found very little need of Missionaries and in the Colonies of Connecticut and the Massachusetts, none at all"—And yet in 1761 there were 30 Salary Men employed by the Society in New-England, 35 in New-York, New-Jersey and Pennsylvania, and only 14 in all the other Continent and Island Colonies, altho' poor blind Heathen Negroes make up the Body of the People in most of these last mentioned.[5]

NOTES: "CENTINEL" II

1. "Dare something big, which merits Chiara or jail or just deserts if you want to be somebody."—Juvenal *Satires* I. 11. 73–74

2. Acts 19:24–41.

3. The Pretender to the English throne was James Francis Edward, the son of James II, Stuart King of England from 1685 to 1688, who had been replaced by William of Orange

in the Glorious Revolution of 1688. Raised in France, and recognized there as James III, he wished to reclaim the English throne after the death of his half sister, Anne (1702–1714). He enlisted aid from the French in an abortive invasion of Scotland in 1708. Englishmen who supported him were often called Jacobins. They opposed the constraints placed on the monarchy by Parliament, objected to the Settlement Act of 1701 which provided for the succession of the Protestant electress of Hanover and her descendants after the death of Anne, and were such high Churchmen that they were accused of plotting to reintroduce the Catholic Church into England.

4. John Tillotson (1630–1694), Archbishop of Canterbury; Thomas Tenison (1695–1716), Archbishop of Canterbury; Benjamin Hoadly (1676–1761), Bishop of Winchester; Gilbert Burnet (1643–1715), Bishop of Salsbury.

5. This quotation comes from Jonathan Mayhew, *Observations on the Charter and Conduct of the Society for the Propagation of the Gospel in Foreign Parts* (Boston, 1764), p. 49, who took it from Noah Hobart, *Second Address to the Ministers of the Episcopal Separation in New-England* (Boston, 1751), p. 126 who cited Thomas Bray, *Life of Dr. Coleman*, p. 142.

6. "With only the name changed, this tale is about you." Horace *Epistles* I. 11. 69–70. The editor is unable to locate the speech by the Bishop of St. Asaph.

Centinel Number III

April 7, 1768

Tantum religio potuit suadere malorum. Lucret.[1]

Having opened the general tendency of Dr. Chandler's Appeal, &c I shall now proceed to make some remarks on the inconveniencies and mischiefs of religious establishments.

The Doctor, as hath been shewn, endeavours to engage "our superiors in England," "the guardians of the national interests" on his side, by endeavouring to make them believe, that without an *Episcopal establishment* here, they must not expect due obedience from the colonies; nay, that the state is not safe. It hath, at all times been the policy of ambitious ecclesiasticks to persuade the civil magistrate, that necessity of state, and even his particular interest required him to interfere in their behalf, and invest them with dignity and power; and that he ought to oblige all persons to Church conformity, and to enforce obedience by civil disabilities and penalties, though such a conduct is obviously an invasion of the rights of mankind, and tends to disturb the public peace, which can only be effectually restored, by removing the iniquitous restraint, which introduced the mischief.[a]

Our blessed Lord was the only lawgiver in his Church. He expressly commands his followers to "call no man father upon earth," and adds, "neither be ye called master, For one is your master, even Christ;" Math. XXIII. 9. 10. words which obviously mean to exclude all religious obedience, or claims to dictate to conscience on the footing of human authority; yet how commonly have Church governors, under all establishments, assumed the place of God, and demanded submission, as sinful as the exercise of the power was unjust and impious. Indeed the Church of Rome, by setting up a pretended *infallibility* have a more specious tho' false pretence to contend for uniformity.

In short, whoever peruses ecclesiastical history, ever since the time of Constantine, will find it contains little else than the follies, absurdities, frauds, rapine, pride, domination, rage, and cruelty of spiritual tyrants; who practised every artifice to persuade, or cajole the temporal rulers to support their measures. They told them that as the Kings of Israel were bound, under that very singular kind of government, a theocracy, to preserve purity in religion, so were Christian Princes obliged, on pain of damnation, to root out error; even by racks and tortures, sword and fire. How ill this horrid doctrine became the followers of the meek and holy Jesus, who refused with indignation to call for divine judgments on the schismatical Samaritans, needs not at this day to be explained. Now the same spirit, which not content with the many thousands already contributed for the establishment of a Bishop, calls for aid from every quarter, even for a tax on all other denominations, in provinces where the Episcopalians are not a fortieth, perhaps not a fiftieth part of the community; the same spirit, which represents the body of the people as disaffected to government and dangerous to the state, and would disable them from holding civil offices; the same spirit that unchurches all their christian neighbours, merely for the want of a particular form of Church government, no ways essential to christianity; and because they make no pretensions to a certain whimsical *uninterrupted succession* of Bishops from the Apostles, which counteracts the principles of the reformation, and can serve only to sanctify the tyranny of their order; this spirit would, beyond a doubt, carry the base of ecclesiastical domination as high as every *Laud* and his brethren did, or as far as Doctor *Sacheverell* contended for, if the civil magistrates could but be deluded once more to lend his aid. Indeed, as a great writer speaks, "it requires an uncommon degree of grace and virture in the clergy, not to abuse so dangerous a power."[3]

Thanks be to our wiser statesmen, of late *spiritual power* has been kept within bounds and Dissenters in England have been suffered to worship God peaceably according to their consciences; and many of the clergy of the establishment, with a truly christian temper, have written and preached in favour of toleration. It is evident, however, that to maintain the toleration, and support the rights of conscience, the government has been careful to promote in the Church men of moderation only, and at the same time, has thought it expedient to prevent the convocation from meeting to do business for fifty years past.[4] They fear there is still enough of the old leaven left, to work up abundance of mischief, whenever times shall permit; and on this account dare not hazard the least alteration in anything established, either as to doctrine, discipline, worship or ceremony, however necessary.

Although the body of the established clergy have taken the liberty of departing from the ancient doctrines, as set forth in the *thirty-nine articles*, yet they are tenacious of the words of their service book, and of every rite, mode and ceremony to the last degree.[5] They would disturb the public peace, and set the populace in an uproar with the old cry, *The Church is in danger*, if an Iota in outward form should be taken away. Rather than suffer ecclesiastical authority to be explained, and regulated on a scriptural footing, they choose to let matters, however repugnant to christianity, continue in their present state; and are deaf to the loud complaints which many good men among themselves, make of the necessity of some alteration. They may write *candid disquisitions*, &c. and shew unanswerably wherein great amendments and improvements ought to be made in the worship of their Church, till they are tired; but the people educated in a narrow attachment to forms, and from their infancy, taught to look on every part of their own, as essential to the true worship of God, are easily led to shut their ears against every proposal of alteration, and to revile the authors as betrayers of religion: an incurable evil this, arising partly from the use of forms, but especially from the rigid manner in which governors in Church and state almost ever since the reformation, have pressed uniformity.

I would not be understood to assert that the principles of the episcopal Churches tend more particularly to these abuses, than those of others; but it is the fault of human nature, which cannot bear great power with equinimity, and perhaps is most apt to abuse it in religious matters. The high rank and large revenues of the Bishops in England must tempt them, however, into this error more easily, than the leaders in Churches, whose influence depends on personal qualifications only.

The Doctor strongly hints the need of an establishment in the colonies for the purposes of discipline, his words are "Churches are set up against Churches, and those who are rejected by one are received by another." (31) This complaint comes somewhat unexpectedly from a missionary of the society: The Doctor would do well to explain the discipline of the rest, by receiving, with open arms, their outcasts or deserters; how many of these are among the missionaries, I leave the Doctor to tell? On this subject I would likewise ask him, how the primitive Churches managed? They had no coercive aid from without, nor did they stand in the least need of any; yet their discipline was rather severe: for if a Church-member had not esteemed it his honour and felicity (next to pleasing God) to stand well with his fellow-christians, his preference in their assemblies would have given them no satisfaction. Far from seeking to enlarge their society by courting the rich and great, or attracting the herd of nominal professors into membership, by winking at their irregularities and vices, they chased out of the Church all backsliders and scandalous persons without reserve. At the same time the terms of communion were as large as the great head of the Church had left them; unembarrassed with the trifling niceties of modern uniformity which by fixing men's zeal on modes, and ceremonies, habits and gestures, has diverted them from the weightier matters of the law, whilst forbearance, charity, and other christian virtues have been neglected and forgotten.

Religious establishments are very hardly kept from great corruption; but if the provision made for the clergy be large, and the leaders are enabled to live in grandeur, it is not likely they should long continue pure. Ambitious worldly-minded men, who seek the fleece, not the well-being of the flock will insinuate themselves into the chief offices; their example and influence will mislead or discourage others, who in better company might have been usefully employed; the industry and vigilance of the spiritual guides in the proper business of their function will be relaxed; and that skill in their profession which practice, study, and attention alone can give, will not be attained. Secure in their salaries, they may look on it as superfluous to be further active, than just to keep up some decent appearance of duty. Thus preacher and people will indolently go to sleep, and forget the important messages and warnings of heaven, which, from the intervention of earthly and present objects, are but too apt to escape our attention, under the most diligent administration of God's world. And should the evil proceed yet further, and the clergy, instead of being "examples to their flock," set before them patterns of *irregular living, open immorality*, and *daring wickedness,* will it not be readily granted that there can be no religion at all among the zealots for an establishment so enormously corrupted; of which yet we want not dreadful instances in church history, as well as our own daily observation.

But still worse than this: there is no probability of religion's being reformed under these ecclesiastical polities. Nothing less than a state convulsion effected the reformation, in most of the countries where it took place. Generally the body of the established clergy, instead of promoting, violently opposed it, by the help of those very emoluments and advantages which had been granted for the support of religion; and in some kingdoms they succeeded: And even since that glorious period, have we not seen the like difficulties stand in the way on every occasion? Bishop Burnet very pleasantly says, in some of his writings, "we acknowledge our church liable to *err* in the general, but when you come to *particulars* we are *always* in the *right*."[6] Under the specious pretence of keeping out dangerous innovations and errors, no mistakes or corruptions, however hurtful or disgraceful, are allowed to be corrected. "One might as well say churches and chappels need no repair, tho' castles and houses do; whereas commonly to speak the truth, dillapidations of the inward and spiritual edifices of the church, are in all times as great as the outward and material."[b] But above all the most dreadful evil is the danger of persecutions; which worldly minded men, to gratify their own pride and lust of power, are forward on proper occasions to practice; and which weak men with better intentions, are too apt to be led into. We too readily think ourselves secure from error, if we have the wise, the powerful, and the many, in our opinions. Those who differ from us we conclude must be obstinate and perverse; and are without much difficulty brought to look on it, as an act of charity as well as duty, to administer some wholesome restraints and severities to such manifest heretics. Thus is the pride of supposed right opinion nourished under establishments, till from one step to another in the practice of hardships on dissenters, we easily proceed to inquisitions, tortures, and death. For if penalties can be justified in religious matters, perhaps the most violent may be the most merciful, as well as effectual. "Imprisonments, fines, and whipping, serve only to irritate the sects, without disabling them from resistance, but the wheel, the gibbet, and the stake must soon root out, or banish, all non-conformists."[c]

Such are some of the mischiefs which spring from the civil powers medling with religion. Beware! O beware then my countrymen, of countenancing this mistake! Your fore-fathers and predecessors fled from the tyranny of religious establishments; and do you resolve "to stand fast in the liberty wherewith Christ hath made you free, and be not entangled again with the yoke of bondage,"[d] let not "cunning crafty men, who lie in wait to deceive,"[e] persuade you there are any other terms of salvation, besides faith and repentance, much less lead you to think modes of discipline are to be accounted essentials. If "all things be done decently and in order" among you, but especially "if they be done to edification," you want neither an *unbroken succession*, nor an *indelible character* in your pastors and teachers. You should have virtue enough to treat them with reverence whilst they deserve it, but so much discretion at the same time, as to keep any order whatever, "from lording it over God's heritage."

Dr. *Warburton*, the present bishop of Gloucester, although strenuous for civil establishments in religion, concedes that no such institution can be useful, unless it includes the major part of the people.[f] On this footing, who with any good face can claim it in Pennsylvania? surely not the missionaries; tho' it is one of the "unparalleled hardships" which the doctor says "demands speedy relief." But this will be more strikingly apparent when the Doctor's monstrous exaggerations of the number of their followers comes to be considered on some future occasion.

INTERNAL NOTES: "CENTINEL" III

[a] "Equality among subjects is the great source of concord." Hume.[2]
[b] Bacon, *on the peace of the church.*[7]
[c] Hume.[8]
[d] Gal. 5:1.[9]
[e] Ephes. 4:14.[10]
[f] See Divine Legat. Vol. 2. And Discourses on principles of nat. and reveal. religion, Vol. 2.[11]

NOTES: "CENTINEL" III

1. "Such evil deeds could religion prompt." Lucretius, *De Rerum Natura*, i. 72
2. The editor is unable to locate the source of this quotation.
3. The editor is unable to identify this "great writer."

William Laud, Archbishop of Canterbury from 1633 until 1641 under Charles I, represented a High Church group who wanted more Roman Catholic tendencies to remain in the Church of England. After filling important secular positions with men of his persuasion, he launched a drive for uniform adherence to Church of England doctrines and practices, thereby incurring opposition from the Puritans. When he extended his activities to Presbyterian Scotland in 1637 by requiring the adoption of a new prayer book modeled on the English Book of Common Prayer, the Scots fought back. To pay for this war, Charles I was forced to reassemble the Parliament in 1640, which demanded reforms and precipitated the Civil War. Laud was executed in 1645.

Dr. Henry Sacheverell became a symbol of High Church interests during the reign of Queen Anne, when he preached a sermon in 1709 against Parliamentary rights acquired from the monarchy in the Glorious Revolution of 1688. His attack and subsequent trial in the House of Lords heightened the conflict between the High Church Tory advisers to Queen Anne and the Whig-dominated Parliament.

4. When the Hanoverian family ascended the English throne it looked to Whigs as its main support. It sought to make the Church of England another safeguard for the Whig system of government by appointing Churchmen of similar principles and political loyalty to bishoprics. These men did not want to stir up dissension by raising religious controversies. Thus, some of the acts against dissenters were either officially relaxed or unofficially ignored. Those High Church bishops appointed by Anne opposed this trend whenever convocations of the clergy were held, so such meetings were not called from 1717 until 1855, with the exception of one attempt made in 1741.

5. The Thirty-nine Articles set forth the doctrines of the Church of England. Henry VIII's Six Articles were increased by Parliament in 1571 on the recommendaton of a convo-

cation of clergy in 1562 and, at the desire of Elizabeth I, were designed to be broad enough to allow various interpretations.

6. The editor is unable to locate the exact quotation in the writings of Gilbert Burnet.

7. Francis Bacon, *Certain Considerations Touching the Better Pacification and Edification of the Church of England, The Works of Francis Bacon*, (4 vols., London, 1740), 4:474. The quotation should read: "[T]hey may as well tell me that churches and chapels need no reparations, though castles and houses do: whereas commonly, to speak truth, delapidations of the inward and spiritual edifications of the church of God are in all times as great as the outward and material."

8. David Hume, *The History of England from the Invasion of Julius Caesar to the Abdication of James the Second*, (6 vols., Boston, 1858), 3:419. The quotation should read, "Imprisonments, fines, confiscations, whippings, serve only to irritate the sects, without disabling them from resistance: but the stake, the wheel, and the gibbet, must soon terminate in the exterpation or banishment of all the heretics inclined to give disturbance, and in the entire silence and submission of the rest."

9. Galations 5:1.

10. Ephesians 4:14.

11. William Warburton, *The Divine Legation of Moses Demonstrated, on the Principles of a Religious Deist*, (3 vols., 9 books, London: 1742), Vol. 2. Warburton, *The Principles of Natural and Revealed Religion*, (2 vols., London, 1753), Vol. 2.

Centinel Number IV

April 14, 1768

Tantane animis caelestibus Ira *Virg.*[1]

As the Proposal of introducing Diocesan Bishops into British America is an Innovation, which would probably affect the religious and civil Liberties of his Majesty's American Subjects, I shall not be terrified from offering my Objections, meerly because Doctor Chandler has been pleased to call it Persecution. (Appeal, Page 82.) The good Gentleman knows that all the Rejecters of Episcopacy have distinguished themselves in the Cause of Liberty, and that their Principles of Church Government are Principles of Freedom. He ought not therefore to think it Persecution, if they, jealous of their liberty, should oppose this dangerous Innovation; the very mention of which recalls to our Minds the unrelenting Rigors of episcopal Tyranny: the heavy Fines, Imprisonments, and Persecutions which peopled the savage Wilds of America; and forced many Thousands of our Forefathers to seek a peaceful Retreat from the Cruelty of their Fellow-Christians, amongst more hospitable Indians. These Refugees have not yet forgot the Groans and Blood of the many Myriads of oppressed Puritans, which cry beneath the Alter "how long O Lord"! The List of sixty thousand Persons that suffered in England on a religious Account, betwixt the Restoration and the Revolution; nor the severe Penalties inflicted on them, for worshipping God according to their Consciences; by which they suffered in their Trade and Estates near two Millions in the Compass of a few Years.[2] These Instances of Episcopal Tyranny, which should fill every Reader with Horror, extort from the Doctor himself, notwithstanding his Fondness for ecclesiastical Power, the modest softened Concession, "that there have been formerly some Instances wherein the Power of our Bishops has been strained too high" P. 91. And lest we should be led to imagine, that he, out of his abundant Charity, had acknowledged too much against his Church, he endeavours to wipe off the Reproach from her, and cast it rather "on the Times, in which neither the natural Rights of Men, nor the religious Rights of Christians, were so well understood, as in the present Age." "For even then," he says, "the Spirit of the Church of England, like that of the Gospel, was more *peaceable, gentle, and easy to be intreated*, than that of any other national Church." This may serve to give us some Idea of the Doctor's comparatively peaceable and gentle Spirit. But I hope we shall have a still more peaceable and gentle Spirit to reign in America: Indeed he labours to persuade us, that when his so much wished for Bishop comes, he will bring it with him, "for the Times" he says, "are much mended in this Respect." P. 90—Excuse us, good Sir, if we think, that however the Spirit of the Times be much mended, the Spirit of your Church, and her Bishops, is not yet so much mended, as to free us entirely from any Fears of Oppression by their extensive Powers.

In considering the peaceable Spirit of the Rulers of the Church of England now, or in some following Paper, I may have Occasion to point out some Things that do not favour much of the Spirit of Moderation and Candour. However I would be understood through the whole, not to intend any Reflection on the Laity of that Communion, nor on all the Clergy. The Moderation of some is well known: they have endeavoured with a truly Christian Spirit, not only to bear a constant Testimony against the numberless Abuses, which have arisen from the Powers of the Clergy, but are endeavouring to bring about a Reformation in many Things, which they candidly acknowledge to stand in need of it. Far be it from me to lay that to the Charge of those Men, which they, as well as we, acknowledge to be unjust and tyrannical. But there are others of a very different Character and Temper, especially among the Clergy, who have been distinguished by the Name of High-Church; and who according to Doctor Chandler, compose the Body of that national Church, who have not as yet Candour enough to admit of such a Reformation. Page 96 and 97.

Although the Wings of these High-flyers have been cropt, and their exorbitant Powers limited in some Degree, by the salutary Restraints of some modern Statutes; yet we know it was much against their Wills, that such merciful Laws were made. They must therefore give the World some more substantial Proofs of their peaceable forebearing Temper, than their Advocate Doctor Chandler's Word, before we can believe that the Spirit of Persecution is not yet alive in that Church, and would not flame out again in all its wonted Rage, if they were but allowed to exercise the Powers they claim.

Until that flagrant Abuse of the Sacrament of the Lord's Supper, occasioned by the TEST Act, shall be removed out of the Churches of England and Ireland, we must believe, good Doctor, that you not only *would* but *do* persecute your Brethren, and cut them off from the natural Rights of serving their King and Country, in all important Places of Power and Trust; unless they can concur with you, not only in what they look on as a superstitious Mode of administering that divine Ordinance; but also in prostituting that sacred Rite to secular, nay to worse than secular Purposes; by making that which was instituted as a Test of our Fidelity to the King of Kings, a Test of our Allegiance to our earthly Sovereign. That this is Persecution, the Doctor himself will help me to prove, Page 82, "To punish us for our religious Principles when no Reasons of State require it, is Persecution in the strictest and properest Sense. Whatever Evil is inflicted on us, on Account of our Principles and Practices, is properly Punishment, and every Good we are deprived of, is equal to an Evil inflicted. As such Treatment has the very Essence of Persecution, so it can have only its Source in an intollerant persecuting Disposition." The sacramental Test is therefore a standing Monument of the persecuting Spirit of the Church of England; even in the Judgement of Doctor Chandler, unless he be hardy enough to attempt assigning Reasons of State to change that "which has the Nature of Persecution, and arises from an intollerant Spirit," into a salutary Regulation. When he produces Arguments to convince Men, who are the least conversant with the Rights of Men or Christians, that it is reasonable and necessary, that so large a Body of his Majesty's Subjects, as the Rejecters of his beloved Hierarchy in England and Ireland, who have always distinguished themselves for their Loyalty and Attachment to the present Royal Family, should have such an unheard of Stigma fixed upon them, that they are deprived of the common Privileges of Subjects; then, and not till then, will the Doctor be able to wipe away the Reproach from his Church. But it is hoped, he will never subject his Knowledge of the Rights of Mankind, nor his own Christianity to the Suspicions which must arise from such an Attempt. The Doctor would indeed in some Places appear charitable enough to allow that they are as loyal and good Subjects, as the Episcopalians themselves are. "There are," says he, "many British Subjects both at Home and in the Plantations, who reject Episcopacy, and yet are warm Advocates for our happy civil Constitution. It is therefore rash and injurious to charge any with disaffection to the Government, at this Day, because they dissent from the national Religion." Page 115. Whether he means that of South or North-Britain, is not distinguished; but it is most likely the former, as very few of his

Brethren, the *Dissenters in Scotland*, are Friends to the present Government.

What Reasons of State can there be alledged, why so many of his Majesty's loyal and faithful Subjects, should be deprived of their natural and undoubted Rights? Possibly the Doctor's fertile Imagination, will furnish us with some, which have hitherto lain hid from the Penetration of Men of inferior Genius and Invention. When he condescends to do this, and thereby attempts to wipe off the Offence which his Church continues to give by the Profanation of the Lord's Supper, and the Denial of civil Rights to as good Subjects, as those who join her Communion, it will be time enough for me to give them a thorough and Impartial Examination. But till this shall be done, the good Doctor will not take it hard, that we fear the Spirit of Persecution is still alive in his church, and ready to operate, with its native Violence, whenever an Opportunity shall offer. There is no Way at present for the Doctor to evade the Force of this Argumentation, transcribed from his *Appeal*, unless he boldly cuts the Knot, and asserts, that none who reject Episcopacy, have any natural Right to civil or military Offices. He has indeed such an Expression on Page 109; but it betrays such an unacquaintedness with the Rights of Mankind, and savours so much of a persecuting Disposiion, that Charity would incline us to think it fell inadvertently from his Pen, when he was solacing himself with the glorious Prospect of the Clergy and People of his Church engrossing all honourable and profitable Employments throughout the Colonies. The Doctor surely will not vindicate the Expression, but from a Regard to his Character for *Moderation,Candour*, and *Catholicism*, retract it without Delay.

But this is not our only Reason for concluding that the Spirit of the Bishops, and inferior Clergy, (as they are called) is not like the Spirit of the Gospel, peaceable, gentle, and easy to be intreated. Nor is it owing to the gentle Temper of the Constitution of their Church, that the Rejectors of Episcopacy are not treated as harshly now as formerly. The *Act of Uniformity* breathes a very cruel and slavish Spirit. It enacts that "whoever shall declare, or speak any Thing in Derogation, or depraving of the Book of *Common Prayer*, or any Thing therein contained, or any Part thereof, he shall, for the first Offence, suffer Imprisonment for one whole Year, without Bail of Main-prize; and for the second Offence be imprisoned during Life." Weak must the Church have appeared, which stood in need of such a Support! But we are assured by divine Authority, that "the Gates of Hell shall never prevail against the Church of Christ." This famous Act however has been often called, and I doubt not Doctor Chandler himself has long esteemed it a grand Pillar of his Church. But who envies him the Honour of belonging to a Church, that must be supported, if supported at all, by such a notorious Infringement of the Rights of private Judgement; such a Prohibition of a fair and candid Examination of her Principles and Discipline; and such a Restraint on the Freedom of Speech, essential to British Liberty? Here I can safely Appeal to the impartial World, and even to the Conscience of the Doctor himself, whether this be not a very unjust and persecuting Law.

I might easily proceed to shew, that the *Canons* of the Doctor's Church do not bespeak a very charitable Temper; but this I shall have more Room to enlarge upon in some future Paper—Z

NOTES: "CENTINEL" IV

1. "Does Wrath so great reside in heavenly hearts?" Virgil, *Aeneid* I. 11.

2. After the restoration of the Stuart line to the English throne in 1660 in the person of Charles II, a series of harsh religious acts was passed which laid the basis for later persecutions against noncomformists. Some of the more well-known laws which comprised this Clarendon Code were the Corporation Act, which barred anyone from municipal corporations who refused to take the sacrament according to the usage of the Church of England; the Act of Uniformity, which authorized the old prayer book; a Quaker Act, which inflicted severe penalties on worshippers of that persuasion; the Conventicle Acts, which forbade worshipping in non-Anglican forms; and the Five Mile Act, which forbade any dissenting minister from living or visiting within five miles of any corporate town or place where he had served as a minister. The Test Act, added in 1673, required that anyone holding military or civil offices must take the sacrament according to the rite of the Church of England.

Centinel Number V

April 21, 1768

They shall put you out of the Synagogues; yea the Time cometh, that whosoever killeth you will think that he doth God Service.—John 16, ii

In my last I began to examine the peaceable and gentle Spirit of the Church of England, and now shall endeavour to trace it a little farther. The Canons of your Church, Dr. Chandler, do not seem to us to breath a very gentle Spirit. Your 4th, 5th, and 6th Canons solemnly denounce—"that whosoever shall affirm that the Form of God's Worship, contained in the *Common Prayer* hath any Thing in it repugnant to the Word of God,—or that any of the 39 *Articles* are in any Part erroneous, or such as may not with a good Conscience be subscribed, let him be excommunicated *ipso Facto*, and not be restored, untill he repent and publickly revoke his wicked Errors." Does not this bear hard on the Rights of private Judgement, and the indispensible Duty of every Christian to examine the Scriptures, "to see whether *these Things be so or not*."[1] In the Judgement of an inspired Apostle, the noble Baereans were justly commended who searched the Scripture, and by that infallible Rule judged of the Truth of the Doctrines that were preached to them. But the highest Censure of the Church is inflicted by the Church of England on the Person that would presume to judge for himself and pronounce his Judgement, if it should happen to be against any thing contained in your 39 Articles, Common Prayer and Forms of Ordination. Yet there are many Things therein, acknowledged by your own most learned Divines, to need Alteration, as is abundantly evident from their *Candid Disquisitions*, &c. And Dr. Chandler himself, speaking of some of the Laws, which relate to the spiritual Courts, which are imagined to bear hard upon British Liberty, says, (P. 96) "it is probable that these and all other ecclesiastical Laws, as well as our Liturgy and public Offices, and our Translation of the Bible will be reviewed, as soon as it shall be thought that there is good Sense and Candour enough in the Body of the Nation to admit of it."

It is indeed pleasantly ridiculous to see the most zealous Advocates of the Church of England, and her brightest Ornaments excommunicated *ipso Facto* by the gentle, peaceable Spirit of their own Church, merely for confessing what all the Christian Churches as well as themselves know to be true, that there are many Things in their Church that need Reformation and Amendment. By the Force of these Canons the Dr. himself is really an excommunicated Person, if we can believe the learned Primate Dr. Wake, who says, concerning an Excommunication *ipso Facto* "that there is no need in the Case of an Admonition, as where the Judge is to give Sentence, but every one is to take Notice of the Law at his Peril, and to see that he be not overtaken by it, and that there is no need of any Sentence to be pronounced, which the Canon itself has passed, and which is by that Means already promulged upon every one, as soon as he comes within the Obligation of it."[a]

If these Canons do not breath a persecuting Spirit against the Rejecters of Episcopacy—I am sure they breath a very ungrateful Spirit against the most valuable Members of that Church, who would willingly wipe off at least some Part of that Reproach which they are sensible has lain heavily upon her ever since the Reformation. You know Reverend Doctor that the Rejecters of your Form of Church Government have been calling upon your Church to reform many Things, some of which the best Men among yourselves have confessed to need Reformation for more than a Century past; and is there not yet good Sense and Candour enough in the Body of your national Church to admit of such a Reformation? If this is the Complexion of your Church what must we expect from the plenary Establishment of such a Church among us, as has not good Sense and Candour enough in the Body of it to admit of the Removal of such Things as have been justly complained of so long a Time, as an unrighteous Persecution of their Brethren and even unchristian Violation of the Rights of Conscience and private Judgement? The Doctor's Conjecture, "it is probable that there will be a Reformation in some Things in his Church" gives us but very slender Encouragement to submit to his American Episcopate; when we know it is at best just as probable that there will be no Reformation in that Church, which has so long continued to persecute her Brethren, and yet has not good Sense enough in the Body of it to remove the Persecution. We rather conclude, that as she has encroached so long on the Rights of Conscience and oppressed her fellow Christians where she has the Power in her hands, she would continue to give sensible Proofs of the same peaceable and gentle Spirit in America if she was clothed with the same substantial Proofs of her Moderation, by restoring her fellow Christians to the full Enjoyment of their civil and religious Liberties, and by abrogating the penal Laws which oppress their Consciences, we promise them we shall entertain fewer Jealousies of the exorbitant Power of her Bishops being exercised in the Colonies.

Pray Doctor is it an equal Thing that all Denominations of Christians, should be taxed for the Support of Episcopal Ministers in the Provinces South of Pennsylvania; especially when we consider that thereby some Ministers of that Communion are enabled to revel in Luxury and Wantonness, who, as Dr. Chandler expresses it, "are such Wretches as are not only a Scandal to the Church, but also a Disgrace to the human Species?" Must not this be a Grief and a Burden to such Christians as have any Regard to the Promotion of the Redeemer's Kingdom? And must it not be peculiarly grievous to other Denominations to support a Church in which the pure Worship of God is corrupted and obscured with human interventions, while they "teach for Doctrines the Commandments of Men."[3] Pray Dr. would you not think it an unrighteous Oppression if the Members of your Church, were Taxed for the Support of the Church of Rome; I can safely appeal to your own Conscience, whether you would not think so, notwithstanding all your fond Partiality for her, which leads you in a very Christian like Manner to unchristianize the Foreign Protestant Churches with the Church of Scotland and the Dissenters in England, in order to secure to yourselves the unenvied Treasure of an *uninterrupted Succession*? Remove therefore this Instance of Oppression out of your Church and shew us that you have as much Moderation as the Churches established in New-England, who oblige no different Denominations to pay for the Support of their Clergy, but every one supports its own. Believe me Doctor, had your Clergy united together in addresses to your Superiors at home to obtain a Deliverance for the Rejecters of Episcopacy in the Southern Colonies from this Yoke of Bondage laid on them for the Support of your Church you would have given a more substantial Proof of your Moderation and Regard to the Rights of your fellow Christians than you have lately done in your Application for an American Episcopate. Do you expect we can lay aside all Jealousy of a Church which we see oppressing all others both in England and in the Colonies in such Flagrant Instances; regardless of the Rights of Reason and Conscience where she has the Power to oppress; or that we can peaceably submit to a Scheme which threatens us with a still farther Loss of our Civil and Religious Liberties.

Thus we have examined the peaceable and gentle Spirit of the English Episcopal Church, and still find in her the mournful Relicts of her ancient persecuting Spirit, and from thence conclude that neither her Spirit nor that of the Times are so much mended, as to pave the Way for an easy and safe Introduction of the beloved Hierarchy, among those whose Ancestory abandoned their native Country and all the tender Endearments of Relations and Friends to escape her Ecclesiastical Rage and Persecution.—Nor is the Spirit of her Bishops so much mended as Dr. Chandler would persuade us. Did not almost all the Bishops in Parliament Vote against the Repeal of the Stamp-Act and use their Influence to rivet the Shackles on the Colonies which our Enemies had formed. Can we then expect that those, that are so regardless of the Property and civil Liberties of their fellow Subjects, would be tender of the Rights of conscience; or that those who so lately manifested a Disposition to enslave as in one Instance, would not also oppress us in another?

But this is not the only Indication of their present peaceable and gentle Spirit. The Episcopal Congregation in New-York is established by Law and incorporated; when the Presbyterians there applied lately for a Charter, did not the Bishop of London appear against them and use his utmost Endeavours to render their Application fruitless and ineffectual?[4] With what Pretext then can the Episcopalians complain that they do not enjoy the same Privileges with other Denominations of Christians in the Colonies; when themselves think it no Injustice to prevent others from obtaining the same Privileges with themselves. Nor this is not all, the Legislature of the Province of Massachusetts-Bay, moved with Pity and Compassion for the poor Savages in America, who continue in deplorable Ignorance of the Way of Salvation through a Redeemer, lately by Act of Assembly erected a Society in Boston, to spread the Gospel through these benighted Tribes; when this Law went Home for the Royal Approbation, the pious Archbishop of Canterbury appeared in Person, and made use of his extensive Influence to have it repealed.[5] Why should the highest Dignitary in the Church of England oppose so well meant a Design for the Conversion of the Heathen? What have these poor Wretches done to deserve so heavy a Stroke from his Grace? Was he afraid that the known Zeal of the Clergy and Society of Boston, would engage with Vigor in carrying so good a Work into Execution, and thereby bring a Reproach upon a Society in England erected for the same Purpose, who for more than half a Century past have been squandering away large Sums of Money collected for the Relief of those Savages, in the Support of a Body of Missionaries whose usual Feats are some few Conversions from other Denominations of Christians to their Communion? His Grace can best tell what were his Motives to this Conduct, but at present it must appear very strange to us at this Distance, that his Grace should have so little Compassion for the Souls of those poor Out-casts of the human Species; so little Zeal for the Promotion of Christianity, that he would rather suffer the heathen Tribes behind us to continue in their deplorable Ignorance without God in the World, and Strangers to the Covenants of Promise, than that they should be instructed in the Doctrines of the Gospel by Protestants of a different Communion.

You will excuse me, Dr. Chandler, that I presume to think you also have imbibed a small Portion of the Spirit which seems to have influenced your charitable Primate, and that, though the Times are mended, you have yet no great Abhorrence of Persecution; for in Page 31 you lament that "Excommunication however it was dreaded in the purest Ages of Christianity, has lost much of its Force in this, wherein Alters are set up against Alters, and Churches against Churches, and those that are rejected by one may be received by another; a Disposition to slight the highest Punishment which the Church can inflict has become general, and there appears to be no Remedy, but *in the Use of* Reason and Persuasion." A lamentable Case truly! that your church has lost her Discipline, and that there is no way to restore it but by Reason and Persuasion! What a Pity is it that the penal Laws formerly executed in England and Ireland against Dissenters, are not in force in America; and that *spiritual Courts* aided by the *secular Arm* are not introduced to restore primitive Discipline. Then might we see some more success follow the good Doctor's labours among the *Heathen* in , and about Elizabeth Town; and refractory Quakers, Baptists and Presbyterians, who never claimed any relations to the CHURCH, solemnly cast out of it, and brought to *due* obedience by fines, imprisonments and outlawry. Then, indeed, might there be some good prospects, "that the word of God would mightily grow and prevail in" New-Jersey, &c. as well as "New-England, *according to the Liturgy of the Church of England.*"[b]

Thus we see that neither the Spirit of your Church nor of her Bishops and Clergy, nor of the Times, if we believe Doctor Chandler, is so much mended as to free us from Fears of Oppression, upon the Introduction of an American Episcopate.—Z

INTERNAL NOTES: "CENTINEL" V

[a] See App. in Behalf of the King's Supremacy. p. 22.[2]
[b] See Dr. Philip Bearcroft's *Sermon, in 1744, before the Society for propagating the Gospel.*[6]

NOTES: "CENTINEL" V

1. Acts 17:11.
2. William Wake, *An Appeal to all the True Members of the Church of England in Behalf of the King's Ecclesiastical Supremacy* (London: 1698), pp. 22–23. The quotation should read: "[I]n such a Case there is no need of any Admonition, as where the Judge is to give Sentence; but every One is to take notice of the Law of his Peril, and see that he be not overtaken by it. And Secondly; That there is no need of any Sentence to be pronounced, which the Canon it self has pass'd; and which is by that Means already Promulged upon every One, as soon as he comes within the obligation of it."
3. Matthew 15:9.
4. See "Centinel" I, note 3.
5. See "Centinel" I, note 3. The Archbishop of Canterbury was Thomas Secker.
6. *An Abstract of the Proceedings of the Society for the Propagation of the Gospel in Foreign Parts, 1744* (London, 1745).

Centinel Number VI

April 28, 1768

Liberty is a most tender Plant, that thrives in very few Soils; neglected, it soon withers and is lost; but is scarce ever recovered. Nothing less than a supreme Regard to this inestimable Blessing, could have induced me to undertake the disagreeable Task of a Disputant. I conceived it was dangerously attacked by Doctor Chandler and his Associates in their Attempt to introduce diocesan Bishops among us, and my Design was to shew the manifest Tendency of this Innovation, to undermine and demolish this religious Freedom by which these Northern Colonies are so remarkably distinguished from every other Country; and under the Auspices of which, joined with an excellent Frame of civil Government, they have beyond all Example grown up and prospered. In some future Papers I shall pursue the Subject; but at present, I wave it, to make Room for the following Letter, just received from an ingenious Correspondent; who considers the Manner in which our civil Liberties must be violated, by this Scheme of an American Episcopate. As his Reasoning appears to be clear and demonstrative, I shall be much obliged to him for the Continuance of his Correspondence.

To the Author of the CENTINEL.

Sir,

At a Time when the Liberties of America are at Stake; when Claims are set up destructive of our Rights as free-born Subjects, we cannot be too much on our Guard against any Measure, that has a Tendency to give Colour or Strength to those Claims: Nor ought we to give it the less Opposition, because it may have been undertaken with a different Design.

In this Light I view the Application for an American Episcopate, lately made, by some of the Missionaries from the Society for propagating the Gospel. I would fain acquit the Applicants of any Intention to infringe *the civil Rights of the Colonists*; and yet I am clearly of Opinion the Application has a direct Tendency to this and therefore ought to be opposed.

I shall not enter on any Dispute about *uninterrupted Succession, the Divine Right of Episcopacy*, &c. These are Subjects to which I am altogether a Stranger. I apprehend Christianity can well consist with the Enjoyment of civil Liberty; and that a man may worship God and be "accepted with him" without becoming a Slave, or parting with the Rights of a British Subject. It is not more lamentable, than true, that the Clergy of all Denominations, and in every Age, have discovered a Fondness for Power, and have seldom been scrupulous about the means of procuring it; nor have they used it with Moderation when obtained. This might be improved as an Argument against every Attempt they may make to encrease their Power. But waving this, I shall at Present consider the Subject in another View, and endeavour to shew that the Application of Dr. Chandler and his Brethren, is in itself a dangerous Attack upon the civil Liberties of this Country. If this can be made evident, I hope the Missionaries will not only decline every Attempt of the like Nature for the future, but that they will, from a Regard to the Liberties of the Colonies, unite with their Fellow-subjects in opposing any Steps that may be taken, in Consequence of the Application already made; and that the Doctor will admit, that the Opposition, neither arises from a Spirit of Persecution, nor from Disaffection to Monarchy.

It is well known, that the far greater Part of those who first settled the Northern Colonies, left their native Country, and took Shelter in the Wilds of America, in order to be free from the Persecution of Ecclesiastical Rulers, and to enjoy the Liberty of worshipping God in a Way agreeable to their Consciences.[a] Although they disclaimed the Jurisdiction of Ecclesiastical Courts, they retained their Allegiance to the King, and claimed the Protection of the British Crown. In Conformity therefore to the Principles of the British Constitution, to which they strictly adhered, they accepted from the Crown a Grant for the Lands they settled, and Charters declarative of their Rights and Privileges.

In Consequence of these Grants, both they and their Posterity ever since, as free-born Subjects, have always claimed, and do still claim, not only the *sole Right of disposing of their Property*, but also *of making, with the Consent of the Crown, such Laws and Regulations, as they think most convenient, for their internal Police and Government.*

Without the full Enjoyment of these Rights, it is impossible for them to preserve the least Shadow either of *Liberty or Property*. For what *Property* can any Man have in that which another can by Right take and dispose of as he pleases?[b] Or what *Liberty* has he, whose

Conduct must be regulated by the Pleasure of another? A Government without the Consent of the Governed, is with me, the very Definition of Slavery.

It is readily granted that the Colonies are dependent States, united under one Head; and with the other British Dominions, form one entire Empire. It is also admitted, that the Parliament of Great-Britain, as the supreme legislative Power, has a superintending Authority to regulate and preserve the Connection between the several parts and Members of the Empire. But this does not imply, either a Power for disposing of the Property of the Subjects in the several inferior legislative Jurisdictions; nor of making Laws, for their internal Government. Both of these, by the constitution and Charters of the several Colonies, are lodged, where Nature and Reason and Justice point out that they ought to be lodged; with the Representatives of the People.

Sufficient Caution is taken that this Power may not be abused. The Laws in the Colonies must be made "as near as conveniently can be, agreeable to the Laws and Statutes and Rights of the Kingdom of England."[c] They must receive the Sanction of the Governor, or the King's Representative: And even after that, a Power is reserved to the Crown of repealing, within a limited Time, any Law that may be enacted.

Every Application[d] therefore, to any other than the Legislatures of the respective Colonies, for Laws or Regulations relative to our internal Police, I consider as an Attack upon the Liberty of the Colonies. The Regulating of Church-Discipline, and establishing particular Forms of Religion is certainly a Matter of internal Police. If the Parliament, or any other Power upon Earth, may establish in the Colonies any Form of Religion, or the Hierarchy they please, they can grant to the Members of that establishment what Immunities and Exemptions they see and inflict Penalties upon such as do not conform. If they may, without the Consent of the Colonies, establish Bishopricks and Bishops among us, they may appoint Revenues for their Support, erect Spiritual Courts, and enforce Obedience to the Authority and Jurisdiction of these Courts. And if the People must yield Obedience to such Laws and Establishments made not only without, but against their Consent, I would gladly know wherein their Liberty can consist.

In vain did our ancestors leave their Native Land, and fly into the Wilderness to avoid Spiritual Tyranny, if those who established it in England, can extend it to America. In short, if the Parliament is to interfere, and regulate one Part of our internal Police, why not every Part? If they among whom we have no Representatives; who from the Distance between them and us, must be unacquainted with our Condition, Circumstances, &c. they in whose Election we have no Choice, over whose Conduct we have no Check, as the Laws they make for us, will not affect them; if our Superiors in Britain, can bind on us religious Establishments and rule us by Laws made at the Distance of three Thousand Miles, we may boast of our Liberty, as we please but it is no more, than

"The baseless Fabrick of a Vision."[e]

I am, Sir,

Yours, &c. A. B.

INTERNAL NOTES: "CENTINEL" VI

[a] It must be acknowledged, that it was the *unhappiness* of New-England and the adjoining Parts, to be first planted and inhabited by Persons who were generally disaffected to the Church by Law established in England; and many of them had taken Refuge in those Parts, on Account of their Sufferings for Non Conformity here at Home"—*Account of the Foundation, Success, &c. of the Society for propagating the Gospel.* Anno 1706; Page 10.[1]

That it was their unhappiness thus to suffer is plain enough—but that it was the unhappiness of the Northern Colonies to be settled by *conscientious Non-Conformists* is not so clear.

[b] See *Locke* on Government.[2]

[c] The Words of the Charter from K. Charles 2d. to Penn.

[d] Dr. Chandler, in his Appeal, tells us "Application has been made to our *Superiors;*" and in sundry Places he calls upon the "*Nation*" to establish Episcopacy in America. Who these Superiors are, he does not Explain: but by the Nation, he must Mean the Parliament; for the Nation has no Mode of Acting, but by its Representation in Parliament.

[e] Shakespear.[3]

NOTES: "CENTINEL" VI

1. *An Account of the Society for Propagating the Gospel in Foreign Parts,* (London: 1706), p. 10.
2. John Locke, *Of Civil Government, Second Treatise.*
3. William Shakespeare, *The Tempest,* act 4, sc. 1, line 148.

Centinel Number VII

May 5, 1768

To the Author of THE CENTINEL

Sir,

I have already endeavoured to shew from the principles of Liberty, that the British Parliament ought not to interfere in the civil Police of the Colonies; and that any Application to that august Body, directly or indirectly, to make Laws for us, or to establish among us any Form of Church-Discipline, deserves to be treated as an Attack upon our civil Liberties. I shall further evince this, from the Sentiments of those who gave, and the Conduct of those who received, the several provincial Charters: This will tend not only to enforce the Arguments already advanced, but to give a clearer View of our Constitution, by tracing it back to its first Principles.[a]

Before I proceed, it may not be amiss to offer a few Reflections on the Nature of Charters.

I have heard it advanced by Men, who ought to know better, that the People derive their Rights and Liberties from the Charters granted by the Crown. Nothing can be more groundless than this. A People derive their Liberty from God, the Author of their Being.[b] When for the Sake of Security and other Advantages they enter into Society, and form Governments, individuals part with some of their natural Rights, freely giving up such as are inconsistent with Government, and invest their chief Magistrates with such Power as is deemed necessary for the Defence, Protection and Security of the whole. Hence it appears, that Obedience and Protection are relative Terms: Where the one is not granted, the other is not due.

It is to be observed, that different Nations, according to the Degree of Strenth, Valour, Understanding, and public Virtue, or Vigor of Spirit, that prevailed in them, have surrendered more or less of their natural Rights. But as Power is of an encroaching Nature; ever on the Watch to extend its Sway; and ever tenacious of what it has obtained, hence it comes to pass, that the wisest and best Nations, those endowed with the greatest Degree of Ability, Bravery, and public Spirit, have often found it difficult to guard against the Encroachments of their Rulers, and to defend their Liberty against the Attacks of wicked Princes.

Our Ancestors, whether we trace our Origin from the ancient Britons, Picts, Scots, Saxons or Angles, preserved an unconquerable Love of Liberty. Though they paid a ready Obedience to Government, and revered the just Authority of their Kings, yet they kept the legislative Power in their own Hands; and obliged their Princes to swear, "that they would hold, keep and defend the just Laws and Customs, *quas vulgus elegerit*", (which the People should choose).[c] But as some of their Kings, influenced by wicked designing Ministers, endeavoured to subvert the Liberties of the People and to establish arbitrary Government, it became necessary to reduce them to Reason and to ascertain the Limits of their Power. This gave Rise to Charters; which are no more than solemn Declarations of the Rights inherent in the People, and the Privileges they are intituled to under that Government to which they are Subject; and which being granted, or in other Words acknowledged, and subscribed by the King, or supreme Magistrate, bound his Power, and limit his Prerogative. Of this Nature is that commonly called *Magna-Charta*; the great Charter of England; which is only an Abridgement of the ancient Laws and Customs of the Realm. Of the same Nature is the Petition of Rights, granted by King Charles the first, and confirmed at the Revolution. Charters therefore, are not to be considered as mere Matters of Favour, conferred by the Grace of the Prince, but Declarations of the Rights and Privileges inherent in the People.[3]

Thus at the Settlement of a Colony far distant from the Mother-Country, when the King grants a Charter to the Colonists, with Power to make Laws for their good Government, it is not to be supposed, that they derive that Power from the Charter. It was inherent in them as Freemen. They enjoyed it before in their native Country. They carried it with them. And when settled in the new Country might have exercised it, though no Charter had been granted.[d] It was prudent indeed to receive a Charter, in order to settle their Rights, to direct the Mode of exercising their Privileges, & to ascertain the Bounds of Royal Prerogative with Regard to them, and the Authority of the Crown to which they acknowledged Allegiance.

For my own Part, I am sorry the Charters which have been granted are not explicit enough. It is indeed to be lamented, that the Prerogative of the Crown, or the Privileges of the People should ever be liable to Dispute, in any single Branch of either. By means of this, the Public has often suffered great Inconveniences. Had the Rights of the People been fully and clearly expressed in these Charters, according to the Spirit of the English Constitution, and the Ideas that even then prevailed in the Minds of People, it might have prevented Claims that have lately been set up, and Disputes that threaten the Peace of the Empire. Lesser Matters in Government may be reformed without any ill Effects, while the ancient Constitution remains entire; but when the very Nature of the Government is attempted to be changed, and the Foundations of it to be overturned, it is hard to say, what may be the Consequence.

It is a first Principle in the Constitution of England, that the Happiness of the Subject is the End of Government, and that the Safety of the People is the supreme Law. As then the People are supposed to be the best Judges of what will promote their own good, and most interested in what concerns their own Safety, it is an established Maxim, that no human Laws, can, or ought to bind them, unless made with their consent. This is the glorious Privilege of Britons; a Privilege of the most inestimable Value so essential to Liberty that without it, a State can make no Pretensions to Freedom.

Whatever Reason there might be for granting particular Indulgences to those who with great Danger, Fatigue and Expence undertook to settle Colonies in the Wilds of America, and thereby to extend the British Dominions, and encrease the Power, Wealth and Influence both of the Crown, and Inhabitants of Britain, yet surely there could not be the least Shadow of Reason for depriving them of the Privileges of the British Constitution. Had there been the most distant Prospect of this, it is not to be imagined, that Freemen, much less Men of Rank & Fortune, such as many of the first Adventurers were, would ever have hazarded the Attempt. Far different were their Views. In going abroad to settle Colonies, they considered themselves intituled to all the civil Rights and Liberties of British subjects, at the same Time that they were freed from the Oppressions of Ecclesiastical Courts, as well as from some particular Customs, Tenures and Usages, which by the Common and Statute Law, were confined to certain Districts in England.

Thus in every Charter granted to the Colonies, the Rights of English free-born Subjects, are confirmed to the Colonists: and in particular a Power of making Laws for their internal Government. It is indeed provided, that the Laws so made shall not be repugnant to the Laws of England: a Provision founded on Wisdom and good Policy. For a Similarity of Manners and Customs is a great Bond of Union among Subjects of the same King. In some Charters, particularly those granted to People who left their native Country from religious Motives, a Liberty of Conscience in the Worship of God, is allowed to all Christians, except Roman Catholicks.[e] The only Stipulation in Favour of any particular Denomination, is that found in the Charter granted to *William Penn*; which provides, that "If any of the Inhabitants of said Province (*Pennsylvania*) to the Number of Twenty, shall at any Time hereafter be desirous, and shall by any Writing or by any Person deputed by them, signify such is their Desire to the Bishop of London for the Time being, that any Preacher or Preachers to be approved of by the said Bishop, may be sent unto them for their Instruction, then such Preacher or Preachers shall and may reside within the said Province, without any Denial or Molestation whatsoever." But even this supposes in the People here, a Power of establishing by Law any particular Church or Denomination of Christians they see proper; and the utmost this Reserve can be construed to mean, is no more than this, that in Case of an Establishment, the Preachers above-mentioned shall be *tollerated*.[f]

Thus were the Colonists left to the Enjoyment of the Rights and Liberties of British Subjects, and their Power of making Laws for their internal Police acknowledged and confirmed. Accordingly no sooner were they settled in this new Country, than they exercised this Power in its full Extent; particularly in Relation to Church-Government and religious Establishments.[g]

The Conclusions therefore, which I would draw from the Premises are these; that the making of Laws for internal Police, is essential to Liberty; that this Power is by the respective Charters, confirmed to the Legislatures of the several Colonies, and has been accordingly exercised by them; and that the regulating or establishing of religious Denominations, is a Part of this internal Police: for any Persons therefore, to apply to any other than the Legislatures of the Colonies to which they belong, for an Establishment, or to other Public Support or Preferrence of their Sect, is very derogatory of the Authority of those Legislatures; injurious to the Rights and Liberties of Americans; and subversive of the Constitution of their Country—. "There is a Way which seemth Right unto a Man, But the End thereof are the Ways of Death."—
Prov. XIV. 12[6]

I am, Sir,

Yours, &c.

A. B.

INTERNAL NOTES: "CENTINEL" VII

[a] "I wish the Maxim of *Machiavel* was followed; that of examining a Constitution at certain Periods, according to its first Principles; this would correct Abuses and supply Defects." Lord Cambden's Speech, &c.[1]

[b] Ad eo Libertas, a quo Spirites. "We are born free, as we are born rational: Age that brings one, brings the other too." *Locke* on Govt. 61. Again, "voluntary Agreement gives political Power to Governors, for the Benefit of the Subjects, and secures them in the Possession and Use of their Properties." Ibid 173.[2]

[c] See the *Coronation Oath*.

[d] Thus the former Colony of Plymouth in New-England acted for many Years without Charter or Commission.—*Hutchinson's* History of Massachusetts.[4]

[e] See the Charters of *Massachusetts Bay, Connecticut, Rhode-Island*, &c.

[f] King Charles and his Council saw that *William Penn*, a Person of Note among the Quakers, had asked a Grant of Land in North-America, with Powers of Government, as an Asylum for his Sect, then grievously harrassed and persecuted for Non-Conformity to the established Religion. They observed, that Laws destructive of Liberty of Conscience, had been made in the Colonies already settled, *even by those who had fled from the like Tyranny themselves*; and they might easily suppose that the Quakers would in like Circumstances, act the same Part; they therefore took care to secure to such few Episcopalians, as might take up their Residence in this Quaker Settlement, full Liberty of Conscience. To the Honour of the *Friends*, it ought however to be mentioned, that the Precaution was altogether needless; for the *Charter of Privileges* from *William Penn* to the People established *unalterably* an entire Liberty in religious Matters; declaring that no one shall ever "be compelled to frequent, or maintain any religious Worship, &c. against his Mind." N.B. This is also established by *Act of Assembly*.

[g] As in *Virginia, Maryland* &c., where the Episcopal Clergy are supported by public Tax and in *Massachusetts-Bay, Connecticut* and *New Hampshire*, where the Congregational and Presbyterian Ministers are maintained by legal Assessments, to which however neither Baptists, Quakers, nor Episcopalians are contributory.—The Church of *Ireland* derives her Establishment, Articles, Forms, &c wholly from Irish Acts of Parliament; no Arch-Bishop or Bishop of the Church of *England* has any Jurisdiction over her; and in some lesser Matters, she differs from her sister Church.[5]

NOTES: "CENTINEL" VII

1. The editor has been unable to locate the speech referred to here.

2. John Locke, *Of Civil Government, Second Treatise*.

The complete quotation should read: "Thus we are born free, as we are born rational; not that we have actually the exercise of either: age that brings one, brings with it the other too." Ibid., paragraph 61.

The complete quotation should read: "Voluntary agreement gives the second, namely political power to governors for the benefit of their subjects, to secure them in the possession and use of their properties." ibid., paragraph 173.

3. The Magna Carta, signed by King John (1189-1216) in 1215 under pressure from barons, churchmen and townsmen, granted security for the rights formerly exercised by these classes and imposed limitations on the encroachments by royal authority which Henry II (1154–1189) had begun in an effort to centralize the English government.

The Petition of Right, reluctantly signed by Charles I (1625–1649) in 1628, circumscribed the powers of the monarch by forbidding him to levy any tax or loan without parliamentary consent, to imprison anyone without a specific charge, to billet soldiers in private houses, or to declare martial law in time of peace.

4. Thomas Hutchinson, *The History of the Colony and Province of Massachusetts-Bay* (3 vols: Boston, 1764), 1, chapter 1.

5. In 1768 the Anglican church was established in Virginia, Maryland, South Carolina, North Carolina, Georgia and, partially, in New York.

6. Proverbs 14:12.

Centinel Number VIII

May 12, 1768

My Kingdom is not of this World.—St. John's Gospel, *XVII. 36.*

To the Author of the CENTINEL.

Sir,

My View in these Letters is not to combat a religious Denomination, nor to oppugn the theological Opinions of any Man or set of Men, but to defend the Liberties of my Country. Had any other Society of Christians applied in the same Manner for an Establishment, I should have thought it my Duty to object to it, and, as far as my Influence could extend, to oppose the Design. Bishop, Priest, Presbyter or Pastor have no Magic in them to justify with me, any Attempt prejudicial to public Liberty.

It is very unfortunate that any Dispute should be raised in America, at a crisis when union of Sentiment and Design, seem especially necessary for preserving our civil Rights.[a] A ship's Crew quarreling in a Storm, or when an Enemy is within Gun-shot, does not argue a greater Degree of infatuation. For what Purpose, or with what View it is started at this crucial Time, I do not willingly allow myself even to conjecture. For the sake of their Country, their Posterity, and themselves, I hope the Friends and Lovers of America, will consider themselves no further concerned in this Dispute, than as it relates to civil Liberty.

For the Debate, as I view it, is not concerning a Bishop, nor concerning episcopal Discipline, but about the Manner of introducing the Bishop, and establishing that Discipline in America.

It is evident from sundry Parts of the *Appeal*, that Application has been made to our Superiors in Britain to procure an Act of Parliament to establish Episcopacy in the Colonies.[b] But it must be allowed, that whether the present Attempt "for establishing an American Episcopate," was begun by some of the Missionaries, or set on Foot by the Society for Propagating the Gospel, who, as Dr. Chandler says (page 53) "have *ever been watching* for seasonable Opportunities of exerting themselves to obtain it," they could have not hit upon a Time more unfavourable to American Freedom. However, I hope the Friends of the Colonies, whether of the Episcopal, or any other Church, will unite in opposing an Attempt, which is in itself an open acknowledgement of the Claims which the Enemies of America have lately set up, and which are totally subversive of our Rights and Liberties.

Suppose the Application had been made to the Parliament of Ireland, or to the Legislature of Virginia, to establish Episcopacy in New-England, in what Light would it have appeared? Or suppose Scotland were at this Day a separate Kingdom and the Presbyterians of Pennsylvania and Maryland should apply to the Legislature of that Kingdom, to establish the Kirk of Scotland and her Discipline in America, how would the Application be resented?

The British Empire consists of several Provinces united in Allegiance to one Prince. The Legislative Power of and for each Province, consists of the King or his Representative, with the Deputies of the People in that Province. Tho' Great-Britain is now united in one Legislative Body or Parliament, it was, not many Ages since, divided into several Districts, with distinct Legislatures in each. At that Time it was not pretended, that the Laws of one, bound the Subjects in another Province. Each, with the Consent of the Sovereign, or his Representative, enjoyed the Right of Legislation for itself. Britain, since its Union into one Legislative Body, has acquired greater Power; but whether it has thereby acquired a *Right* to make Laws to bind the other Parts of the Empire, remains to be proven. There is certainly a Difference between *Power* and *Right*; nor does the one follow as a Consequence of the other. For if Power gave Right, then would the strongest have a Right to whatever he pleased to seize on: and "the High-way Man would have a Right to my Purse, who demands it with a Pistol at my Breast."[3]

But why shall not the Episcopalians be upon an equal footing with their Neighbours?[d] I answer, are they not on an equal footing? Are they not permitted, as freely as any other Denomination, to form a "voluntary Society"[e] for the public Worship of God, in the Way they think most agreeable to him.

"They have no Bishop to ordain the inferior Clergy, to govern the Church and confirm Adults." What hinders? Perhaps it may be said they cannot have a Bishop, unless sent from England, because the *Succession* must not be *interrupted* and that he can not be sent from England, placed in a Diocese, and endowed with a Revenue according to his Rank, without the Appointment of his Majesty, as supreme Head of the Church, and without an Act of Parliament.

Before I answer to this, I should be glad to see the Edict by which Christ has enjoined the unbroken Succession of Bishops.[f] Next I would be glad to know how the Christian Church was supplied with Bishops for the first three Centuries, when there was no civil Power imposed to establish them. Whether a settled Revenue is essential to a Bishop; or whether the Church of England in America (as it is called) is so peculiarly different from all other Christian Churches, that even under the surest and freest State of religious Liberty, it can not enjoy the "Form of its Ecclesiastical Government and Discipline, without an Act of Parliament to establish it."

Religion and Government are certainly very different Things, instituted for different Ends; the Design of the one, being to promote our temporal Happiness; the Design of the other to procure the Favour of God, and thereby the Salvation of our Souls. While these are kept distinct and apart, the Peace and Welfare of Society is preserved, and the Ends of both answered. But by mixing them together, Feuds, Animosities and Persecutions have been raised, which have deluged the World in Blood, and disgraced human Nature.

In the middle and eastern Governments of North-America, the Legislatures have, with great Wisdom, taken care to keep the Church distinct from the State. They have made Laws to secure to the People in general and to each Member in particular, the full Enjoyment of their civil Rights, Interests, and Properties; and have armed the Magistrate with Power to enforce the Execution of these Laws. But at the same Time individuals are left at full Liberty to unite themselves into Societies[g] for the public Worship of God, in such a Manner as they judge acceptable to him, and effectual to procure eternal Life and Happiness. This indeed may be disagreeable to those, who complain, that "Altars are set up against Altars, and Churches against Churches, and that those who are rejected by one, may be received by another;"[h] but certainly Nothing can be more consistent with Reason and Religion, or more agreeable to the sincere Lovers of Liberty.

How long shall we enjoy the Happiness of this Constitution, if Establishments can be imposed on us without our consent, is very uncertain. Let us therefore with one Heart and with one Mind unite in Support of our common Rights, and resolve to stand fast in the Liberty wherewith Christ hath made us free, and be not entangled with the Yoke of Bondage.

I am, Sir,

Yours, &c.

A. B.

To what this spirited Correspondent has here said, I have added some Notes, to shew that if the Episcopalians in this Country are under any Difficulties, they arise from themselves; either because they have adopted some confined Notions concerning the Episcopal Character; or from an arbitrary and needless Association of State Establishment with Church-Government in their Ideas of it; or lastly from an assuming Disposition, which prompts them to claim the Superiority over their Neighbours, who reject Episcopacy.

For if the same Privileges, which other Denominations enjoy, would satisfy their Clergy, why did not the Episcopal Ministers of New-York and New-Jersey, instead of sending seven Petitions to England for Bishops, proceed to chuse one of their Number to be their Superior, and voluntarily agree to be governed by him. Thus their Hierarchy might have been compleated, without lordly Revenue, state Appointment, or giving ground of Jealousy to others. The Moravian Bishops, who stand on this Footing, never gave any Umbrage.[4]

But a voluntary Episcopate, in the primitive Way, or as other Societies enjoy their forms of Discipline, will not satisy the Missionaries. *They* and their People are *the Church, the American Church*; as it were, emphatically and exclusively; all others are Hereticks or Schismaticks. *They are the Church of England in America*; nay, *the national Church*, and of the national Religion; and must be raised upon the Depression of all other Churches, whose Members are already termed Dissenters,[i] and roundly denied any natural Right to Civil or Military Offices.[j]

These extravagant Claims of some of the Missionaries, in behalf of about twenty five thousand of their People, dispersed among a Million or more of British Subjects, who are settled between Nova-Scotia and Maryland, are very alarming; especially as many of the Episcopal Laity are utterly averse to the invidious Scheme. But the Course they take to obtain what they seek for, by applying to England for an Act of the State in their Favour, is most presumptuous, unconstitutional, and subversive of Liberty and Justice.

How these enterprizing Geniuses came to be authorized to transact for all British America, or at least for all the Episcopalians in it, does not appear. It is very remarkable, the Bustle about Bishops seems to be confined to Colonies generally settled by People averse to Prelacy, in which "it would, (as Dr. Chandler himself confesses, Page 47) without Dispute be improper to have any:" whilst in Virginia and Maryland, where a numerous Episcopal Clergy are provided for under Acts of Assembly, and where the Pleas of Usefulness and Necessity would have some Meaning, there is little said concerning them. Doubtless if the People of those Provinces, who are generally Friends to the Episcopal Church found it expedient to compleat their religious Establishments, they would pass Laws for the Purpose, and carefully ascertain and limit the Duties, Privileges, and Authority of these spiritual Superiors; which from the peculiar Circumstances of the Colonies; from the Uncertainity of the Law of this Subject; but especially from the encroaching Disposition which this Order of Men has shewn in all Ages, would be absolutely necessary.

If the Propriety of establishing Diocesan Bishops in the Colonies was ever so apparent and the Right of Parliament to interfere in our internal Police ever so clear, yet the Colonists would scarce think it prudent to have an Affair so delicate, and so nearly connected with public Liberty, regulated in England. The People there, very remotely interested in the Consequences, would probably leave it to the Clergy themselves, to form the Plan; as seems to have been the Case, at the Close of Queen Anne's Reign, when the Design of *establishing an American Episcopate by Act of Parliament*, was on the Carpet before. But I hope we are not so infatuated as willingly to trust this momentous Affair to such interested Management. Let us then speak and act for ourselves and be watchful that our Rights and Privileges be not violated, under the specious Pretence of advancing the Interests of Religion.

INTERNAL NOTES: "CENTINEL" VIII

[a]This affair seems to have risen in the Time of the Stamp-Act. How some People love to fish the troubled Waters!

[b]Appeal. Page 52.—We are told, "An Order was obtained from the Crown for *a Bill to be drawn and laid before the Parliament, for establishing an American Episcopate*; but when the Affair was a fair Way of being speedily accomplished, the Death of Queen Anne that excellent Princess," put a stop to it. And we are further informed that "in the Beginning of the next Reign," (George the first) "the Attempt was renewed, and the Prospect of Success was most encouraging; but it proved abortive." The Archbishop of Canterbury, and the Bishop of London had on this latter Occasion proposed, that part of the Lands in St. Christophers, which had belonged to the French Clergy, should be applied to support two Bishops; one to be settled in the Islands, the other on the Continent of North-America.—Page 80, we are assured "no Reason has been given to suspect a Departure from the general

Plan aimed at." Again, same Page, it appears that his Majesty is to fixt the Places of Residence for the Bishops.

[c]Locke.[1]

[d]See Appeal, Page 42

[e]Ibidem, Page 30. "The Church considered with relation to Civil Power, is in the very Nature of it a voluntary Society," says Dr. Chandler.

[f]*Eutichius*, elected Patriarch of Alexandria, A.D. 933. says "That the twelve Presbyters constituted by Mark in the See of Alexandria, chose one of their Number to be Head over the Rest, and the other Eleven laid their Hands on him, blessed him and made him Patriarch."—Jerom, more ancient than he, relates, that "At Alexandria from Mark to Heraclius and Dionisius Bishops the Priests always took one of their Number, whom they set in the highest Place and called him Bishop."—arch-Bishop Cranmer, a great Name in the Church of England, in his Answers to Edward the VI. says, "That tho' in the Admission of Bishops; there be divers comely Solemnities used, yet they be not of Necessity, but only for good Order and seemly Fashion; his Ministrations are good without them."—Again, "He that is appointed a Bishop needeth no Consecration by Scripture, for Election and appointing thereunto is sufficient." See Stillingfleet's *Irenicum*, Cap. viii-No Protestant Church, save those of England and Ireland, makes any Account of this unbroken Succession of Bishops.[2]

[g]In some of the Colonies indeed, one religious Society is forbidden, not on Account of Religion, but on Account of certain political Principles, which are supposed to be inconsistent with the good of the State. How far the Fears which those Governments have conceived against that Society are well-founded, I will not undertake to say. In *Pennsylvania*, where it is tolerated, no inconveniences have arisen. However, it is not to be denied, that the Magistrate has a Right to prohibit the propagating of Opinions or Doctrines, which are contrary to human Society, or to those moral Rules, which are necessary to the preservation of human Society.[3]

[h]Dr. Chandler's *Appeal*.—Page 31.

[i]See *Appeal*, throughout.

[j]Ibid: Page 109.

NOTES: "CENTINEL" VIII

1. This quotation is a summary of the paragraph which should read:

"Nor does it at all alter the case to say 'I gave my promise,' no more than it excuses the force, and passes the right, when I put my hand in my pocket, and deliver my purse myself to a thief, who demands it with a pistol at my breast." John Locke, *Treatise of Civil Government*, chapter 16, paragraph 186.

2. Edward Stillingfleet, *Irenicum. A Weapon-Salve for the Churches Wounds, or the Divine Right of Particular Forms of Church-Government.* (London, 1662), chap. 8, para. 2, p. 392. p. 392.

3. Several of the colonies passed laws against the Roman Catholic religion on the supposition that its adherents followed orders from the Pope even when they conflicted with civil laws.

4. The Moravian church, a radical pietistic sect, was organized in Germany in 1722 by Count Nicolas von Zinzendorf, came to Pennsylvania in 1736, was active in the revivals of the 1740s, and organized a hierarchy in which bishops were chosen to officiate only among the Moravians. The Mennonite church also maintained voluntary bishops.

Centinel Number IX

May 19, 1768

The abuse of Power, has in all Ages, furnished the most copious Fund of Materials to the Moralist, and to the Historian, and has ever given the greatest Perplexity to the Legislator. Private Persons doubtless affect the public Weal by their Vices and by their Crimes; but standing singly and alone, their Transgressions are easily corrected. Whereas those who by the Advantages of Birth, Fortune, Office or superior Abilities are enabled to influence others, and to direct the public Views and Councils, are not without Difficulty and Address kept within the Bounds of Law and Justice. The Passions and Prejudices of Men are constantly leading them into one Mistake or another; and the Remonstrances of Reason and Duty alone, are but feeble Restraints. In order therefore to curb the Licentiousness of leading Men, it hath been found expedient, to distribute the Powers of Government among the different Orders of which the Community is composed, as to excite, and employ those of one Rank and Interest, to correct the Irregularities of another.

Although this may seem to lay a Foundation for constant Debate and Faction, yet even this is a small Inconvenience compared to the galling and oppressive Yoke of Absolute Monarchy; or even the jealous Severity of an aristocratic Senate. But the common Disadvantages of the mixed Forms of Goverment, will be found neither very considerable nor lasting, in Case the Distribution of Power is made with Judgement. The old Roman Policy was deficient in this Respect. The patrician and plebian Orders in that Republic, wanted a third Estate to moderate between them: which Defect the King in the British Constitution admirably supplies; whilst our popular Branch, acting by Representatives, their Assemblies are more deliberate, and less factious, than at Rome, where the People appeared in Person.

The Circumstances of the British Colonies, just rising out of the Difficulties of an infant State, do not admit of such a regular Distribution of Power. To forward the full Settlement of a new Country, such a Division, and Diffusion of the Lands is Necessary, as shall leave the Profits wholly in the Hands of those who cultivate them. Hence our Laws for making partition of real Estates among all the Children of the Family; and for the ready Sale of Lands to satisfy Debts, equitable in themselves, are even political in such a Country as this: but they render the Rise and Establishment of an upper Rank among us, difficult, if not impracticable.

In this State of Things, it behooves the People of North-America, to consider fully what political Consequences and Effects the Introduction of diocesan Bishops among them may produce. By Dr. Chandler's Account of them, as smooth as he writes, we find they are not to be mere voluntary Bishops, such as the Moravian Church has, but Prelates commissioned by the Nation, as branching from the ecclesiastical Establishment in England. Nor are these American Bishops to be suffered to tarnish the Splendor of their Brethren at home, by being left to the precarious Maintainance of the Episcopalians here; as was the Case in the primitive Times of the Christian Church. But Thousands of Pounds sterling have been laying up and accumulating at Interest, for above half a Century past, as a Fund for supporting one or two of them.[a] Besides this, it is intimated that many Persons in England, stand ready to contribute to this Use, as soon as the Scheme shall be put in Execution. Hereafter, great Matters may be expected from the Crown Lands, which it is proposed to set apart for the Benefit of the American Hierarchy; but till the further Settlement and Improvement of the Colonies, shall raise these to a proper Value, "*the general Tax on the Country,*" which Dr. Chandler speaks of, Page 107, may supply all Deficiencies.

This Scheme of the Episcopal Missionaries and their Patrons, the Society for Propagating the Gospel, whatever they intend by it, would be likely to have great influence on civil Government and public Liberty; and therefore, whether we consider the Thing itself, or the Method taken to obtain it, our most serious Attention cannot but be awakened on this Occasion.

In their Zeal for their Hierarchy, these Gentlemen, possibly, have not considered what they are about, in this View. Or if any of them have glanced so much beside their own Concernments, as to have perceived the obvious Effects of their Proposal on political Affairs, they may have reconciled to themselves the Pursuit of so dangerous a Measure, by the Prospect of the spiritual Advantages they expect will flow from it.

For my part, I have often esteemed it a great Advantage to the northern Colonies, that their Clergy have very little Weight in Government. This is owing to the moderate Salaries paid them;

to their Debates and Divisions about the Modes and Circumstantials of Religion; and to the want of general Connection among themselves, and with the Churches established in Britian. By their Dissentions, we are secured from the Usurpations and Encroachments they might otherwise make as a Body; for one Denomination carefully watches another, and sounds the Alarm on Occasion of any Schemes that may be devised to the Prejudice of the Public. This also keeps up a Spirit of Free-enquiry, and prevents the ill Effects of a fond superstitious Credulity.

But here is a Measure proposed, that directly tends to form and combine this Order of Men into a regular and powerful Band; and to put them under the Direction of superior Officers, invested with great Powers over the rest. It is also calculated to connect them by Uniformity, Establishment and Interest with the Church established in England.

It was formerly proposed that the Clergy, on account of their Wealth and Influence, should be considered as a fourth Estate in Parliament, but this happily did not take Place.[b] Among us, they must be much more than a separate Estate; they can have no equals in the Colonies. Whilst for Civil Government the British Dominions on the Continent are already divided into seventeen Provinces, the Episcopal Clergy (who may before long, by proper Management, and the Aid of Acts of Parliament, be augumented to three or four Thousand in Number) will be collected and disciplined under twenty or more Bishops, and a Primate appointed from home. What restraint or check will there be on the Views and Schemes of a Body so well compacted, so weighty, so well established by, and so well allied to powerful Hierarchies in Europe. Without an Order of Nobility to stand on equal Footing with the Prelates; without Courts of common Law, of Jurisdiction extensive enough to issue Prohibitions and correct the Proceedings of the Archbishop and his Suffragans, when they exceed their proper Limits; as the Spiritual Courts in England frequently do; without a General Assembly of the Colonies, or other Association for civil Purposes, in what Circumstances must the Laity be to guard themselves against the ambitious Designs of the spiritual Power? In short they must lie entirely at the Mercy and Moderation of the Clergy. And what these are, let Spain, let Italy, let the History of England, in papal Times, and even since the Reformation, under the Government of the House of *Stuart*, picture out to the Readers.[c] Men in all Ages and of every Character are much the same in regard to the Abuse of Power; and their Conduct when they get above Controul, loudly proclaims the Necessity of attending to the proper Distribution of it in every free Government, that would preserve its Constitution.

INTERNAL NOTES: "CENTINEL" IX

[a]Dr. Chandler from Recollection instances six Gifts or Legacies, some of them of 50 Years standing, which amount £4500 sterling; doubtless there are many smaller ones. These having been at Interest, must now make a very considerable Fund; of which about £826 only appear to have been expended for a House at Burlington. See Appeal, Pages 108 & 50.[1]

[b]*Gilbert*, on the Exch. 48.[2]

[c]"It hath been a great Mistake among us, that the Papist Religion is the only one, of all Christian Sects, proper to introduce and establish Slavery.—Other Religions have succeeded as effectually as ever Popery did." *Lord Molesworth's* Account of *Denmark*: He instances in that Kingdom; yet he observes the Super-intendants or Bishops there, have no Temperalities, nor any Power over the other Clergy; being only *Primi inter pares*, First among Equals.[3]

NOTES: "CENTINEL" IX

1. An unknown benefactor, probably Archbishop Thomas Tenison, gave £ 1,000 in 1718, Dugal Campbell bequeathed £500 in 1720, Lady Elizabeth Hastings presented £500 in 1741 and Bishop Benson of Gloucester left a legacy in 1752.
2. Sir Geoffrey Gilbert, *A Treatise on the Court of the Exchequer* (London, 1758), p. 48.
3. Robert, Lord Viscount Molesworth, *An Account of Denmark as it was in the Year 1692*, 5th ed. (Glasgow, 1745), chapter 16, p. 179.

Centinel Number X

May 26, 1768

—Brethren, who came in privily—to spy out our Liberty, which we have in Christ Jesus, that they might bring us into Bondage.

—*St Paul to Gal.* ii. 4.[1]

The Clergy, whenever Opportunity has offered, have appeared as apt to pervert Power, as other People, and their Conduct too plainly proves that "we have the Treasure of Religion conveyed to us in earthen Vessels."[a] This should teach us to distinguish carefully between the Schemes of ambitious Ecclesiasticks, and the true Interests of Christianity. If this be forgotten, the Laity will soon be reduced to spiritual Thraldom, and the Ministers of Religion, neglecting their proper Duties, will become Competitors with the Magistrate, for civil Power.

These are far from being Conjectures only; our own History, not to recur to those of other Nations, abounds with numerous Instances of this Temper in Men, who are by Profession, abstracted from worldly Business. Even the Monks, who apparently renounced all Intercourse with Society, and pretended to retire to Cells and Deserts, could not resist the Temptation of exercising the extensive Influence, which their sanctified Character among the credulous Multitude, gave them.

In fact, this Order has ever been found to consist of speculative men, clear-sighted to their own Interests, adhering closely together, and pursuing their Views with Steadiness. As an incorporate Body that never dies, they build for Ages, and their Fabricks almost always affect, often endanger the Welfare of the State. The large Revenues, Privileges, Immunities and Jurisdictions, which they claimed and exercised in the Days of Popery, rendered them formidable to the civil Magistrate, and invested with excessive Powers a Body of Men, who never want a plausible Pretence for making other Usurpations. That System had indeed been the Work of many dark Ages, when the Ignorance, Barbarism, and Superstition of Rulers and People, afforded the most commodious Opportunity of puting their Schemes of Aggrandizement into Practice. Whoever looks into the History of those Times, will be apt to conclude, that the Priests had imagined all Mankind were made for their Advantage, and that the Christian Revelation was considered by them, as a cunning Fable, invented for the Benefit of the Clergy.

Although Popery has been abolished, still the Clergy "are Men of like Passions with others."[b] It does not yet Appear, they have got above the Temptations to Pride & Arrogance, which are apt to be excited and gratified by dictating the religious Faith and Principles of the People. Ambition, and a Lust of unbounded Rule with the other Passions and Disorders of the human Breast, are by no means, in our Days, confined to the Laity: and therefore, the present Ministers of Religion have no better Claim to extensive Authority, than their Predecessors.

The ecclesiastical Scheme that has been pursuing, as to the Colonies, is this; the leading Clergy in England, desirous of encreasing their Power, and of building up a mighty Hierarchy in the British Empire, are labouring to bring the Colonies under their Dominion, by every Device they can think of. Many Circumstances seem favourable to this Scheme; most of the Provinces South of Pennsylvania, & the W. India Islands, have by their own Acts of Assembly, provided a regular parochial Maintenance for the episcopal Ministers. The like has been obtained by Artifice in some few Districts of New-York, and an Attempt has lately been made to extend it.[4] In Nova-Scotia, Episcopacy according to the Church of England, is declared to be established; but as it might put a total Stop to the settling of that new Province, no Tax for supporting the Clergy, is yet levied on Dissenters. Attempts have been made, more than once, to get a legal Assessment in the lower Government of Pennsylvania, for the same Purpose.[5] And as establishing Lands for pious Uses, is not restrained by the Laws of the Colonies, as in England, and most other Countries in Europe; and as the old Statutes made against granting Lands to the Church, are not supposed to extend here, Measures are taken to advance the Interests of the designed Hierarchy, by making Acquisitions of this Sort. Accordingly Instructions have been procured from the Crown to the Governors of New-Hampshire to grant a Proportion of every new Township to the Society for Propagating the Gospel; and a like Practice has been begun at New-York.[6] In that City and its Suburbs the Lands of the episcopal Church are extensive and valuable; and if the

Place continues to increase, they must in Time become an immense Estate. The Dodrington Plantation in Barbados, which is vested in the said Society, for the Purpose of supporting a College, is suffered to extend and accumulate in a most rapid Manner. To these might be added the Funds of the Colleges of New-York and Williamsburgh, the numerous Glebes and Manses of the Clergy in America, and the designed Tracts of Land for the future benefit of the Bishops, and for perfecting the Scheme; which hereafter may become of enormous Value, when taken, with the above Particulars, into one Computation.[7]

That Nothing may be wanting to perfect the Spiritual Kingdom, the most vigorous Attempts have been making for above half a Century to episcopize the middle and northern Colonies, which were settled by Non-Conformists, and for this Purpose a large Fund has been employed in sending out Missionaries to these People, as if they were Heathen, and utterly void of all Gospel Knowledge. But as it has ever proved a difficult Matter to change an Ancestorial Religion,[c] especially where Prejudice and old Debates stand in the Way, the Progress of this Part of the System is by no means answerable to the Expence and Pains, it has cost; especially as these Missionaries have had no superior Advantages, as to greater Strictness of Life, Pungency of Address in enforcing their Doctrines, or Novelty as to the Subjects of them; Therefore two or three Bishops with State Appointment, and Lordly Revenue are now proposed in Order to forward this "grand Affair."[d] The well disposed People in England have been formerly amused with the Design of converting Indians, and by this Argument, they were induced to contribute largely to the Fund of the Society. They are now told, the Reason why no more has been done in this important Business, is the want of well endowed Bishopricks in the Colonies;[e] tho' it is evident they never engaged seriously in the Matter. In short, tho' the Society has debarred others from doing it to Purpose, the Conversion of the Indians in both Cases is a meer Pretence.

There are now upwards of five hundred and fifty parish ministers in New-England; suppose all the colonies settled equally with that country, and equally furnished with religious Teachers and all these of the Episcopal Denomination, with Diocesan Bishops, and Primate subordinate to a Patriarch at Lambeth; what a mighty Body would this Connection form, what Colony could pretend to govern the Clergy within its Limits, whilst such a *Imperium in Imperio* subsisted? At present the Episcopal Colonies find it difficult enough to oblige these People, who interest the Bishops of England in their Pretensions on every Occasion, to submit to any

Acts of Assembly that may affect them:[f] but combined by a regular Plan of Discipline authorized by Parliament, they will no longer be Subjects, but Lords and Masters over every Jurisdiction in America.

It may pass with Children and the blinded Devotees of the Order, "that no such temporal Powers will be exercised here, as have been claimed and exercised in England; nay that the American Bishops, are even to be reduced much below the Standard there; to have no Power over the Episcopal Laity much less over Dissenters; to have no Courts,[g] &c. But none who know the Nature of Man, or have considered the Transactions of past Ages, can pay the least Regard to such Declarations. Can it be believed by any Man in his Senses, that the leaders of a Body of Men, who by their Offices, Endowments, Polity, Connection and Alliances must unavoidably have great weight in Public Affairs, will be so mortified to worldly Considerations, as to renounce the Influence and Power, their high Stations must give them? No such Instance has ever happened in Church or State, since the World began. Some rare Instances indeed may be quoted, of Individuals, who being possessed of high and dangerous Authority, have had the Magnanimity to renounce it; but of Bodies-Politic, Senates, or other Combinations of Men, we meet with none; Large Assemblies or Orders of Men are not diffident of their Capacity to exercise Power, or if some among them should be so, the more assured Majority overrule the few squeamish Brethren; besides the odium of severe Measures, being divided among so many, it has less effect in Restraining their Proceedings.

The recapitulation of the temporal Advantages, which the Episcopal Clergy have obtained in the Provinces, is not made with an invidious design; but merely to alarm all People against the grand scheme of Spiritual Dominion, that seems to be planned for this Country. If Church-Discipline is to be regulated by the Legislatures here, I shall be in no great pain for Civil Liberty on this Account; tho' it might be prudent to put some Limits to the Church possessions of all Denominations. They neither serve any purpose to Religion, nor Government; but often prove mischievious to both: Without these, the Clergy could never be an Object of much Distrust to the Magistrate;[h] nor would it be worth his while to interfere in Religious Matters, as he often does, to his own Loss, and the Corruption of Christianity, by debasing it into a political Engine. But when the Church enjoys large Revenues, her Officers become too important Members of the Community, to be suffered to go loose, and unconnected with the State; and the Magistrate, for his own Safety, must establish the prevailing Sect, by which he offends and perhaps distresses others, and loses the Affections of many good Subjects.

Can it then be prudent, or safe, or consistent with good policy, quietly to suffer "this Yoke of Bondage to be put on our Necks, which neither we nor our Fathers were able to bear."[i] If the Power of the Crown, the Weight of the Nobility, and the National Influence collected in Parliament, have scarcely been able on some Occasions to restrain the Hierarchy at home, what must be the Consequences of a like plan of Discipline extended through, and independent of the Colonies; where, for want of the Constitutional Ballances of the Mother Country, the influence and weight of the Clergy, must enable them to enforce every claim to Power and Independence, which *Laud*, or the highest flyers of the Church of England have ever started.[11]

INTERNAL NOTES: "CENTINEL" X

[a]Corinth. IV. 7.[2]

[b]Acts XIV. 15.[3]

[c]This has been very much the case of *Ireland*, where, setting aside the Scots and English settlers, the alteration among the Natives has been very inconsiderable, notwithstanding the Protestant Establishment has subsisted above 200 Years. Perhaps less precipitation and severity in this Business, had been better. Any Nation, especially one claiming to be free, would resent extremely an Attempt to impose a new Religion, to which there was no predisposition in its People; but in that Kingdom, on the contrary, the rude uncultivated Inhabitants, were to the last degree attached to a Superstition, from which they suffered the greatest Injuries. No wonder State-convulsions followed, and that when these were punished by Confiscations and capital Penalties, general Rebellions and Massacres followed. —Thus was the Protestant Religion discredited by its imprudent Friends in the Eyes of the Irish, and its Prospects effectually hindered.—Is not the present Policy toward the Canadians wiser and more humane?

[d]In *Appeal*, Page 49, The Schemes of an American Episcopate, is so stiled.

[e]One Chapter of the *Appeal* is wholly employed on this Topic.

[f]The most remarkable Instance of this sort, that I now recollect, happened in Virginia, some few Years since, on Occasion of an Act of Assembly commonly called the Two-Penny Act. It affected all Salary men Civil and Ecclesiastical: the civil Officers submitted to the Legislative Regulations; but the Clergy revolted; and applying to England, by Means of their great Friends, the Bishops, got the Act Repealed, with expressions of Royal Displeasure to the Governor for passing it.[8]

[g]See Dr. Chandler's *Appeal*, Pages 79, 80, 81, 94, 95.

[h]Mr. Hume observes, that when the Abbey and Churchlands, which had been seized by Henry the VIII and given to the Nobility, were confirmed to them by Act of Parliament (1st and 2d. of Philip and Mary) the Power of the Papacy was effectually Suppressed; for tho' the Jurisdiction of the Ecclesiasticks was restored, *their Property, on which their Power depended* was irretrievably lost, and no Hopes remained of recovering it. See his His. Eng.[9]

[i]Acts, 15. 10.[10]

NOTES: "CENTINEL" X

1. Galatians 2:4. The complete verse is, "And that because of false brethren unawares brought in, who came in privily to spy out our liberty which we have in Christ Jesus, that they might bring us into bondage."

2. II Corinthians 4:7. The complete verse is, "But we have this treasure in earthen vessels, that the excellency of the power may be of God and not of us."

3. Acts 14:15. The verse should read, "We also are men of like passions with you."

4. A New York law, passed in 1693, provided public support for Protestant ministers in the four southern counties of that colony. The royal governors interpreted that law to mean support for Anglican ministers only. See footnote 6 below for the attempts to extend this support.

5. Under William Penn's charter, twenty male adherents of the Church of England who would promise to provide a house and church (and after 1740 a glebe) could petition the SPG for a missionary, whose stipend could be augmented by local subscriptions. In many cases, the stipend, house, church, and glebe received inadequate local funding, leading the missionaries to apply for support from the legislature of the Three Lower Counties.

6. Governor Benning Wentworth followed these instructions by setting aside land in each of the one hundred and twenty-eight new townships for a glebe for the first minister's private property and for an endowment for the SPG. When New York received jurisdiction over this land, now known as Vermont, the Society wanted to retain these grants and urged that New York make similar reservations for the Society in all future land grants. The controversy was just beginning in 1768.

7. The most recent attempt to enlarge these land holdings came from Sir William Johnson, Northern Commissary for Indian affairs, in January, 1768. He offered 20,000 acres of land to support a bishop if the Crown would grant an equal amount. The Dissenters did not yet know that the King's government would refuse the offer.

8. The controversy, commonly called the "Parson's Cause," which arose over the Two-Penny Act of 1758, was a bit more complicated than the "Centinel" suggests. It involved not only the medium of payment to the clergy but also the vestries' right to church patronage and the authority of the House of Burgesses to alter a provincial law confirmed by the Crown. Since 1696, the Burgesses had set the clergy's annual salaries at 1,600 pounds of tobacco. The Crown confirmed the acts which implemented this arrangement which could not be altered without permission of the English government. Because of the smallness of the tobacco crops after 1753 and the subsequent rise in the value of tobacco, a series of acts were passed which allowed the vestries to pay their ministers in money. The Virginia clergy protested to England, got the acts disallowed, and elicited a judgment against Lieutenant Governor Francis Fauquier for allowing the passage of laws which altered acts already confirmed by the Crown. The ministers did fail in their attempt to lessen the power of the vestries to control church offices. The controversy which raged from 1758 until 1764 exposed anticlerical and anti-English sentiments which were eloquently presented by Patrick Henry as counsel for the House of Burgesses.

9. David Hume, *The History of England from the Invasion of Julius Caesar to the Abdication of James the Second*, (6 vols., Boston, 1858), 3: 411–12.

10. The complete verse is, "Now therefore why tempt ye God, to put a yoke upon the neck of the disciples which neither our fathers nor we were able to bear."

11. William Laud, Archbishop of Canterbury. See "Centinel" III, note 3.

Centinel Number XI

June 2, 1768

It was remarked in a former Paper, that if the Jurisdiction of Parliament to interfere in the internal Police of the Colonies, was ever so well established, yet it would be extremely dangerous for us to have so very delicate a Part of it as Church Polity, regulated by that respectable Body; especially as the Proposal has come from the Clergy, speaking as they pretend, in behalf of a Million of American Episcopalians. The Members might indeed afford it as much Attention as they usually give to American Business;[a] and whilst they incautiously adopt the Financier's Scheme for taxing us, they might as readily receive from the Clergy, a System of Faith and Discipline for the American Church. If it had the outward Appearance of the Religious Establishment of England, they would scarce examine further, but agree to it without a Vote; and, however, unsuitable and inconvenient to the Circumstances of this Country, they would doubtless consider any Complaints from America, as humoursome, if not factious, and highly inconsistent with the Submission and Reverence due to the Supreme Legislature.

However highly we may think of the Wisdom and Justice of the British Senate, yet we cannot but see strong Marks of their sustaining a quite different Character in considering Home Affairs, from what they do in providing for us. It is easy to perceive, that when the Subjects within the Realm, and consequently the Individuals of the Legislature, are to be affected by the Parliamentary Proceedings, the Debates are serious and lively, the Scrutiny into the Consequences of the Business proposed, strict and curious; and the Appearance of Interest and Feeling, visible to all. Hence their Statutes in these Cases being penned with Care and corrected with Caution, usually become lasting Monuments of the Prudence of the national Councils.[b]

But this is by no Means the Case, when a Bill is brought in to bind the Subjects *without* the Realm, for the Benefit of those *within* it. Here the Character of the watchful Representative no longer appears; the Business if at all attended to, and not treated as a Thing of Course, is only regarded as it affects the superior Kingdom: Whilst the People in the subordinate States and Districts of the

Empire, are left to learn their inferior Situation from the crude and mistaken Provisions of the new Statute; which without really serving the real Interests of any Part of the British Dominions, tend to distress and enslave the distant Subjects.

There is a most remarkable Instance of this, in the very different Conduct of the Parliament towards the Admiralty Jurisdiction in England, and in America. The Proceedings in this Court, being before a single Judge, *according to the Course of the Civil Law*, have ever been looked on, and treated as repugnant to the free Constitution of England, which making the People Judges of one another, has provided in the best Manner for the Liberty and Safety of the Subject. Trial by Jury, is indeed that happy Mode of administering Justice, which having survived the various Changes and Convulsions of the State, has been preserved and handed down to us; and GOD grant we may be able to transmit to our Children! To the Admiralty Law, therefore, the Temper and Policy of our Ancestors have always shewn Aversion and Jealousy. They seemed rather of Necessity to endure, than of Choice to encourage it.

Accordingly the common Law is the Law of the Land, and the Civil and Canon Law are no further permitted than to give Relief in Cases to which the other is wholly inapplicable, or which it does not provide for.[c] They who would draw any Thing out of its Jurisdiction, must intitle themselves well, says Lord Raymond. If the Admiralty undertakes to judge in Matters manifestly without their Limits, the Judge and Party[d] prosecuting, are treated as offending against the Statutes of *Premunire* devised against the foreign Jurisdiction, of the Pope, by which they forfeit their Lands and Goods and the Protection of the law, and are to be imprisoned. But if this Court takes Cognizance of a Matter of a mixed Nature, partly within their Jurisdiction, and partly not; or should so little trespass their Boundaries, a Prohibition will be issued from the King's Court, to correct, or wholly stop further Proceeding.[e] It may not be amiss to remark here, that the Courts of the Clergy, the *spiritual Courts*, are under the same wholesome Restraint,[f] and the Canon Law is suffered to operate no further than the Law of the Land has adopted it[g] which is extremely necessary, as otherwise we might be led into the endless Mazes of that arbitrary System.

Not content with this, sundry Acts of Parliament have been passed to circumscribe, and as it were to naturalize this Jurisdiction. It is by meer indulgence, that Mariners are suffered to sue, in the Admiralty, for their Wages; it being expressly against an old Statute, which had rather too severely forbid it. Lord Hale contends, that the Court of Kings-Bench, had certainly a concurrent Power with the Admiralty in Case of Felonies done upon the narrow Seas, or Coast, as though it were high Seas, because within the King's Realm of England; but says, this Jurisdiction of the common Law, was interrupted by a special Order of the King and Council, 35 Ed; 3d, and that since 38 Ed; 3d., it does not appear, that the King's Courts have taken cognizance of Crimes committed on the high Seas.[h] However as Trade began to extend, and Tryals for capital Offences, before this unconstitutional Jurisdiction, more frequently to occur, the Nation would not endure it; and therefore, by two Statutes of Henry the eighth,[i] a Commission of Oyer and Terminer was ordered to issue out of Chancery, directed to the Judge of Admiralty, and others, to inquire of, and punish all Traytors, Pirates, Robbers at sea, and other marine Felons, *according to the Course of the common Law*; which Practice continues to this Day. Again, by a modern Statute,[j] it is provided, that if any one be feloniously stricken, or poisoned upon the Sea, and dies at Sea, or beyond Sea, the Fact shall be triable in any County, *according to the Course of common Law.*

Thus have the Legislature, and the Judges of the Land, wisely concured, in curbing and qualifying this arbitrary Mode of judging, as far as it relates to the mother Country. If we enquire what has been the Conduct of Parliament towards admiralty Jursidiction in the Colonies, we shall find it has been the Reverse; and that a Court, whose Powers have ever been carefully circumscribed within the Realm, has been favoured with new, and extraordinary Jurisdiction in America; that Matters quite foreign to its Nature are made cognizable there; and all Restraint and Superintendency of the Common Law taken away.

As to Pirates, and other Sea-felons, they and their Accessories are to be tried in the Colonies, before a Bench of Judges, appointed by Commission under the great Seal, or Seal of the Admiralty,[k] *according to the Course of the Admiralty,* that is without a Jury; and the Charters of the Provinces are set aside as far as they interfere with this Court; which is the more extraordinary and dangerous, inasmuch as the Judges are the respective Governors and Councils; who in case of the absence, or want of Members to make up a competent Number, are directed to associate such Captains in the Navy, Masters of Ships, or Merchants they see fit; contrary to the very Nature of the Office of a Judge, which is a trust of personal Confidence and Skill, and may not be put over to others. How arbitrary is this Revival of the Admiralty Jurisdiction towards Americans! How loose and dangerous the Exercise of it!

This, it may be said, was only restoring the proper Jurisdiction of the Admiralty. But why should a Jurisdiction be revived in the Colonies, which had been found intolerable in the mother-Country? The Laws of Trade, have however introduced a new one; which was first craftily slipt into the Act of Navigation, by directing that Vessels seized by Ships of War for Breach of that Statute, should, in the Colonies, be proceeded against in this Court;[l] other Cases were left to the Cognizance of the Law of the Land. By an Act of William the Third,[m] this new Authority was extended; and ever since it hath been the usual Course for the Parliament to refer the Execution of any new Statutes, passed for regulating our Trade, to the same Judicature; so that heavy Penalties, even the Forfeiture of Ships, and their Cargoes, are often adjudged here.

Yea, such a favourite is the American Admiralty, that the British Legislature, on assuming a Power to tax the Colonies, has given much of the Business of the Court of Exchequer, which is a Court of common Law, to this arbitrary Tribunal.[n] And, not content with bringing it ashore at our Sea-Ports, and enabling it to scourge our Merchants, they have sent it up into our Forrests, and directed that the Penalties imposed on such Persons as shall destroy his Majesties Pine-Trees in New-England, New-York, and New-Jersey, shall be recoverable in the Admiralty.[o]

Can any Thing more fully manifest the Difference between a *virtual* Representative, and a *real* one? Does it not sadly expose the Hardship, the Authors of that *ideal* Character, were reduced to, when they seriously advanced such a wretched Argument for binding America by Acts of Parliament? Is there any sympathetic Affection in these suppositious Delegates, for the Subjects without the Realm? or the least Attention shewn to their Interests? Or, is it any Wonder, that Ministers of State, are able to procure the parliamentary Sanction, to whatever they draw up for the Colonies, without Enquiry or Debate?

This may Account for a most extraordinary Statute; that has been passed the very last Sessions of Parliament, which gives a new Blow to our Rights as Englishmen. By this, Provision is made for erecting three or four Admiralty Courts on this Continent, each to have Jursidiction over two or more Provinces; by which the constitutional and wholesome Superintendency of the common Law over the Civil, is wholly evaded, as there is no Court of King's Bench in America, of equally extended Jurisdiction.

The Pretence of this new Measure might be, that the Multitude of Judges of Admiralty and their Officers, left without to spunge upon the Colonies for a Living, had been a long and just Subject of complaint, and could not be well remedied, except by lessening their Number, and giving proper Appointments to those which remained. Suppose the Matter placed in this Light, and what Member, not well acquainted with the internal Affairs of this Country, could have any Objection against a Regulation, in Appearance necessary, and for ought he could see, attended with no dangerous Consequence, not even the least Inconvenience.

It is scarce necessary for me to remark on this indignant Treatment of a loyal, a useful, and a numerous Body of British Subjects. But can any good Man in his right Senses think of an Application to "our Superiors in England" for an ecclesiastical Constitution, after this View of their Conduct towards us in the important Business of Admiralty Law.

INTERNAL NOTES: "CENTINEL" XI

[a]Witness the Success of Captain Cole, in getting the free Exportation of Rice restrained, for his own Purposes; the Blunders in the late regulating Statutes, concerning the Word Ireland; as mentioned in the Patriot *Farmer's* Letters.[1]

[b]How different the late regulating and revenue Laws for America! hence the several Repeals; the Inconsistencies and want of precision, observable in most of them.

[c]Burn's Eccles. Law. Preface.[2]

[d]If one Libel in the Admiralty for a Thing done on the Land, and it appeareth upon the Libel to be so, and they notwithstanding hold Plea of it, a Premunire lyeth on it; but if the same do not appear on the Libel, then a Prohibition only shall Issue.—2 Leonard, 183, Sir Richard Buckley's Case. 13 Richard II. Cap. 5th., 15 Richard II Cap. 3, 2d. Henry IV, Cap. 11.

[e]Roll's Abrid. 532, 533.[3]

[f]Henry VIIIth. encouraged the Judges on all Occasions to interpose in Ecclesiastical Causes wherever they thought the Law or Royal Prerogative concerned. A happy Innovation says Hume, tho' at first invented for arbitrary Purposes. See his Hist. Eng.[4]—The Clergy objected afterwards that since all Church as well as State Jurisdiction flowed from the King, it was strange he should correct his Ecclesiastical Power by his Civil; not considering the Difference between the Law of the Land, and the arbitrary Nature of the other. Archbishop Laud frightened the Judges in his Time from this Practice.

[g]Burn's Eccles. Law. Preface.[5]

[h]His: Pleas of Ct: Vol: 2, Pages 14 and 15.[6]

[i]Stat. 27, Henry VIII, Cap: 4–28 Henry VIII, Cap: 15—These Statutes do not alter the Offence or make that Felony which was not so before, but leaveth it as it was before the Statute, viz. Felony by the civil Law, but give a means of Tryal by the common Law: Molloy, 74.[7]

[j]Stat: 2, Geo. III. Cap: 21.

[k]Stat 11 & 12, Will. III Cap: 7–6th. Geo. I, Cap. 19–8 Geo. I. Cap. 18.

[l]Stat. 12. Char. II, Cap. 18.

[m]Stat. 7 & 8 Will. III. Cap. 22–5 Geo. II, Cap. 24–6 Geo. III, Cap. 13.

[n]See Stamp Act etc.

[o]Stat. 8 Geo I. Cap. 12–2 Geo. II, Cap. 35.

NOTES: "CENTINEL" XI

1. John Dickinson, *Letters from a Farmer in Pennsylvania to the Inhabitants of the British Colonies* (Philadelphia, 1768), Letter VIII.

2. Richard Burn, *Ecclesiastical Law,* (2 vols., London, 1763), "Preface."

3. Knightley D'Anvers, *A General Abridgment of the Common Law (Compiled by Henry Rolle) Alphabetically digested under proper titles.* (4 vols., London, 1705–1737), 1: 532, 533.

4. David Hume, *The History of England from the Invasion of Julius Caesar to the Abdication of James II, 1688.* (6 vols., Boston, 1858), chapter 30, p. 196.

5. Burn, *Ecclesiastical Law.*

6. Sir Matthew Hale, *Historia Placitorum Coronae: The History of the Pleas of the Crown.* (2 vols., London, 1736), 2: 14, 15.

7. Charles Molloy, *De Jure Maritime et Navali: or, a Treatise of Affairs Maritime and of Commerce.* (3 books, London, 1682), Book I, chapter 4, para. 15.

Centinel Number XII

June 9, 1768

In my last Publication, I stated the Conduct of Parliament towards the Admiralty Court in England, and compared it with their very different Behaviour towards it in America. I think it a very remarkable and alarming Instance of the mischievous Effects, that must follow from "our Superiors" in England undertaking to make internal Regulations for the Colonies. If they should listen to the Missionaries, and attempt to provide for us a religious Establishment, they would probably do us much more Harm, as the Subject is of more Importance. Every Circumstance leads to this Conclusion.

No Body of Men is interested in supporting undue Stretches of Power, or Abuses in the Admiral's Court, and it is not improbable, that on proper and reiterated Representations, the Ministers of State might do us Justice, in Respect of that arbitrary Judicature, or other Instances wherein our Rights have been violated; at least it would be in their Power to do it. The Success of the People of Ireland, in procuring the Limitation of their Parliaments, and the Independency of their Judges after long Endeavours, ought to inspire our Attempts, and never suffer us to despair of recovering our Rights.[1]

But if the Clergy once gain an Advantage, let the Inconveniences, or Oppressions it brings on the Laity be what they will, there is no coming at Redress. These People have the Artifice of making a Zeal for Orthodoxy, and a Regard for their own Interests go Hand in Hand. By asserting their Claims and Encroachments to be of divine Right, under Establishments they tie up the Hands of the Magistrate, and make it dangerous for him to reform the most acknowledged and most pernicious Abuses.[a] Thus, when other Arguments have failed, Forms of Church-Government, particularly Diocesan Episcopacy;[b] the uninterrupted Succession of Bishops;[c] Tythes;[d] Exemption of the Clergy from civil Authority &c.[e] have, at one Time or another, been stiffly maintained to be of divine Right: and this, when once instilled into the zealous, but ignorant and more numerous Part of their Flocks, has generally enabled them to support the most unreasonable Usurpations, and to baffle all Attempts at Reformation.

The Risque we should run, would be heightened by another Circumstance: The *Successors of the Apostles* in England, whose Power over their inferior Clergy, whose Revenues, Dignities, and Seats in Parliament, necessarily give them great Weight, would find themselves interested to have every Power, every Privilege they enjoy, as far as possible, extended to their Brethren, the American Bishops. The Example of a reduced Episcopate in the British Dominions, they could not but esteem dangerous to their own Jurisdiction, and they must of Course be induced to exert all their Endeavours, and to watch every Opportunity, which a weak Administration or other favourable Conjuncture, might afford, to advance and aggrandize the American Hierarchy; in which, from the Experience we have had of the Disposition of same, and the Inattention of most of our *virtual* Representatives, there is too much Reason to fear they would succeed to their Wishes; at least no Argument can be drawn from the Watchfulness of the Laity of England, over the Clergy there, that a like Caution would subsist as to the Clergy of the Colonies: Witness the Case of Admiralty Jurisdiction.

Let us for a Moment suppose that Dr. Chandler's Scheme, as exhibited in Italicks, in the 79th. Page of his *Appeal*, as "without *Reservation* or *Equivocation*, the exact Plan of an American Episcopate, as it hath been settled at Home;" viz. "That the Bishops to be sent to the Colonies shall have no Authority, but purely of a spiritual and ecclesiastical Nature, such as is derived altogether from the Church and not from the State.—That this Authority shall operate only on the Clergy and not on the Laity, nor Dissenters of any Denomination.—That the Bishops shall not interfere with the Property or Privileges, whether Civil or Religious, of Churchmen or Dissenters.—That in particular they shall have no concern with the Probate of Wills, Letters of Guardianship, and Administration, or Marriage-Licences, nor be Judges of any Cases relating thereto; but that they shall only exercise the original Powers of their Office as before stated, i.e. ordain and govern the Clergy, and administer confirmation to such as desire it." Let us suppose, I say, that the Word of Dr. Chandler, a private Missionary, is to be taken in this most important Affair; and that the Bishops would, *at first*, be sent over with such limited Powers, what Security have we, that they and their Successors, for any long Time, would remain contented with such Limitations: In a Word, that they would continue such harmless, inoffensive People, as the Doctor represents them? Has this Order of Men been remarkable for such quiet unambitious Conduct? Or have they usually been free of a Disposition to intermeddle in worldly Matters? Does not their Apologist, *Dr. Chandler* intimate the very Reverse, when he says, Page 110, "Should the Government see fit hereafter to invest them with some Degree of civil Power, worthy of their Acceptance, none would be thereby injured?" Is it reasonable to think that the American Prelates, would ever be easy whilst in a Condition inferior to the superb, court-favoured, law-dignified Bishops of England; especially, as the Connections between them, would always keep alive the Hopes of the former, of arriving at the same Authority and Importance.

A late Writer (said to be of high spiritual Dignity beyond the Atlantic) assures us, that as the Bishops intended for America, are "to be appointed by the Crown, the smallest Attempts towards an oppressive Enlargement of spiritual Power would be immediately crushed with Indignation by the Legislature; and that the Moderation of the Clergy and the Watchfulness of the Laity over them, is much more likely to increase than diminish."[f] This is plausible, but not solid. However, at present we shall suppose, that under such Directors of the national Councils as have of late presided, there has been a Discovery of so much Wisdom and Integrity; *of so tender a Concern for the Interests of the Colonies; of so delicate an Apprehension of injuring their constitutional Rights,* as leaves no Room to fear any oppressive Enlargement of *spiritual* or *any other Power,* during the Continuance of such an *happy* Guidance of public Measures: Yet Times may change; Men of a different Stamp may be employed; who knows what another Reign may produce? Whatever may be promised now, yet Reasons of State, (which Dr. Chandler already holds out to our Superiors) it may be said, require more to be done for this *new-fangled* Hierarchy; for a Bishop without Authority over the Laity, is really a Novelty, which no Denomination of Christians that allowed of a regular Ministry, ever before thought of. Either sole or assisted, the Bishops or Pastors of all Sects have exercised it as of scriptural and unalienable Rights; nor can there be any Church of Christ on Earth, without this, or somewhat equivalent to it.

When the Bishops (to carry on the Supposition) shall be once quietly settled among us, we shall be told by Dr. Chandler, or some equal Advocate for the Order, "that the Church in America is in a most wretched and deplorable Condition, perishing for Want of common Necessaries, and under such Diseases, as must prove fatal to her, if much longer neglected; that she only requests, that proper Remedies may be provided for her Sufferings, leaving it to the

Wisdom of her Superiors, *whether any Thing further* is to *strengthen* and *improve* her Interests."[g] In short, she only asks, what cannot be denied by Christian Rulers, to a Christian Society connected with the State, what all other Denominations enjoy; a Power to exercise Discipline over the Laity. "The People are sensible of the Want of this Power over them, and find themselves free from all Restraints of Ecclesiastical Authority: And tho' the Church, as far as it has relation to civil Power, is in the Nature of it a free Society, yet after Men become Members, the Laws of the Church are in Force against them."[h] It is true, this was at first given up, but we find, we "are a Body without Strength, liable to be destroyed by innumerable Accidents";[i] in short, we are under an "unprecedented Hardship"[j] without it.

This granted, (how can Dr. Chandler talk of giving it up) the Necessity of Civil Co-action, or the Aid of the Magistrate to enforce the Censures of the Clergy, may be easily urged. Those, who are rejected by one "Church," it can be said, "are received by another." A Disposition to slight Excommunication, "the highest Punishment the Church can inflict, has become general; in this Age, the Voice of Reason will not be heard."[k] Civil Incapacity, and the Writ from the King's Court for imprisoning the excommunicate Persons,[l] are the only Remedy; and why should not the American Church be enabled to reduce obstinate Offenders to Obedience, as well as the Mother Church of England?

Suppose the Heirarchy invested with this Support, which by Virtue of her *Alliance* with the State, she will claim as her Right;[m] the next Demand will be, that all *Dissenters* be considered as *virtual* Churchmen, and made liable to Censures accordingly; for Discipline is evaded and the Church undermined. Then "a Tax on the Country to support the Bishops will be wanted;" for their Rank requires greater Revenue than can be raised by charitable Contributions, and it cannot be expected that the Mother Country will maintain the Clergy of America. And if a Tax can be justly levied for the Prelates, why not for the Parish Ministers; "it would be no mighty Hardship, nor can be, who would scruple to pay a Tax for this or *any Use* the Legislature of his Country should assign, deserve to be considered in the Light of a good Subject or Member of Society."[n] Nay the Security of the Church, in a Country abounding with Dissenters, indispensibly requires, that the *sacramental Test* should be extended to America; the Argument if much more forcible here, than in England, where the Non-Conformists are not thought to exceed one eighth of the People. "This can be no Hardship on Dissenters, as indeed they have no natural Right to any Degree of civil or military Powers."[o]

What Parliament could have the Conscience, "after such signal Displays of the Divine Favour towards the British Nation, whose Arms in America have triumphed over all that opposed them, to refuse to erect on that Ground some suitable Monument of religious Gratitude; and what so proper, as the further Security and Support of the *true* Religion in America. Other Nations have taken equal Care for the Establishment of ecclesiastical, as of civil Government in their most distant Colonies. In the French and Spanish Colonies, we find Bishops; and in Canada a compleat ecclesiastical Establishment under an Episcopate."[p] These Things will not cost the Members any Thing, nor in the least injure them: They are constitutional; agreeable to what is allowed at Home, and if they had been wrong, we should doubtless have given them up.

How insiduously, how easily might priestly Dominion thus steal in upon us and advance, is too manifest from Church History. The Reader will see, that Dr. Chandler has helped me to make out the Progress of the Scheme, by a Number of Seemingly useless Expressions dispersed through his Appeal. These are prudent Reserves for another Day; when the Words, *if, now,*[q] *at present, in the present State of Things,*[r] and *hereafter,*[s] may be of great Use, however *unmeaning* they may now seem to a careless Reader. This scheme of our Missionaries reminds me of the Instructions, which Pope Boniface gave to Austin and his Fellow-Missionaries, sent to Britain to convert the Saxons to Christianity and the Welsh, who were Christians already, to a proper Sense of the Pope's supremacy, (an essential Article, it seems they had *unfortunately* left out of their Creed) "you are," says his Holiness, "to move cautiously; let them not see all we aim at, lest we gain Nothing."[8]

INTERNAL NOTES: "CENTINEL" XII

[a]"I do not recollect any Instance in History since the Days of the Apostles, where the Reformation of Religion, in any material Point, hath been brought about by the Clergy in general." *Essay on Spirit,* Pref.—said to be Dr. *Clayton's,* late Bishop of the Church of Ireland.[2]

[b]Dr. *Bancroft,* in 1588, first preached up, in the Church of *England* after the Reformation, that Bishops were of divine Right, and Order superior to Presbyters. It surprised his Hearers. Archbishop *Whitgift* said, he rather wished, than believed it to be true.[3]

[c]In the Debate between Dr. *Hoadly,* then Bishop of *Bangor,* and the Nonjurors, the Doctor, with great Success, refuted this Whim.[4]

[d]When the Quakers fought for some Relief from Parliament concerning Tythes, the Clergy set up a Claim to them on this Ground.

[e]Thomas a *Becket,* Archbishop of *Canterbury,* in a Letter to the Empress *Matilda,* told her, "that an Exemption for Clergymen from all civil Justice, was one of the Privileges purchased by the Blood of Christ for his Church." *Lord Littleton's* Hist. Hen. II.[5]

[f]Answer to Dr. Mathew's Observation on Charter and Conduct, &c[6]

[g]See Dr. C's Appeal, P, 40, & 59 for these Quotations.
[h]Appeal, P. 29.
[i]Ibid 30.
[j]Ibid 77.
[k]Appeal, 30, 31.
[l]This Writ issues in 40 Days after Excommunication, in Case the Offender continues obstinate.
[m]*Dr. Warburton* insists on this, as the just claim of every established Religion.—Div. Legat. Book ii. Sect. 5.[7]
[n]Appeal, Page 107.
[o]Ibid. 109.
[p]See *Appeal,* Pages 45, 58, 59, for these Quotations.
[q]Page 110.
[r]Ibid. 105.
[s]Ibid. 110, 111.

NOTES: "CENTINEL" XII

1. Until 1760 the Irish parliament, subordinate to England, had been managed by corrupt "undertakers" whose main goal seemed to be directed toward earning favors from English landholders. After 1760 they began to raise their demands and, by 1768, had forced such concessions as limiting the duration of parliament to eight years, granting Irish judges the security of tenure, cutting down pensions, and introducing habeas corpus into the country.

2. [Robert Clayton], *An Essay on Spirit* (London, 1751), "Dedication." Clayton was Bishop of Clogher.

3. John Whitgift, archbishop of Canterbury, died in 1604 and was succeeded by Richard Bancroft.

4. Benjamin Hoadly began a debate in 1717, commonly known as the Bangorian controversy, by asserting that God's favor depended solely on sincerity in conscience and action rather than on any particular method of religious observation or interpretation of God's law. Therefore the Church of England, according to him, had no authority to enforce particular doctrine or discipline. The controversy elicited over 200 pamphlets from fifty-three writers.

5. George Lord Lyttelton, *The History of the Life of Henry II,* 2nd ed. (5 vols., London, 1767), 2:451–52.

6. [Thomas Secker], *An Answer to Dr. Mayhew's Observations* (Boston, 1764), p. 56.

7. William Warburton, *The Divine Legation of Moses Demonstrated, on the Principles of a Religious Deist,* (3 vols., 9 Books, London 1742), vol. 1, book 2, section 5.

8. Boniface VIII, Pope from 1294 until 1303, attempted to reassert the papacy's temporal supremacy over the state, especially in England and France. Boniface clashed with Edward I over whether the clergy had to contribute to the support of the state or be tried in secular courts. The pope lost the conflict.

Centinel Number XIII

June 16, 1768

There seems to be something perverse in human Nature, that prompts Men to give partial and unfair Representations, when it suits their Purpose. They conceal Truths, extenuate Faults, and diminish or magnify Difficulties as it serves their Turn, or contributes to carry their Designs into Execution. The Client loudly proclaims his Wrongs, and magnifies his Pretensions, while he industriously conceals from his Lawyer some of the strongest Circumstances that operate against him.

Doctor Chandler seems, in his *Appeal*, to labour under this Infirmity: he complains that the Episcopal Church in America suffers unparalleled Hardships: he insinuates, that the Complaints which he makes are the Complaints of a Million of British Subjects in America, suffering under unprecedented Hardships; and that all the Episcopal Clergy and Laity are joint Petitioners with him and his Friends for an American Episcopate, on the Plan he has mentioned. Whereas, in Fact, the People were never consulted on the Measure, nor were they ever heard to complain. The whole was concerted and carried on by a few Missionaries (whom the Doctor stiles the Clergy) of New-York and New-Jersey met together in a *voluntary* Convention. By what Right they assume such Power it may be well to enquire.

According to the English Constitution, every Part of his Majesty's extensive Dominions, where Governments are established, has a Power to take Care of Religion in a Way suited to the Genius and Persuasion of the People. At the Reformation, the English Parliament formed their Articles of Religion, and invested their King with all Power, as well Ecclesiastical as Civil, and modelled Church Government according to their Pleasure. They afterwards by the Act of Toleration made Provision for Dissenters from the established Church. The Legislature of Scotland, (after that Kingdom became a Branch of the British Empire) took Care of Religion in their own Way and established Church Discipline on a Plan different from that of England, which Plan was afterwards confirmed by the British Parliament when both Kingdoms were happily united.[1] In Ireland, though the religious Establishment be nearly the same as the English in Worship and Government, the Legislature claims the sole Right of establishing Articles and Canons, and of regulating the Affairs of their Church as to them seems best.[2] In some of the British Colonies in America, one Religious Denomination, in others another Denomination of Christians have been the peculiar Care of the Government; while in some, by the Constitution of the State, all enjoy equal Privileges.

I would therefore be glad to know by what Authority the Missionaries of New-York and New-Jersey, in Violation of the Constitution of the British Governments, and of the Rights of their fellow Subjects, usurp a Power of acting for all Episcopalians in America; of forming a new Plan of Episcopacy for them; and of petitioning "our Superiors" in Britain, that this *Plan* may be established in his Majesty's American Colonies by the British Legislature? Who commissioned them to act? They will not pretend to say, they exercise this Power by *Divine Right,* or as inherent in them? Who then, entrusted them with the Care of Religion in America? Or who, for Instance, empowered them to intermeddle with the State of it in the West-India Islands? Do the People either Clergy or Laity there complain of "unparalleled Hardships?" With regard to the Clergy in the Islands, an honourable Provision is made for their Support by the respective Legislatures. And if the People think themselves aggrieved, they know where to apply for Redress. They have Governors and Assemblies, in whose Power it is to regulate the Affairs of the Church in their respective Districts and to rectify what they think amiss in its Polity. Or, if they had not this Power, is it to be imagined that so respectable a body of his Majesty's Subjects, were they groaning under intolerable Grievances, as the Doctor represents, would not have addressed his Majesty, for Relief themselves rather than have entrusted so important an Affair with a few Missionaries in North-America, who are ignorant of their Laws and Circumstances? Let the World then judge whether the Petitions sent Home by the Missionaries of New-York and the Jerseys, and the *Appeal* published by Doct. C. as far as they respect the Islands, are not an insolent Invasion of the Rights of others, and a busy intermeddling with their Laws and Constitutions without their Consent or Approbation.

The same may be said of Virginia and Maryland. Have the Clergy or Laity of these Provinces ever complained of "unparalleled Sufferings" or empowered the "Missionaries met in a voluntary Convention," to complain in their Name? Are they not the best

Judges, when an Episcopate is necessary, and what Plan of Episcopacy will best suit themselves? At least are they not as good Judges as the Members of the Convention at Amboy? If an Episcopate be necessary to "ordain, and govern the Clergy and to administer Confirmation to such as shall apply for it," the common Appendages of Episcopacy are not necessary; but may and must be varied, as the Laws and Constitutions of different Governments may require. And to the Body of the People, to the Assemblies and Governors does it belong to regulate these Appendages. These Governments have provided for the Maintainance of the Clergy, in a Way most agreeable to themselves, and when they think it necessary to have a Bishop, they will, doubtless, fall upon Measures to have one. But what Right the Missionaries of New-York and New-Jersey have to publish Complaints in the Name of these People, while they themselves are silent, or to represent their Sufferings as intollerable and their Grievances as unparalleled, while they themselves express no Uneasiness, I cannot well comprehend.

But the Presumption of the Convention which voluntarily met at Amboy and took upon themselves to act as Representatives of all the Members of the English Episcopalians in America seems greatly heightened when we consider first that it was illegal according to the Canons of their Church, secondly, that none of the Laity met in it, and thirdly, that it was composed of but a Part of the Missionaries. Not above one or at the most two of the Episcopal Clergy in Pennsylvania (if I am well informed) met in Convention or were taken into their Consultations; and very few from New-England. The Episcopal Clergy in Pennsylvania are Men of too much Understanding to complain without Reason, and too well acquainted with the Charter and Laws of the Province, not to know that they enjoy the same Liberty as any other religious Denomination. They claim no Superiority over their fellow Christians, nor do they consider themselves in a State of Persecution, merely because they are not established by Act of Parliament, and their Opinions and Practices made a State Religion in Preference to all others. They know that a Difference in Religion does not deprive a subject of his "natural Right to any civil or military Power." And as to the Laity they are contented with the Privileges which they enjoy in common with their fellow Subjects.

Should any One ask who these Gentlemen are that met in this voluntary Convention and assumed to themselves such mighty Powers; I blush to think of the Answer that must be given. Certainly some Respect should have been had to Governors, to the

Members of his Majesty's Council, to the Representatives of the People in Assemblies met. They at least ought to have been consulted, before Application was made to his Majesty for an Episcopate, and before a Plan was concluded on different grounds from what was ever known in the Christian Church.

It might have derogated too much from the Dignity of this voluntary Convention, to have consulted with *Dissenters* on the Occasion, yet where those who reject Episcopacy are more than thirty or forty for one that prefers it, as is the Case in some of the Eastern Governments, thinking People will admit that some Regard should be had to them.

Upon the whole, then, it is evident, that neither the Addresses requesting an Episcopate, nor the bitter and indecent Complaints, of unprecedented Hardships and unparalleled Sufferings, are the Voice of the Clergy and Laity of the Episcopal Churches in America: Neither do they complain of a Want of Government, because they have not a Bishop residing among them. Agreeable to the Constitution of their Church, they consider themselves under the Care of the Bishop of London as their Pastor, and the King as the supreme Head of their ecclesiastical Polity. Their Worship they regulate by the Canons and Rubrics, their Discipline by the Laws of the Community to which they belong, and their Faith by the Articles of the Church of England. The Distance of their Governors does not in their Opinion destroy the Regularity of their Government, nor tempt them to demand a Change, and until the Doctor convinces us that *near a Million* of British Subjects in America have commissioned him and his Associates to petition and complain, we must vindicate so respectable a Body from the Proceedings of the *Convention*, who by assuming an Authority and Power never delegated to them, would pass themselves upon the World for Men of Importance.

NOTES: "CENTINEL" XIII

1. See "Centinel" I, note 2.
2. See "Centinel" XII, note 1.

Centinel Number XIV

June 23, 1768

Among the various and extraordinary Arguments, which Dr. Chandler makes Use of to promote his favorite Scheme of an American Episcopate, there is none he seems to lay more stress on, than that which he draws from the great Increase, and large proportion in numbers of the Professors of the CHURCH among the Colonists. This he carefully states: This he insists on again and again, in his Appeal. Having acknowledged, that "formerly Bishops were not greatly wanted, even in the Provinces settled chiefly by Episcopalians, as the Beginnings were small; and that it would have been, without Dispute, improper to have sent them to Provinces settled by people averse to Episcopal Government," it lay upon him to shew such a Change of Circumstances in America, as would make it reasonable to "settle" a general Episcopate there; for altho' it is manifest the numbers of People in the British Plantations are greatly increased, yet "our Superiors" in England, might not be apprised, that in the Non-conformist Colonies, the Professors of the Church of England are, at length, become so respectable in Point of Numbers, as to make it reasonable to extend the long projected Establishment of Episcopacy, even to those Parts, where formerly "it would have been, without Dispute improper" to have done it.

An Argument, on which so much dependence is placed, deserves to be well examined; and he rather, as we have seen that the Doctor full of Zeal for *Holy Church*, is apt to press Matters too far, and to forget mentioning all the Circumstances necessary to enable his Readers to form a right Judgment of what he offers to Consideration. Thus in calculating the Number of Petitioners for establishing an Episcopate in the Colonies, he takes in the People of the Sugar Islands, the Southern Colonies, altho' never consulted in the forming or forwarding the *Seven Petitions*, drawn up by the Missionaries of New-York and New-Jersey; because Members of his Church abound in those Parts, and every Episcopalian, as a true son of the *Church*, must, in the Doctor's judgement, be at least a *virtual* Supplicant on this important Occasion.

This method of exaggerating Facts, being the Doctor's *Foible*, it shall be my present Business to consider this Argument drawn from the increased Numbers of his *Church*, and the Use he makes of it.

He says, Page 56, "A general Survey was made in 1762, of the proper British Subjects in America, and communicated by a Gentleman of Veracity; that it was then found, (exclusive of the new Colonies ceded by the last general Treaty of Peace) they amounted to between two and three millions in the Colonies and Islands. Of the Whites, the Professors of the Church of England were about a third Part.—The Presbyterians, Independents, and Anabaptists not so many.—The Germans, Papists, and other Denominations amounted to more." He adds, "The Blacks in our Islands and Colonies were found, in the above mentioned Survey, to be 844,000; That many of these, it is to be feared, are not Christians at all; yet, they may be said in an *imperfect* Sense to belong to the religious Class of their Owners, who are chiefly Churchmen." Just before, he has these Words; "should be said, that the Church of *England* in *America*, contains *now* a Million of Members, the Assertion might be justified. It is not easy to ascertain the Numbers exactly in a Country so widely extended, unequally peopled; but from general Calculations, it has been frequently said of late Years, that the proper Subjects of the British Crown in *America*, amount to three Millions." Elsewhere (Page 89) we are told, "that of the Inhabitants *of this Country*, a full Third belong to the CHURCH: and a considerable Proportion of others, are professed Episcopalians, who cannot consistently be supposed to have an Aversion to Bishops." And on page 77 he speaks of the Complaints of *near a Million* of British Subjects, suffering unprecedented Hardships and intolerable Grievances, for Want of Bishops; and argues, that it is absurd, insidious and ungrateful, to entertain any Suspicion, that the Administration and *Legislature* will treat so large a Number of Subjects, with such cruel Partiality, as to deny their Request.

This is the Amount of what Doctor Chandler has advanced on the Subject. Let us now examine what it amounts to. It may not be material to dispute the general number of People, here said to be, in the British Plantations, nor the particular Account of the Negroes included in it; even tho' there might be some Inaccuracies in the Survey referr'd to. But it is of Importance to ask, why *all* the American Colonies, except *Canada* and the *Floridas*, are here considered in one View, and brought into one Calculation. Why Countries, so disjointed and so remote from each other, as many of them are, should for the Purposes of spiritual Polity, be treated as capable of a convenient Connection under Bishops? Is it possible, that such an ecclesiastical Superior placed at New-York, or elsewhere on the Continent, could be of any more Service to the Islands, than his *Grace* of London now is? Or, suppose two of these Lords spiritual placed on the Continent, and one in the Islands, at *Jamaica* for Instance, as the largest, (for three Bishops are the most says their Apologist, that have been mentioned), he must have a strong Eye[a] to see how the Clergy behave at *Barbados*, and the other Islands, which are at the Distance of five or six Weeks sailing from Jamaica. Yet these Places, and People, distant and different from each other, in Climate, Customs, Circumstances and Religious Sentiments, are all proposed to be included in one Plan of Church Discipline, and that too a newly projected one.

I wonder this zealous Advocate for the Proposed American Hierarchy, when he was thus striding over Sea and Land, did not stretch a little further than the Island Colonies, in order to bring some other Country, (*Ireland* for Instance) abounding with Episcopalians into the Survey, in order to counterbalance the great Body of Non-Conformists in North-America; whose Numbers stand so unluckily in the Way of this grand Scheme of the Missionaries. By this Means, they might have been able to say, that the Professors of Episcopacy, in the Dependencies of *Great Britain*, are a great Majority of all the Inhabitants of those Countries, and therefore Episcopacy ought to be established in the middle and eastern Colonies of *North-America*. *Ireland* is as much a dependent State as *Jamaica*, and so much connected with *North-America*. It is true, the major Part of the People in that Kingdom, are Papists; but as they are "professed Episcopalians" and full as good Churchmen, as great Part of the Dr's. Million, *"they cannot consistently be supposed to have any Aversion to Bishops."* In like Manner it might be connected, that Diocesan Episcopacy ought to be established in *Scotland*; for the Professors of the CHURCH, are at least, three Parts in four of the People of *Great Britain*, taken into one Account; *Scotland* containing little more than a Million of People of all Denominations; and the Dissenters in *England* not exceeding a million, among seven or eight, which that Part of the united Kingdom is said to contain. Their Union in Legislation, and their Adjacency, would be additional Arguments, not subsisting in the Case of the Colonies.

The White People in the islands, some few Quakers, Papists and Jews excepted, are all Professors of Episcopacy as established in *England*. It has not yet appeared that they suffer Persecution, nor have we heard them cry out for Relief, on Account of "unprecedented Hardships and intolerable Grievances." If they want an Episcopate in every Island, and will provide for the Support & regulate the Authority of such an ecclesiastical Superior, by Act of Assembly, the Way seems to be clear for them: and till the Crown refuses to concur, there is no Ground for complaint. As they have not offered to do this, we must take it for granted, they are content with the Superintendency of the Bishop of *London*, and do not wish for a Bishop any nearer. The same must be said of *Virginia, Maryland* and other Southern provinces, where the Professors of the Doctor's Church have the upper hand; notwithstanding Dissenters are numerous in those Parts and increase daily. The Power, which established Parishes and taxes for the Episcopal Clergy, must be able to guard the CHURCH against all Persecution, and to give its Dignitaries, residing in *America*, as soon as the respective legislatures, who are the best Judges, find them necessary. How is it possible, then, that "*near a million* of People" "in *America*," are "suffering for their religious Principles and denied the same Privileges, as all other Denominations enjoy?" Is it ingenuous, is it consistent with the Character of a Minister of the "true Religion" to represent the Episcopal Churches of *America* in general, as in Distress and under Persecution?

Tho the People of the English Islands, and of the Episcopal Colonies have been lugged into this Business, yet we find, they have nothing to do with it. They have neither been Petitioners with the Dr. and his Brethren, for Bishops; nor are they distressed and persecuted. As the Missionaries are the sole Petitioners, so are they and their Followers the only People who can have any cause of Complaint.

But even as to them, the Charge is most unjust and ungrateful: Unjust to their Neighbors, and the civil Governments under which they live; Ungrateful to their Superiors and Fellow Subjects in England. They are here called on to shew any Instance, wherein they are denied *equal* Privileges with others. In three of the *New-England* Governments, where a very lax kind of Religious Establishment has obtained, the Episcopal Ministers are entituled to that Part of the Tax levied for supporting the Clergy, which arises from their own Church Members. In the City of *New-York* and in some of the Counties of that Colony, part of the Poor Tax is taken to maintain their Ministers. In *Rhode-Island, New-Jersey,* and *Pennsylvania*, they are on a Footing with the most favoured. And in all the Old Colonies, North-East of *Maryland*, they have Ministers called Missionaries, (a Name peculiar to such as are sent to instruct

Infidels) supported for them by the charity of well-disposed Persons in *England* and *Ireland*, and in the reformed Churches of *Holland, Germany*, and *Switzerland*; at an Expence of between Three and Four Thousand Pounds Sterling, per annum.

It is some of these pretended Missionaries, and these only, who have raised all the late Clamours for Bishops; who are restless and unwearied in their Endeavours to procure an Establishment over the Body of the People, among whom they reside. So unreasonable are they, that not contented with being the most favoured, they would have their Discipline extended over all other Denominations, by Act of Parliament; tho' their Church be not a fortieth Part of the Community. The State of Episcopacy in the Old Colonies North-East of *Maryland*, is nearly this. These Districts having been at first settled by People of non-conformist Opinions, chiefly Refugees from the Persecutions of the Bishops in England, the few Professors of the Church of *England*, who settled among them from Time to Time, would have almost generally joined with, and been undistinguished at this Day from the other Protestant Communions, had it not been for the *Society for propagating the Gospel*, or rather *for propagating Episcopacy*. To their "*indefatigable Application and amazing Perseverance*," we will readily allow, it is owing, that there are above *five* or *six* such Congregations in all the Country above particularized. What indeed are their Societies, for the most Part, but little Parties, not deserving the Name of Congregations, utterly unable to support their Preachers. At this Day, there is not City, Town, or Place, throughout the middle and eastern Colonies, except *Philadelphia*, where the Professors of the church of *England* support their Clergy, without Help; whilst other Denominations, unassisted, maintain their Pastors, to the Number of Eight or Nine Hundred; except it may be the Papists.

The inquisitive and accurate Dr. Stiles, of *Rhode-Island*, in his Discourse on *Christian Union*, tells us, he found the Episcopalians, in all *New-England*, did not exceed 12,600 Souls; yet they had 30 Ministers, and 47 Places of Worship. This was in 1760. The People of other Denominations appeared to be 487,000; and they maintained above 600 Pastors, exclusive of the public Instruction among the *Friends*.[1] The Case is much the same in *Pennsylvania*. The Rev'd. Mr. Craig, of *Chester*, who has resided a long Time, and in different Parts of the Province, in his Letter to the Society in 1764, says, "that of the People of the Province, who as some calculate are 300,000 Souls, *he can safely affirm not one fiftieth Part, belong to the Church of England*; and that his Communicants in his three Congregations, were 15 only". The Rev'd Mr. Thompson, itinerant Missionary in the Counties of *York* and *Cumberland*, acquainted his venerable Patrons the same Year, that his People within those Counties, did not exceed 202 Souls; altho' it is well known those Districts contained at that Time, Thirty or Forty Thousand Inhabitants. And the Rev'd Mr. Murray of Berks County, complained that his People at *Mollattin* were reduced by Removals, to Twenty-nine Families; that he despaired of seeing a Church built within his Mission; and expected soon to be reduced to the Society's Allowance for his Support.[b] The Episcopal Societies in *New-York* and *New-Jersey* are in very little better Circumstances. At *Colanzie*, in *West-Jersey*, stands a Church, but there is not the Shadow of a Congregation in the County. At *Salem* the Episcopal Cause is almost as low. It would be tedious, as it is needless, to multiply Instances to illustrate this Matter: Suffice it to say, that it is in the Cities and some of the larger Towns only, that their Congregations are numerous. Yet the Episcopal Church in the non-episcopal Colonies, never was in such outwardly flourishing Circumstances: And no Wonder; the *Society's* expensive Interposition, could not but have some considerable Effects. It has brought it from Nothing to Something; it has kept the Professors of the Church of *England* together; and, as many like cheapness, even in the way to Heaven, some have joined them from other Churches, who were well enough pleased *to have Ministers maintained for them*, by good-natured People in England, and elsewhere. How unjust, how ungrateful then, are these Missionaries of *New-York* and *New-Jersey* in their Complaints of hardships, Grievances and Persecutions. They are unjust to their Fellow Subjects, among whom they reside: Ungrateful to their Patrons and Benefactors in Europe: and their Behaviour must reflect severely on their own Characters, wherever this Unfairness and Disingenuity shall be opened up.

But the Artifice of bringing all the old Colonies and Islands into one View and Computation, is not the only or chief Ground of Complaint against Doctor Chandler, in his Management of this Argument. It is indeed but a small Instance of his *Infirmity*, compared to one I shall now mention.

No one will assert, that the Whites of the Doctor's Church in America, amount to "*a Million nearly*." We may safely say, they are not half that Number. In all our Islands, the white People do not come up to 90,000; and on the Continent, the Professors of the Church of *England* cannot be four Times as numerous. Where then did the Dr. get above 500,000 of his *Churchmen*? Only among the Negroes, those *virtual* Episcopalians, who chiefly belong to Episcopal Owners. An attentive Reader will perceive this, altho' the Dr. seems loath to speak it out plainly. Behold a Crowd of Negroes, in the Islands, and Southern Colonies, almost all of whom "are not Christians at all," slipt into the Episcopal Scale, in order to balance in some Measure, the dead Weight of Non-conformists in the Northern Colonies: and yet it kicks the Beam! Behold at least 500,000 *virtual Churchmen*, virtuously petitioning by their Friends the Clergy of *New-York* and *New-Jersey* for Bishops! What low Artifice is this! How unbecoming the Clerical Character! Well may Deists represent Dissimination, as a Vice of the Order: Such Behaviour, but too well justifies the Charge.

Are Bishops then to be introduced into, and imposed on the Non-episcopal Colonies, *which were granted as Asylums from the Power of proud Prelates*, by the Force of such wretched Arguments, as this we have been considering: it must not, it cannot be: "It is absurd, injurious and ungrateful to entertain any suspicion, that the Administration and *Legislature* will treat so large a Number of good Subjects with such cruel Partiality" as to put them "under a Yoke, which neither they nor their Fathers were able to bear," merely to exalt a little Party, some of whose Clergy affect Importance, and make a great Bustle, proudly arrogating to themselves the Name of CHURCH, as if all Christianity was confined within their narrow Pale. It may be Time enough a great while hence, to think of "settling" Episcopacy (the Doctor uses this as a softer Term than establish) in this Colonies, if Numbers are to determine the Point. It would be fair, however, that the Episcopal Colonies, should try the Experiment of importing Bishops first; at least, whilst they neglect providing for ecclesiastical Superiors, the Rejectors of Episcopacy may be well excused in opposing their establishment among them, by an Act of the State.

INTERNAL NOTES: "CENTINEL" XIV

[a]Dr. C. talks of the American Bishop, having the inferior Clergy, "Under his Eye." Page 35.
[b]See *Society's* Abstract for 1765, for these and many other Accounts of a similar Nature.[2]

NOTES: "CENTINEL" XIV

1. Ezra Stiles, *A Discource on the Christian Union* (Boston, 1761), p. 113. Stiles was a Congregational minister in Newport, Rhode Island, and later president of Yale College from 1778 until 1795.

2. *An Abstract of the Proceedings of the Society for the Propagation of the Gospel in Foreign Parts, 1765* (London, 1766). George Craig, SPG missionary settled at Chester, Pennsylvania; William Thompson, SPG missionary in York and Cumberland counties in Pennsylvania; and Alexander Murray, SPG missionary in Berks County, Pennsylvania.

Centinel Number XV

June 30, 1768

Nothing has occasioned greater Mistakes, nor given Room for warmer Debates, than the varying and unsettled meaning of Names and Terms. A Word, which in one Age, has served to convey a particular Idea, at some succeeding Period, has been understood in a very different Sense; and controversial Writers have seldom been so candid as to state the Difference: More eager for Victory, than Truth, they have often disingenuously layed hold of such an opportunity, to carry their Point with the ignorant and the prejudiced; whilst every Thing has made against them, except the Construction and Sound of the Sylables.

It has been remarkably the Case of the Episcopal Character in the Christian Church. Many, who have no Idea of a Bishop, separate from the Appendages of the Office in some Hierarchies, when they read any Thing in the New Testament concerning this Minister of Religion, apply it without Hesitation to Prelates of the Establishment they are best acquainted with; and wonder at the Perverseness of those who differ from them. Few Professors of Christianity deny Bishops to be of divine Institution; but the Difficulty lies in adjusting their Rank and Powers. The Roman, the Greek, and other Eastern Churches hold, that Bishops are of *divine Right*, an order superior to Priests; and that although they are Presbyters, they have also a higher Character, and are distinguished from the other Clergy, in like Manner, as the Apostles in the Infancy of the Church, were superior to the common teachers of the Gospel. The Protestant communions abroad, Lutheran and Calvinist have rejected this Opinion as unscriptural, and as having been the Source of much Abuse and Corruption. The Sense of the Protestants of the German Empire on this Point, is set *forth* in the Articles of the League concluded at *Smalcald* in 1530; in which they assert the Power of Ordaining to belong, by divine Right, to Presbyters. Accordingly, the Lutheran Super-intendents are only *first among Equals*, or standing Presidents of the Councils of the Clergy. It is almost needless to observe that the Churches of the *Reformed*, and the Church of *Scotland*, are agreed in the Abolition of all Prelacy; for with them every parish Minister is a Bishop. In *England* the established Church has never explicitly declared herself on the Point; if we attempt to deduce her Judgement from her Conduct, we shall find it unsettled; yet more favourable to the Distinction of Order in later Times, than formerly.[a] The first Reformers in England, with Dr. Cranmer at their Head, perfectly agreed with their Brethren the Protestants abroad, and held Presbyter and Bishop to be the same in Scripture. As they looked on Church Polity to be mutable, in much the same Manner as Civil Government, they thought it very allowable for Presbyters to waive their Rights, and for the Sake of better Order, to submit to Superiors of human Institutions.[b]

It is plain enough to all unprejudiced Persons, that in the New Testament, Bishop, Pastor, Overseer, Presbyter and Elder, are used promiscuously, to describe one and the same Office; and there is nothing any where and of an upper Order in the Christian Ministry. As Churches were gathered in different Parts of the Roman Empire, chiefly in the Cities at first, the People chose their Instructors by common Suffrage; and the Apostles and Evangelists, such as *Paul, Silas, Barnabas,* and *Timothy*, by a solemn imposition of Hands (a Ceremony derived from the Jews) invested these Persons with the Pastoral Office. The Choice of the People was the main Point, the Solemnity of setting apart being "not of Necessity, but only for good Order and seemly Fashion."[c] Of these Bishops, there was, it seems, one or more in every Church or Congregation, as the Number of Converts, and the Prospect of new Additions required. At Ephesus, for Instance, we find two, if not several Elders, who are expressly called Bishops;[d] and Titus was directed to ordain Elders in *every* City of Crete, who are spoken of as invested with all the Episcopal Office.[e] It was a long Time before the original Christian Congregations in the Cities became so numerous as to make it necessary to divide their Assemblies; they kept together till meer Inconveniency forced them to it. Not having equal Success in proselyting the country People, the Difficulty was less felt. And when at length they allowed new Places for holding Assemblies for public Worship, they considered them as *Chapels of Ease*, and the People as Part of the original Congregations. The Number of Pastors was in this Manner necessarily increased within the Parish or Diocese, and it became, in Process of Time, orderly to have a President at the Meetings of the Consistory; to whom, by Degrees the Name of Bishop was restrained. This Head-Presbyter, however, was only *Primus inter Pares*, First among Equals; the affairs of the

Congregation being managed by him and his Brethren, with the Concurrence of the People. As it was natural for the Christians in the purer Ages of the Church to place the most respectable of their Elders in the Chair, it is easy to conceive, how superior Abilities and Character on the one Hand, and undissembled Love and Respect on the other, might conspire to give a fatherly Pre-eminence to a primitive Bishop. His Age and Standing, not to mention the Sufferings which many of them endured, would unavoidably command this, and every other Expression of Reverence, which the Members of a voluntary Society, unsuspicious of any ambitious Schemes, could give. It would of Course happen that the Bishop and the more aged Presbyters would always be resident near the Mother Church or Cathedral, whilst their younger Brethren itinerated thro' the Parish, labouring from House to House, and in the dependent Places of public Worship: The Bishop would be generally deputed to sit in the Synods and Councils of the Church: And nothing of Importance would be undertaken at Home, without the Advice of a Person of so much Experience and Piety.

In all popular Assemblies, great regard is paid to the Opinion of a few of the best Ability, and most Knowledge, but if great moral Character accompanies these Endowments, the Influence of such Persons is almost unlimited.

Such seems to have been the Rise of the diocesan Bishop; an Office not known in Scripture. The very large Extent of the Dioceses in some Parts, and the general Conversion of the Pagans (probably so called from *Pagi,* a Word signifying the People of the Country) must have increased and confirmed the Superiority of the Bishop. As the People became too numerous to assemble and consider of their Affairs, on every Occasion, the Care of them devolved to the Consistory; and the Duties of instruction calling out the younger Presbyters to different Parts of the District, the Business of discipline now increased, and occuring daily; gradually centered in the Bishop and the aged Elders, who remained with him. Hence rose the Chapter, or that Body of Clergy, who at this Day make a mock choice of the Bishop, and are as a Council to him in some lesser Matters; but in the most important are intirely laid aside.[f]

When Wealth and Corruption entered the Church, and lovers of Pre-eminence got into the Episcopal Sees, that Authority which had been conceded to the personal Character of the former Presidents of the Clergy, was now claimed by, and yielded to their Successors, as their proper Jurisdiction. Instead of flying from a

Station, which formerly had set a Man up as an object of persecution, and which was thought to require an uncommon share of Zeal and Faithfulness to discharge its Duties with a good Conscience, the vain and the ambitious secretly intrigued for Votes, and used every Artifice to arrive at a Dignity, endowed with Riches, and consequently invested with state Influence and worldly Power. These Abuses, of which the Prince had by his insidious Liberality been the chief Author, rising into tumults and even Bloodshed, gave him a specious Pretence, for taking from the people, their Right of chusing their Bishops, and to farther debase the Church & Clergy, by turning Religion into a State Engine.

The See of *Rome* was tainted very early. This arose partly from the great Benefactions intrusted with her Bishops, for the Purpose of sending out Missionaries to the northern and western Parts of Europe; which also served to advance their Influence, and promote their Authority, even under the loss of the Seat of Empire, which was transferred to *Constantinople*. The Bishoprick of *Rome* therefore became early the Object of competition among those who fought after filthy Lucre, and were disposed to lord it over the Heritage of God. The Consul *Pretextatus*, a Heathen, in the Year 466, could say, "if you will make me a Bishop of *Rome*, I will make myself a Christian."

To those who are the least acquainted with Church History, it seems strange to find Dr. Chandler arguing, that diocesan Episcopacy must have been the original Plan of Government in the Church, because of the supposed Difficulty of altering Things connected with Religion. I would ask him, whence came Arch-Bishops and Patriarchs? Whence arose that grand Corruption of Christianity called Popery? The Truth is, the Alteration was gradual, and at the Time of his favourite *St. Ignatius*, the Bishop was, as Primate *Usher* words it, "only different in Degree, not in Order;" as a Lutheran Super-intendant at this Day presides over a Consistory of Pastors.[9] To bring in the Episcopacy of the 1st. and 2d. Centuries, then to support that of the Church of *England*, is plainly begging the Question. It is to treat two Characters as the same, who in fact are as different as the First Commissioner of the Treasury in *England*, and the Lord High Treasurer; or as the Doge of *Venice*, the President of that Republic, and the absolute Duke of *Florence*.

INTERNAL NOTES: "CENTINEL" XV

[a] *In the Reigns of Eliz.* and *James* I. many Divines ordained abroad by Presbyters, were admitted to Parishes in England; but since the Restoration, all the Protestant Ordinations are treated as invalid, and Orders from Diocesan Bishops insisted on.

[b] See *Cranmer's* Opinion in *Stillingfleete's* Irenicum, Cap. VIII, also the Opinions of the Bishop of *St. Asaph*, of *Therieby, Redman*, and *Cox*, who assisted at a select Assembly of Divines in the Reign of Ed. VI.[1]—That learned Expositor Dr. Hammond, says, "there were no Presbyters of an inferior Order to Bishops, instituted by the Apostles.[2]—And Bishop *Stillingfleete* makes this noble Concession, "that there were no Bishops, (meaning diocesan Prelates) during the Apostles Life."—And in another Place, (*Irenicum* Page 276), "I believe upon the strictest Enquiry, *Medina's* Judgement will prove true, that *Jerom, Austin, Sedulius, Primasius, Chrisythom, Theodoret, Theophylact*, were all of *Aesius's* Judgement, as to the Identity, both of Name and Order, of Bishops and Presbyters, in the primitive Church."[3]—The great *Usher* and *Burnet* speak the same Things.[4]

[c] This is in *Cranmer's* Opinion in *Stillingfleet. Iren.* Cap. VIII.[5]

[d] Acts XX, 17 & 28. Express mention is made of Bishops, in the plural Numbers, as residing at Philippi, *Phil.* i. 1.[6]

[e] Epist. *Paul* to *Titus* i. 5–6.[7]

[f] The Bishop grants Orders alone, excommunicates alone, and Judges alone: This seems to be a Thing almost without example, in good Governments; and therefore not unlikely *to have crept in during degenerate and corrupt Times.* The greatest Kings have their Councils.—Whence should this sole Exercise of Jurisdiction come? Surely one may suppose upon good grounds, *from the Beginning it was not thus;* and that the Deans and Chapters were Councils about the Chairs of Bishops at first; and were to them a Presbytery or consistory, and intermeddled not only in disposing of Revenues and Endowments; but much more in ecclesiastical Jursidiction.—We see the Bishop of Rome performs all ecclesiastical Jurisdiction as in consistory—"Of the ancient Mode," we see many Shadows still remaining; as that the Dean & Chapter, for form's sake, choose the Bishop; which is the highest Point of Jurisdiction; and that the Bishop, when he grants Orders, if there be any Presbyters actually present, calls them to join with him in the Imposition of hands; and some other Particulars." Ld. Chanc. *Bacon* on the Peace of the Church, Sect: II.[8]

NOTES: "CENTINEL" XV

1. Edward Stillingfleete, *Irenicum. A Weapon-Salve for the Churches Wounds, or the Divine Right of Particular Forms of Church-Government* (London, 1662), chapter 8, pp. 391, 393.
2. Henry Hammond, *A Paraphrase, and Annotation Upon all the Books of the New Testament* (London, 1702), "Annotations of Philippians," chapter 1, p. 571.
3. Stillingfleete, *Irenicum*, chapter 5, para. 12, p. 276.
4. James Ussher, *The Original of Bishops and Metropolitans* (Dublin, 1641), pp. 45–46. [Gilbert Burnet], *A Vindication of the Ordinations of the Church of England*, 2nd ed. (London, 1688), "Preface."
5. Stillingfleete, *Irenicum*, chapter 8, pp. 392–93.
6. Acts 20:17, 28. Philippians 1:1.
7. Titus 1:5, 6.
8. Francis Bacon, *Certain Considerations Touching the Better Pacification and Edification of the Church of England, The Works of Francis Bacon* (London, 1740), section 2, "Circumstances on the Government of Bishops," p. 447.
9. Ussher, *The Original of Bishops.*

Centinel Number XVI

July 7, 1768

To the Author of the Centinel.

Sir,

The Readiness, with which you published the Letters, I sent you, emboldens me to offer some farther Thoughts on the Subject. I have endeavoured to shew that the Church or rather every Church in *America* has a Right in itself to provide for its own Discipline and Government, that if Civil Laws are necessary for the Support of its Clergy, or for the Regulation of its Members, they ought to be made by the Legislatures of the respective Colonies; and therefore, that any Application to the Parliament of *Britain*, or any Power on Earth, other than the Legislatures of the Colonies, to establish any Sect or Denomination of Christians in his Majesty's American Colonies, is an infringement of the Rights of the People, and as such ought to be resented. I shall now consider what it is, that Doctor Chandler and the Applicants petition for, and hope to convince you that it is not a Minister of Christ, a Publisher of the Gospel, nor an Officer of the Christian Church, but a dangerous Engine of State. This will appear if we consider for what Purposes he is wanted, with what Powers he is to be invested, and in what Manner he is to exercise those Powers.

The Liberty of America has ever been a Matter of Envy to the Bigots and High flyers, as well as to the Favourers and Abettors of arbitrary Power in England. Instances of this might be given, from the Times of *Laud,* and *Bancroft* down to the Time of those venerable *Bishops,* who with one Accord entered their warm Protest against the Repeal of the American Stamp-Act.[1]—And it might easily be shewn, that whenever Attempts have been made at Home to encrease the Power of the Crown, or subvert the British Constitution and the Liberties of the People, the Liberty of *America* has at the same time been invaded. Nor is this to be wondered at; for while America remains a sacred Asylum, the Shackles of Slavery cannot well be fixed upon Britons, nor can ecclesiastical Tyrants exercise arbitrary Sway.

But what is particularly worthy of Observations is, that every Attempt upon American Liberty has always been accompanied with Endeavours to settle Bishops among us. Thus in the Reign of *Charles* I, when *Laud* attempted to subjugate the Colonies, then in their Infancy, he was not content with contriving to complete their Trade by foolish Proclamations,[a] but to complete their Mortification and effect their Ruin, was upon the Point of sending them a Bishop, with a military Force to back his Authority.[b] The same attempt was revived in the latter End of Queen Anne's Reign: and had not GOD in his Providence interposed, and blasted the Designs of the Enemies of Britain, the same Year might have been remarkable for the Downfall of Protestanism, and Introduction of the Pretender, and the Revival of Popery in England, and for the Establishment of Bishops in *America.*[4] The unsettled State of the Nation after the Accession of *George* I. gave the Enemies of that Prince and of their Country some faint Hopes of accomplishing their Design; and, therefore, in the Year 1714, while the Spirit of Rebellion was kindling into a Flame, and the Friends of Popery and the Pretender were forming their Party and preparing to overturn the Government, and the Religion of their Country, the same restless Spirits, who in the last Reign had laboured to get Bishops established in *America,* "renewed their Attempt and made one vigorous Effort to accomplish" what they call their "grand Affair," But (Thanks to the great Over-ruler of Events) the Designs of both "proved abortive." The Rebellion was quashed, and the Scheme of an American Episcopate dropt of Course: Some Persons however still continued to keep Sight of the great Object and as they are always watching for seasonable Opportunities of exerting themselves to obtain it, we find it resumed with great Warmth not long before the Rebellion in 1745.[5]

With what Views a Bishop is so earnestly desired for America, and for what Purposes he is sent, we are now to enquire. "His Authority," we are told, "shall operate only on the Clergy of THE CHURCH and "not on the Laity." The Bishop spoken of in the New Testament is ordered to feed the Flock, and take Care of the Church of God. But the American Bishop is to exercise no Authority over the Laity or private Members of the Church, over which he presides. His Business is to "ordain, *unite,*" *support* and govern the Clergy.[c] Over these his Power is to be absolute. He is to hold no Spiritual Court, P. 95, And yet he is to "have Power to suspend any Clergyman, to deprive him of his Benefice and not only silence and depose him but *excommunicate him from the Society of Christians.*"[d] All this he is to exercise "according to the Direction of and by Virtue of a Commission from the Diocesan,"[e] who may reside at *London, Lambeth,* or elsewhere. This, Doct. C. assures us is "the Plan of the American Episcopate, and that he does not know of a single Instance wherein Reason has been given to suspect a Departure from it." How well this Plan was calculated to answer the Views of a *Laud,* who wants to introduce arbitrary Government into Church and State, is easy to see: Nor will it be difficult to reconcile it with the Schemes of those, who laboured to introduce Popery and the Pretender.

But to add to the Weight and Importance of these Bishops, and the better to enable them to promote the Designs of the Minister, a hint is given that "the Government may hereafter see fit to invest them with some Degree of civil Power, worthy of their Acceptance;" that as "a Clergyman may be made a Justice of the Peace or a Judge of the Quorum; so Bishops may be invested with a proportionable Degree of civil Authority;[f] which can be nothing less than a Member of the upper House of Assembly or Governor of a Province." To this we are told, no one ought to object: For "all that the Happiness and Safety of the Public require, is, that the legislative and executive Power be placed in the Hands of such Persons as are possessed of the greatest Abilities, Integrity and Prudence; and it is hoped, says Dr. C., Bishops will always be *thought* to deserve this Character."

Let us now consider what dangerous Engine of State this might be in the Hands of an enterprizing and ill minded Minister. Where a Man's private Interest is united with the Interest of his Country, it is reasonable to suppose, he will heartily wish that Country may thrive, and will exert himself in Support and Defence of its Liberty! but this is not the Case with those who are sent from another Part of the World, to be Employed in Places of profit and power: Because they can bear no Affection to the Place where they soujourn; their sole Business being to advance themselves by following the Directions of their Principals: Neither will it be the Case with those who are taken into Offices, although Natives of the Land, because they are greater Gainers while they keep their Offices, than they can be by promoting and defending the Interest of their Country.

The People of *America* are to have no Concert in the Election of this Bishop. Over his Actions they have no controul. The Clergy, as they will hold their Livings at his Pleasure, must pay the same implicit Obedience to his Commands, which he himself will always pay to the Minister of State, whose Creature he is, and on whom his Hopes of Preferment depend.

I cannot therefore wonder if the Administration of a B———e or a G———e is distinguished with an Attempt to introduce an American Episcopate.[7] I am, &c. A. B.

INTERNAL NOTES: "CENTINEL" XVI

[a] Rushworth, Second Part, P. 718.[2]

[b] Heylin's Life of Laud. P. 369.[3]

[c] A Confirmation is also mentioned as one of the important Offices of a Bishop, and great Stress seems to be laid on it, by Doctor C. But how high soever the popish Church and its Adherents may rate Confirmation, and the uninterrupted Succession, the Doctor ought to know, that the Church of England, of which he professes himself a Member, considers them in no very favourable Light. "Confirmation, Penance, Orders, Matrimony and extreme Unction are not to be accounted for Sacraments, being such as are grown partly of the CORRUPT Following of the Apostles, partly are States of Life allowed by the Scriptures. 25 Art. of The Ch. of Eng."[6]

[d] P. 33.

[e] C. 80.

[f] C. 3.

NOTES: "CENTINEL" XVI

1. See "Centinel" III, footnote 3 for William Laud. Richard Bancroft, archbishop of Canterbury from 1604 until 1610 under James I was unalterably opposed to Puritan dissenters and demanded that all ministers must conform to the use of the Book of Common Prayer and subscribe to each of the Thirty-nine Articles of the Church of England.

2. John Rushworth, *Historical Collections from the Year 1628–1638* (London, 1706), p. 209.

3. Peter Heylyn, *Cyprianus Anglicus: or, the History of the Life and Death of the most Reverend and Renowned Prelate, William* (London, 1771), pp. 260–62.

4. See "Centinel" II, footnote 3.

5. The rebellion of 1745 was precipitated by the landing in Scotland of the Young Pretender, Charles Edward, son of James F. Edward. He hoped to enlist the aid of the Scots in his fight to recover the British throne. The English suspected that Catholics were also behind the effort. The rebellion was put down by the Duke of Cumberland in such a vicious way that he earned the nickname of "The Butcher." Charles escaped to France.

6. *Articles of the Church of England,* Article 25.

7. John Stuart, third Earl of Bute, was the tutor, confidant, and later unpopular Lord of the Treasury of George III. He served from May, 1762 until April, 1763, when George Grenville replaced him. It was under the ministry of Grenville from 1763 until 1765 that many acts, unpopular in the American colonies, were passed.

Centinel Number XVII

July 14, 1768

Dr. Chandler, in the Name of his Brethren, adduces the wretched Condition of the Episcopal Church in the Colonies, for want of regular Government and Discipline without Bishops, as an Argument for their Introduction. He esteems it a great Grievance, an unparalleled Hardship, and a Disadvantage of greater Consequence than the Want of Confirmation; although he imagines that by that Rite, the gracious Assistances of the Holy Spirit are communicated.

Wretched indeed is the Condition of that Church, which is destitute of regular Discipline: But there is Ground to suspect that the Episcopal Missionaries in America are not more affected with this Consideration, than their Brethren on the other side of the Atlantic, who are in the same wretched Condition, yet make no Attempts to get the Grievance redressed.

The Reformation of their Church in this Article, is not among the *happy Consequences,* which they can expect from the Establishment of Bishops in this Country. The Argument is only thrown out to work on the ignorant, and to excite Compassion among well-minded Persons for their *suffering, persecuted* Church; which their Apologist, Dr. Chandler, artfully represents as "perishing for want of Necessaries." The Missionaries must allow, there is no necessary Connection between the Establishment of Diocesan Bishops in a Church, and the Administration of Godly Discipline: That there may be Discipline in a Church, where there are no prelates; And that there may be Bishops in a Communion, destitute even of the Shadow of regular Discipline. With Respect to the First of these, they see other Churches around them without Bishops, exercising Discipline over their own members, and they know that the Church of England in the midst of all their uncharitable Pretensions to be the *only true Apostolic Church, the Propagators of the True Religion; the best reformed Church in the World, the Preservers of the True Christian Faith, Worship and Discipline,*[a] is solemnly confessing to God from Year to Year, that they are destitute of a godly Discipline, although they are aided by a civil Establishment, and supported by the Authority, Grandeur and Opulence of Prelates and other Dignitaries.

That this is truly the Situation of the Church of England, has been often acknowledged by her most judicious and candid Members. They ingenuously confess, that there is a great Prostration of Discipline in their Church: That it is ruined among them:—That the Distemper of the Times is evidently too hard for it;—That the Discipline of the Church has not been carried to any Degree of Perfection; and now lies under a general Relaxation—That their People are often indulged in all their unreasonable Demands, and disorderly Ways, to prevent their executing their Threats of going to the *Meeting:*—That they have only the Form and Shadow of Discipline, but trust in God, that "these dry Bones will one Day live."[b]—And Dr. Chandler himself gives a like mournful Account of its Discipline. "Excommunication," says he, "the utmost Effect of the Church's Power *in this World,* however it was dreaded in purest Ages of Christianity, has lost much of its Force in this, wherein Altars are set up against Altars, and Churches against Churches, and those who are rejected by one may be received by another. A Disposition to slight the highest Punishment which the Church can inflict has become general, and there appears no Remedy, but in the Use of Reason and Persuasion. But we live in an Age in which Reason will not be heard, nor the Strength of Arguments regarded, although supported by the Declarations of Heaven, on the Subject of Church Discipline."[c] The Doctor and his Brethren know that the *Test* has broken down all the Inclosures of the Church of England, and has laid open her most Holy Things to the most abandoned and profane. Rakes, Debauchees, Blasphemers of God, Infidels and Scoffers at all Religion, are often seen on their Knees at her Communion Tables, eating her Children's Bread to qualify them for a Post: And dare the Clergy refuse them? No; they dare not refuse the most impious Blasphemer that the three Kingdoms afford, when he comes to demand the Lord's Supper, as a Qualification for a Post in the Fleet or Army.

It is also notorious that the English Bishop himself is excluded from having any Power even in his own Court; where a Chancellor, generally a Lay-Man, sits supreme and uncontrolled by the Bishop, and finally determines who shall be excommunicated from or received into Christian Fellowship. If there be any Thing, says a great Prelate of the Church of England, in the Office of a Bishop to be challenged, peculiar to themselves, certainly it should be this; yet it is in a Manner quite relinquished to their Chancellors, Laymen, who have no more Capacity to sentence or absolve a Sinner, than to dissolve the Heavens or the Earth. And this pretended Power is sometimes purchased with Money. Their Money perish with them! Good God! What an horrid Abuse is this of the Divine Authority. But this notorious Transgression is excused, as they think, because a Minister called the Bishop's Surrogate, but is indeed the Chancellor's Servant, chosen, called and placed there by *him,* to be his Cryer in the Court, no better, when he has heard, examined and sentenced the Cause, then this Minister forsooth pronounces the Sentence. Just as if the Rector of a Parish should exclude any of his Congregation, and lock him out of his Church, then comes the Clerk, shews and jingles the Keys that all may take notice he is excluded.[d] It is also well known, that in these Courts, the most scandalous Sinner is suffered to commute, to have Pardon for Money; nay, when he is actually delivered over, and the Devil has him in Keeping, an handsome Sum of Money will restore him again to the soft, indulgent Bosom of the Church. . . . .

. . . . . . At vos
Dicite Pontifices, in sacris, quid facit aurum
Per. sat. 2.[3]

Such is the melancholly Situation of the Church of England with Respect to her Discipline, even in full Possession of an Establishment by Law, and supported by all the Splendor and Influence of Lordly Prelates and dignified Priests. Yet it is said the Episcopal Church in the Colonies suffers *unparalleled* Hardships, for want of regular Discipline, because she is destitute of Bishops. But can the Missionaries seriously believe this Grievance would be removed by the Introduction of Bishops? No such Matter. They declare, by Dr. Chandler, that no Reformation in this Respect will be attempted; that the Discipline of the Church, as far as it relates to the private Members, will be left as it is, under the proposed Episcopate.[e] Discipline was not the Thing they had in view, when they petitioned for Bishops to be sent over them. They are meerly to unite, govern, support and defend the Clergy. More solicitous for the Honour of an useless ecclesiastical Superior to cut a Figure at their Head, than to edify their People by restoring the primitive Discipline of the Church, they propose a mutilated Prelate, such as never yet appeared in the Churches of Christ. It would seem that when these Gentlemen took a Trip to England in their Youth for Orders, they were captivated with the Magnificence of the Episcopal Palaces, the Glare of the Bishop's Equipage, and the Splendor of their Retinues, and have never been able to get over this youthful

Prejudice: but are always dreaming of lawn Sleeves, the square Cap and Mitre; and lusting after the Leeks and Onions of Egypt even in this Land of Freedom and Liberty.

Why then are these pitiful Lamentations made over the Want of Discipline in the Episcopal Church in America, and Considerations drawn from it to induce their Superiors at home to send over Bishops, to rescue their sinking Church from inevitable Perdition. Let us see how prettily the Argument will conclude, when reduced to a logical Form. The Church in America, without resident Bishops, is necessarily destitute of a regular Discipline and Government: "But the Discipline of the Church, as far as it relates to private Members will be left as it is, and no Attempts of this Nature will be made under the proposed American Episcopate." Therefore an American Episcopate is necessary for the Restoration of the primitive Discipline of the Church. One not so well acquainted with the Rules of Logic, as Dr. C. is, would have been apt to suspect that the Conclusion should have been, that it was by no means necessary for the regular Government of the Church, as it would contribute nothing to the Redress of this "intollerable and unprecedented Hardship." Yet notwithstanding the Obstinacy of the Premises, the Doctor it seems was not willing to loose the wished for Conclusion, nor the Opportunity of displaying his Talents in painting his Church in such doleful Colours. In making such bitter Lamentations over her Want of Discipline, he seems to have consulted poorly for her Reputation, and as wretchedly for the Credit of her Clergy, in avowing to the World, that no amendment is proposed in Point of Discipline, except as to the Clergy, the Laity being professedly left out of the Plan.[f]

This being the Case, it is expected that Dr. Chandler, or the next Apologist for his Church, will soften these mournful Complaints, and for their own Sakes prepare a more favourable Account of the State of Discipline in their Congregations, and of the Disposition of the Clergy to reform it: Otherwise the World will scarce believe their Church to be *the best reformed Church in the World; the purest Church under Heaven; the Bulwark of the Reformation; the pure Apostolic Church;* and *the CHURCH* by Way of Eminence and Exclusion, as if there was no other in the Christian World.

By this Time, it must appear pretty plain, that the Argument taken from the Prostration of Discipline in the Episcopal Churches in America, is meerly a delusive Piece of Declamation, no-ways connected with the Scheme of an American Episcopate. Nay, Bishops would rather tye up the Hands of the Clergy, and prevent any thing being done of this sort, if we may judge from what passes in England. Had it not been for Civil Establishments, what could have prevented the Reformation of many Abuses in the Church of England, which every good Member sees with regret? Dr. Chandler, imputed it to the want of good Sense and Candour enough in the Body of the Nation.[9] But in this enlightened Age, especially as the Things which call for amendment have been held up to public View, for more than a Century past, by some of the greatest Men of the established Church, as well as others, in every striking Point of Light; this cannot be the Case. The Root of the Evil lies deeper, and must be sought for in the civil Establishment; by which even the most distant Hopes of Reformation in any thing material, are cut off. Establishments in Religion may make Hypocrites and occasional Conformists, when their secular Interests lead them that way; but never do great Service to true Christianity. This needs not the Chains of earthly Grandeur, nor the Force of civil Power to spread and establish it. High Dignities and Preferments; Mitres and Thrones; Lordships and princely Revenues have ever been injurious to its Interests; and instead of improving, have dreadfully corrupted, and depraved the Religion of Jesus, and robb'd it of its native Glory and Strength. Ecclesiastical History in all Ages lamentably bears Witness to the justness of these Remarks; yet the want of these Things is now made an Excuse for suffering Discipline in the Episcopal Church to remain relaxed and prostrate.

What can the Episcopal Ministers in the Colonies have to say in excuse for themselves, if they criminally neglect restoring primitive Discipline. Dr. C. confesses that Presbyters may have a subordinate Power to govern the Church and enjoy a Right to exclude from the Sacraments all publickly vicious Members. In this Country they are un-restrained by the Difficulties which embarrass the Conscientious parish Ministers in England, their Enclosures are not laid open by a political *Test*; and they enjoy every Power which other Churches in the Colonies have. Why then should they despair of accomplishing what is daily done by others? They profess to wish for it; why do they not attempt it by reason and persuasion, the only rational Way in which it can be brought about? No Discipline was more severe than that of the primitive Church; yet it was all voluntary, and received no Countenance from civil Power.

But in truth; these People are, themselves little affected with the pathetic Complaints they make for want of a regular Discipline. These are thrown out meerly to excite the public Pity, and to screen themselves from the Charge of supine Negligence, in not attempting to restore it; under an idle Pretence that they want Bishops to effect it for them. Yet at the same Time they are so weak and inconsistent, as to declare that no Attempts to restore Discipline, will be made under the proposed Episcopate.

INTERNAL NOTES: "CENTINEL" XVII

[a] Communion before Lent.
[b] White's *Letters to a Dissent.* Gent Lr. 3d. Pages, 12, 13, 14, 17, 22, 28.[1]
[c] *Appeal,* 31.
[d] Crofts, *Bishop* of Hereford, *Naked Truth,* p. 82.[2]
[e] *Appeal,* 26, 31, 95.
[f] *Appeal,* 97.
[g] *Appeal,* 96.

NOTES: "CENTINEL" XVII

1. John White, *The Third and Last Letter to a Gentleman Dissenting from the Church of England,* 2nd. ed. (London, 1745), p. 28. See also White's *A Letter to a Gentleman Concerning the Lives of Churchmen and Dissenters,* 2nd ed. (London, 1743) and *A Second Letter to a Gentleman Concerning the Lives of Churchmen and Dissenters,* 2nd. ed. (London, 1745).

2. [Herbert Croft], *The Naked Truth, or, the True State of the Primitive Church by a Humble Moderator* (London, 1675), "Of Church Government," p. 59.

3. "But you, O prelates, learn what gold can do within the sacred walls."—Persius, *Satires* 2. 68–69.

Centinel Number XVIII

July 21, 1768

When designing Men have any Schemes to execute, which may be prejudicial to the Rights and Privileges of others, Reasons, different from those, which really influence them, are contrived and thrown out to amuse the Populace, and to divert their attention from the Consequences, that may follow from the execution of their Schemes. This seems to be the Policy of the Episcopal Missionaries in their Attempts to introduce Bishops into the American Colonies.

In our last Centinel, we considered their idle pretence of the want of Discipline, as it is urged by Dr. C. as an Argument in Favour of the proposed Episcopate. We will not consider another Artifice to gild the disagreeable Pill, that it may be swallowed without Suspicion, namely that these new Bishops are to have no Power over the Laity.

It is well known, there are among the Laity, many moderate Members of the Episcopal Communion who detest Spiritual Domination, as much as others, and who are as tenacious of their Civil and Religious Liberties, as the Members of any other Church, and therefore likely to be alarmed at this dangerous Innovation. Least these should proceed on the Supposition that to prevent the Yoke from being fixed upon them, it was the safest way to oppose the Scheme of introducing these new Masters into the Colonies, they are first deprived of their natural Right of being consulted on the important Article, and then they are amused with the *false* and *inconsistent* hopes of being entirely exempted from the Jurisdiction of the American Bishops. We call it an inconsistent Hope, as it is contradictory not only to the known Sentiments of the English Episcopal Church, but also to the Sentiments of every other Christian Church in the World. This plan of American Bishops is a mere novel Invention, without any parallel in History either sacred or profane, since the first Establishment of a Church upon Earth; and yet, no doubt, some zealous Clergy will tell us, it is the pure Apostolic Plan. It seems strange, indeed, that the Clergy of the Church of England, who are, doubtless, Dr. C's Superiors at Home, who have settled this Plan, (if, indeed, they ever settled it) should deviate so much from the model of their own and of every other Christian Church, as well as from the Discipline prescribed in the Scripture. A Church, whose Members are exempt from the Government of its Officers, is what no Age can furnish an Example of. The inconsistency, therefore, of this Plan with the known principles of the Church of England, give grounds to suspect that Dr. C. has not given us the Plan, on which Bishops are to be sent to America, with that openness and candour that might have been expected.

But this is not the only Reason we have to suspect, that there is something more at the Bottom, than what Dr. C. seems willing to confess. Sundry passages in the Appeal (where Dr. C. was off his Guard and therefore expressed the true Sentiments of his Heart) seem to convince us, that the Laity must yield Obedience to the new Spiritual Lords, and subject their unpractised Necks to the Ecclesiastical Yoke prepared for them. We shall point out some of these.

"The Church," says he, "considered with relation to civil Power, being in the very Nature of it a voluntary Society, it is left to Men's Consciences, whether they will become Members of it or not. But after they are become Members of it, the Laws of the Church are in force against them, and they are *subject* in Ecclesiastical Matters to the *Authority* of those, who govern it. What the just penalties of Disobedience are, we may learn from the Nature of the Church itself. The utmost effect of its Power in this World is the cutting off and rejecting such Members, as are incurably and dangerously corrupted."[a] Let the World, to which the Doctor appeals, judge how consistent this is with the Declaration, "That the American Bishops are to have no Authority, nor indeed to exercise any Discipline over their own People, the Clergy excepted."[b] Let but the Bishops be once introduced to govern the Clergy, and the Laity will soon hear it asserted, and probably feel it to their Cost, "That from the very Nature of the Church, its Laws are in Force against them, and they are and must be subject to the Authority of those who govern it."

Again Dr. C. tells us, "When Bishops were first proposed or requested for this Country, they were mentioned under the Title of *Suffragans*. This is no ambiguous Term, it has a fixed and determinate meaning in the Laws of England and cannot be mistaken. Suffragan Bishops are the same with those, that were *Chorespiscopi* or Bishops of the Country, in the Primitive Church; and it is their Business to exercise all Offices merely Episcopal, in the remote

Parts of the Diocese, wherein they reside, according to the Direction of and by Virtue of a Commission of the Diocean."[c] Is it then no Part of the Episcopal Charge? Are they not the Flock, over whom the Holy Ghost has made Bishops?[d] If it is a Suffragan Bishop, that is requested for America, whose Power to govern the Laity of the Diocese is fixed and determined by the Laws of England, with what Confidence can Dr. C. and his Brethren abuse the Members of their own Church, with the fond Hopes of being exempted from his Government and Jurisdiction? Is it not an Office *merely* Episcopal to take Notice of and to punish the irregular and scandalous Behavior of the Members of the Church, to take cognizance of scandal and of causes Matrimonial? If these Suffragan Bishops must hold their Commissions from the Bishop of London, or any other Bishop in England, and discharge all Parts of the Episcopal Office in the Colonies, as being remote Parts of his Lordship's Diocese, and if his Power is fixed and determined by the Laws of England, it is plain beyond Contradiction, that the desire of the Missionaries is to have such Suffragan Bishops imported into America, as shall have Authority to exercise all the Powers given them by the Laws of England, although Dr. C. is obliged to confess, that some of these Ecclesiastical Laws bear hard upon British Liberty and need an Amendment.[e] The Colonies in America, it seems, are to be made a Part of some English Bishop's (it may be the Bishop of London's) Diocese, and the Power and Authority of his Suffragan is to be reverentially submitted to, and acknowledged in as full and ample a Manner as is specified in the English Laws, by all that reside in this new erected Diocese. In vain therefore, will the Laity expect (if they disoblige the Clergy) to escape the "utmost Effects of the Church's Power *in this World,*" happy for them, should their Poverty hinder them to *commute* and purchase a Pardon, if they escape her Power *in the World to come;* and if her excommunicated Members are not made to feel, *after Death,* or in the *other World,* the dire Effects of her sore Displeasure. "Excommunication," it is true, has among Protestants; "lost much of the dreaded Force" it once had in the Romish Church, but D.C., it would seem by his modest Hint, is not without hopes or at least without desire of "restoring" it in America. Happy will it be for Americans if "this Power of the Church" be confined to those who willingly "become Members of it." There is Reason to fear, that the Members of every other Communion will feel the Effects of it, in this remote Part of his Lordship's Diocese, when his Suffragan Bishops come over here "with as full and complete Authority over the Clergy as the Laws and Canons direct."[f] For although it may appear miraculous, that a Church should excommunicate or cast out those that never did belong to her; yet we know that the Church of England daily works such Miracles; and we have no Reason to doubt, that the Suffragan who is "to discharge all Episcopal Offices" will exhibit in America the same Evidences of his Apostolic Descent.

But least there should remain any doubt about the Power of this American Suffragan, or the Plan, upon which he was first requested for the Benefit of the Colonies, the whole Affair is settled with sufficient Precision, in the Words of the Supplicants, as Dr. C. has recorded them.[g] Their Request was "that such Governors in the Church should be constituted" in America, "1st, to rule and govern well the People, who are desirous to be committed to their Charge, without which (they are the very Words of the Supplicants) no Wonder if some Members grow remiss in their Duty, it may fall into scandalous Practices; and if Atheism, Deism, &c. prevail over more," "2dly, To protect and defend both Laity and Clergy." Their Power and Business as set forth in the Abstract quoted P. 52 is to "govern both Priests and People according to the Model of the English Church;" This was the Plan, upon which suffragan Bishops were first requested to be established in America; and Dr. C. says, "he knows not of a single Instance, wherein Reason has been given to suspect that a Departure from the same general Plan has been aimed at or desired."[h]

The Power then of these Suffragans is to rule and govern both Priests and *People*, according to the Model of the English Church; to govern well the *People*, who are Members of their Church and put under their Care; to correct remissness in Duty, scandalous Practices, Atheism, Deism, &c. and yet if we believe Dr. C. "their Authority shall operate only upon the *Clergy* and not upon the *Laity*, or Dissenters of any Denomination."

Another Thing I would just remark. It is agreed on all Hands, that the American Bishop is to govern the Clergy. Dr. C. tells us "his Power over them shall be as full and as compleat as the Laws and Canons of the Church direct."[i] and yet that "spiritual Courts will never be established here."[j] What is this, but to say, that an arbitrary spiritual Jurisdiction, unknown in the British Constitution, and abhorrent to the Rights of Freemen is asked and about to be established in America. Alas for the poor Clergy; if, when their Character and Livings are in question, they must hear from the Mouth of a proud Ecclesiastic, sic volo, sic jubeo, stat pro ratione voluntas.[2]

INTERNAL NOTES: "CENTINEL" XVIII

[a] Appeal, p. 30.
[b] p. 95.
[c] App. p. 20. System of English Ecclesiastical Laws.[1]
[d] Acts 20: 28.
[e] App. 95. 96.
[f] p. 31.
[g] See Notes in p. 49, 50, 51, 52.
[h] P. 80.
[i] P. 31.
[j] P. 96.

NOTES: "CENTINEL" XVIII

1. Sir Richard Gray, *A System of English Ecclesiastical Law* (London, 1730), p. 65.
2. "That's what I want, so that's what I bid you. So ('take it on authority')—the will stands in place of a reason."

Centinel Number XIX

July 28, 1768

In clearing up Difficulties and in adjusting Differences that occur in any Society, it is the surest way to look back to the original Principles on which the Founder proceeded; to examine how they and their immediate Successors understood, and how they acted upon these Institutes. This has been acknowledged to be a regular procedure in civil Policy, and in expounding Human Laws: It seems still more proper in revealed Religion, whose Author is infallible. If the Professors of Christianity had made this their Rule, and had oftner recurred to the words of their Lord, and to the writings and practice of his Apostles; If they had always made the Bible their directory in Faith and Discipline; and determined to call no Man on earth Master, abundance of misguided Zeal, angry Contention and cruel Persecution might have been avoided; much confusion in Doctrine and Discipline prevented; and the primitive Simplicity of the Gospel better maintained.

Most denominations of Christians are indeed ready enough to appeal to Scripture, and to be determined by it, whenever they think it favours their Peculiarities. Nay they will torture it by forced Constructions to speak favourably of their distinguishing Tenets, even where it would seem to express a contrary Meaning. But the human inventions and corruptions of some Churcches are so plainly against Scripture or unwarranted by it, that this method of Defence will not always answer. Recourse is then had to Tradition, pretended Apostolic Usage, the supposed Right of the Church to decree Rites and Ceremonies, and to institute new modes of Discipline, (if not to add new Articles of Faith) for the Support of these Innovations: A method by which almost any Absurdity, Error or Usurpation might be vindicated, and the Christian Faith intirely thrust aside, to make Room for the weak or wicked Devices of Men.

In the matter I have now in View, Dr. Chandler appeals indeed to Scripture; though many will think, without good Ground. However he cannot be charged with wire-drawing its meaning, as he adduces no particular Proofs of what he nevertheless roundly asserts. The Passage of his memorable *Appeal* to which I refer is this; "If we carefully examine the Writings of the Apostles, these Things will evidently appear, that our Blessed Saviour before his Ascension committed the Government of the Church *entirely to them;*—That this Government was exercised by *them;*—That they conveyed this power to others, to be communicated successively to others to the latest Posterity;—Particularly that these their Successors, were an Order distinct from, and superior to those now called Presbyters; and that none who were not of this Order, had the powers of Ordination and Government committed to them." But although he does not stay to offer Proof, yet he mentions for Instances, *James* as Diocesan of *Jerusalem; Timothy* of *Ephesus; Titus* of *Crete;* and the Angels of the seven Churches of *Asia.*

It would have been satisfactory to many of his Readers, if the Doctor had pointed out the Passages in the New Testament, which so clearly prove, that the great Head of the Church has committed the Government of it *entirely* to diocesan Bishops, as successors of the Apostles; because so important a Claim ought to be substantially supported. To instruct Mankind in the Doctrines of the Gospel, we indeed find a Charge given, accompanied with a Promise of Power from on high to assist them in doing it. But even supposing this Commission and Promise limited to the twelve, what do they make for the *sole* Authority of modern Prelates. The Apostles were an extraordinary sett of Men; they had no Successors circumstanced as they were: nor after the Choice of *Matthias* in the Room of *Judas*; and the divine Appointment of *St. Paul*, do we read of any new Elections. As they were to be chosen Witnesses of the Resurrection of Christ,[a] it was not possible they could long continue a distinct Order: Their Character and Name accordingly died with the Generation in which they lived.

In ordinary Matters, the Apostles, however, exercised no such *sole* Jurisdiction. They preached and delivered the Christian Doctrines as of divine Authority, and they proved their Mission by Works of extraordinary Nature; such as the Death of *Ananias and Sophira*, the Blindness of *Elymas*, and the like.[1] But in those Matters in which only their Conduct can be exemplary, they did every Thing with the common Voice of the Church. Thus were the Deacons chosen. In this Manner did they proceed in giving their Judgement upon the Controversy at *Antioch* referred to the Church of Jerusalem, concerning the Obligation of the Mosaic Law over the Gentile Converts to Christianity. *St. Paul* upbraiding the Corinthians for remissness of Discipline in a Case of Incest tells them "*that when they were gathered together,*" they ought, "with the *Power* of Christ," to excommunicate the guilty Person. And in his 2d. Epistle, speaking of the same Affair, he says "sufficient to the Man was the Punishment, or Censure, *which was* inflicted by many." What became of the *sole* Authority of the Bishop in these Cases? How came the "Multitude,"[b] the "whole Church,"[c] the "many" to meddle with the Apostolic or Episcopal Rights. Nay, how durst any Teachers at *Antioch* to dissent from, and dispute with *Paul* and *Barnabas*, one, if not both of them, of the superior Order, to whom the Government of the Church, according to Dr. C. had been *entirely* committed? And whatever blame they incurred for Error in Doctrine, how happened it, that they escaped without Censure for Want of due Submission to an Apostle? The great Lord Chancellor *Bacon*, who speaks the general Sense of the Doctor's church from the Reformation till his Time, differs widely from him. His Words are remarkable; I shall give them at large. He says, "on reading the *Scriptures*, I could never find, but that God had left the like Liberty to Church Government as to Civil Government; to be varied according to Time, Place and Accidents: which nevertheless his high and divine Province orders and disposes. For all Civil Governments are restrained from God to the general grounds of Justice and Manners; but their Policies and Forms are left free; so that Monarchies, Senates, and popular States are lawful, and where they are planted ought to remain inviolate. So in the Church, the Substance of the Doctrine is immutable: but for Rites and Ceremonies, particular Hierarchies, Policies and Disciplines of Churches, they are left at large. It is proper therefore to return to the ancient Degrees of Unity in the Church of God, which were one Faith, one Baptism; not one Hierarchy, one Discipline." This penetrating Genius was so far from supporting the Hierarchy of the Church of England, (of which he was a zealous Defender) even from primitive Practice, that he subjoins, "the Times of Persecution were excellent Times for Doctrine and Manners; *but are improper and unsuitable Examples of external Government.*"[2]

That the Apostles conveyed this *sole* Power, which Dr. C. ascribes to them, to others, to be handed down in Succession, is equally destitute of Proof. If they assumed no such Power themselves; if in the ordinary Affairs of the Church, they and the Evangelists and Elders, mentioned in Scripture, exercised none, how could they convey it over to Successors.[d] The Pastors and Ministers of the Church, called by the People and solemnly set apart by the Apostles and Evangelists, had the Power of preaching the Gospel; and, says a great Writer, "there is an Empire in preaching:"[e] But the supreme Direction of the Affairs of the Churches, as assumed by modern Prelates, was exercised by none. The People, jointly with their Elders judged, even in excommunication. This Passage of the Doctor's implies the necessity of an uninterrupted Succession which he had just before asserted very explicitly; notwithstanding the Absurdity of such a Notion, and the many inconveniencies attending it, have been often expressed. Mr. *Locke's* Argument against it is invincible. If, says he, a Society enjoys the Benefit of the Presence of Christ, according to his Promise, that "where *two or three* are gathered together in his Name, he will be in the midst of them," they want neither Bishops by unbroken Succession, nor any Thing else necessary to the Salvation of Souls.[f] Is the Christian Ministry so essential to the Being of a Church, that it could not exist without it? By no means, say very able Divines. Arch-bishop *Cranmer*, had this Question put to him; whether if all Bishops & Priests were dead, it would be lawful to appoint others to preach the Word, and administer the Sacraments? His Answer to this and another Question of like Nature is this, "it is not against God's Law, but on the contrary they ought indeed so to do."[g] The Truth is, the Churches of Christ, as all other Societies, have the Principle of all Power & Privilege residing in the Body, not in the Officers: and are competent to all necessary Points. As in Civil Government, where a Failure of the Royal Family, or other Defect in the Administration is made good by the inherent Power of the Community; so in ecclesiastical, the Church may interpose & supply every Deficiency. All pretensions then of the Officers of the State or Church to indefensible hereditary Right, are only derived from Ambition and Usurpation, and can serve only to set them above controul. If the Claim of a divine Right in Kings "to govern wrong" be inconsistent with civil Liberty and public Happiness; the Opinion that all Authority and Privilege in the Church, resides in the Clergy, and is to be conveyed through an uninterrupted Succession of Bishops as Successors of the Apostles, is destructive of Christian Liberty, and sets the Blessings of the Gospel on a most precarious Footing.

That Bishop and Presbyter are the same in Scripture, has been shewn in a former Paper; and further, that many great Men of the Church of England have thought so. The Instances of diocesan Episcopacy given by Dr. C. have no Countenance from the New Testament; for the Notes subjoined to the Epistles to *Timothy* and *Titus*, in the Opinion of the learned, were added 500 Years after these Epistles were written. *Titus* was left behind at *Crete* to ordain

Elders or Bishops (as they are also called) in *every* City, which would rather prove that he was an Arch-Bishop. But it is evident *Timothy* and *Titus* were Evangelists, employed in spreading the glad Tidings of Salvation to infidel Nations; consequently they had no settled Charge. The Primacy of *Peter* at *Rome*, and the Prelacy of *James* at *Jerusalem* seem much of equal solidity; and rest equally on Tradition. The Angels of the seven Churches in the prophetical language of the *Revelations*; are evidently put for the Churches themselves. But the prelatical Cause labours much, when Recourse is had to such precarious and slender Proofs; which would not be offered, if better could be had.

INTERNAL NOTES: "CENTINEL" XIX

[a] Acts of Apos. 1. 22.

[b] Ibid; vi. 5.

[c] Ibid; xv. 22.

[d] St. Paul, who was an inspired Writer, in giving his Judgement in Matters to which his divine Direction did not reach, could say, "I speak this by Permission, and not of Commandment." I Epis. Corinth. vii. 6.[3]

[e] Dr. Jer. Taylor.[4]

[f] Letter 1st, on Toleration.[5]

[g] See Bishop *Stillingfleet's* Iren. Cap. viii.[7]

NOTES: "CENTINEL" XIX

1. Ananias and his wife, Sapphira, sold some land and held back a part of the price instead of offering it all to the Lord. As a result, both died. Acts 5:1–10.

Elymas, or Bar-jesus, was a sorcerer in Paphos who tried to keep the deputy of the country from hearing the preaching of the apostles, Barnabas and Saul. He was blinded for his effort. Acts 13:1–12.

2. Francis Bacon, *Certain Considerations Touching the Better Pacification and Edification of the Church of England, The Works of Francis Bacon*, (4 vols., London, 1740), 4:475.

3. I Corinthians 7:6.

4. Jeremy Taylor, *Clerus Domini, or A Discourse of the Divine Institution, Necessity, Sacrednesse and Separation of the Office Ministerial* (London, 1655), pp. 11–12.

5. John Locke, *A Letter Concerning Toleration.*

7. Edward Stillingfleet, *Irenicum. A Weapon-Salve for the Churches Wounds, or the Divine Right of Particular Forms of Church-Government* (London, 1662), chapter 8, p. 392.

Anti-Centinel Number I

June 16, 1768

Audi & alteram partem.—Keep both Ears open.

The Person who is injured and persecuted, naturally becomes the Object of Attention and Pity.—The Man who will not support and succour afflicted Virtue, deserves to be afflicted without Succour or Support. Such Considerations as these may plead my Excuse, while I take the Liberty to address the Public in Favour of the Revd. Dr. Bradbury Chandler, who has been maltreated and cruelly abused and persecuted by a certain Writer, who stiles himself the CENTINEL. Not that I have any Doubt of the Doctor's Appeal to the Public carrying Conviction wherever it finds its Way; but as many People may read the Centinel, who have not seen the Appeal, and may thence form Prejudices against the Gentlemen, who have been promoting a Church Establishment in this Country, it seems proper that they should be presented with the Sum of these Arguments, which may be offered in Favour of an American Bishop.

After so eminent a Writer as the Revd. Dr. Chandler, the Reader is not to expect that I should offer any new Arguments on the Subject.

Mecum habito & Novus quam sit mihi curta supellex.[1] I shall be contended with treading faithfully in the Doctor's Footsteps, taking his Arguments as they stand, or sometimes abbreviating, at other Times enlarging them, so as to place them in the clearest and strongest Light, and upon these Arguments we are determined to rest our Cause; they are the Sentiments of a *general Convention of our Clergy*, published after the maturest Deliberation, therefore as we do not think any new Arguments are necessary to support our Cause, so, are we determined not to desert one of those which we have already advanced.—The Prayer of our Petition is to this Import, *That his majesty and the British Parliament would graciously be pleased to send over to America one or more Bishops of the Church of England, and make such Establishment for their*

Maintenance, &c. as may be suited to the Rank and Dignity of their Office. Who could have imagined that any Objection would have been made to a Scheme so moderate and reasonable as this; a Scheme which must be equally profitable to Church and State. It may be of great Use towards preserving the Obedience and loyalty of his Majesty's Subjects in North-America, and is absolutely necessary towards the very Existence of Christianity in this Part of the World. That such is the Importance of an American Episcopate, Dr. Chandler has effectually proved to every Person, who is not hardened against Conviction by the obstinate Prejudices of Education.

It is absolutely necessary towards the Propagation of Christianity in America, the Bishops be immediately sent over to these Parts. *For it is, (says the Doctor) an essential Doctrine of the Church of England, that none can have any Authority in the Church of England, but those who derive it from Christ immediately or mediately. They who receive the Authority immediately must prove their Mission by working Miracles. Those who receive it mediately must derive it from those Persons whom Christ has authorized to convey it, i.e. they must receive it by regular Succession. Man may ridicule the Notion of uninterrupted Succession as they please, but if the Authority of the Clergy derived from Christ (and if it is not, they are no Ministers of Christ) they must receive it in one of the Ways already mentioned, and if the Succession be once broke, and the Power of Ordination once lost—not all the Men on Earth; not all the Angels in Heaven, without an immediate Commission from Christ can restore it.* P. 4th.

All Persons therefore who call themselves Ministers, unless they be truly originated from this immaculate, uninterrupted Line, are Imposters and no Ministers of Christ. *It is as great an absurdity on St. Paul's Principles for a Man to preach the Gospel without being properly sent, as for a Man to hear without a Preacher, or believe in him of whom they have not heard.* Therefore as the Teachers who are not *ordained* by a Bishop, or sent in by him, cannot possibly preach the Gospel, so neither can the People hear the gospel from them. And where there are no Preachers of the Gospel nor any Hearers, there can hardly be any Christianity. If there be any Nations then who have no public Teachers *duely sent* by Apostolic Bishops, we are not to think that Christianity subsists in those Nations. Hence we see the singular Propriety with which Doctor Chandler distinguishes his American Episcopalians by the Name of *the Church, the American Church, the Church in America.*

I confess he might have avoided this seeming Tautology, by calling them at once the Christians in America, or the Christian Church in America; not that he has entirely neglected this accurate Distinction, for, Page 113, he tells us, that *the Cause of the Church in America is the Cause of Christianity*, and who else are entituled to the Name of Christians? What other Church (that of Rome excepted) has a Christian Ministry? The Churches of Denmark and Sweden, the Lutherans and Calvinists in Germany, the Churches of Geneva, Holland and Scotland, are nothing but the Shadow of Churches; they have forsaken, they have shut out the Light of Christianity by rejecting the Gospel Ministry through the only Channel of Conveyance, *the unbroken Succession*. When I think of those Millions of Souls who in this enlightened Age, suffer themselves to perish without Benefit of Clergy, my Compassion is stirred up, my Heart is moved within me.

The pious Mr. Dodwell in his *one Priesthood*, expresses himself in this elegant Manner. *It is*, says he, *the most dreadful Aggravation of the Condemnation of the Damned, that they are banished from the Presence of the Lord, and from the Glory of his Power, The same is their Condition also who are disunited from Christ by being disunited from the Bishop, his visible Representative.*

Some People who abound in a Kind of false Charity, such as would presently sap the Foundations of the Church, will here ask, What then do we make of all Protestant Nations besides the English? Do we in very Deed deny them the Gospel Ministry, and consign them to the Blackness of Darkness for ever? To this we shall only answer by repeating what the Doctor has already said, The Necessity of Episcopal Ordination is an essential Doctrine of our Church.—They who have it not are bound to maintain it, let the Consequences be what they may; we are not accountable for those more than for the Fate of the Mohametans, since they also have Christianity in their Offer, but obstantly refuse to accept of it; and if the Protestant Nations in Europe suffer themselves to perish without the Ministrations of the Gospel, they are so much the more unpardonable, as a very little Care would render it universal. We do not say that those People are deficient in general Acquaintance with the Christian Religion; nor that they fail in Piety, Benevolence, Charity, or any other moral or christian-like Virtue. But they have rejected or lost *Episcopal Ordination*, which *alone* can restore them to the Fellowship of the Church, and entitle them to her Blessings. But how shall they who live in Darkness, shut out from the benign Influence of a Gospel Ministry, receive this invaluable Blessing.

Their Duty is plain; they may readily obtain from England suppose it were but one or two Bishops, and even as a little Leaven leaveneth the whole Lump, so will these Bishops in a short Time convey genuine Ordination to all the Clergy in a whole Kingdom.

Having thus proved the general Necessity of Bishops, towards the Existence of Christianity, I shall next shew that they are peculiarly necessary in America. For since there can be no *christian* Ministers without *Episcopal Ordination*, it is plain that our Clergy must either have Bishops to ordain them here, or they must go to England for Ordination; but the latter is absolutely impracticable, considering the Dangers of the Seas.—It has happened, I don't know by what Fatality, ever since the Affair of Jonah, that the Clergy have been singularly unfortunate at Sea. This is also a general Observation of Seamen, who doubtless are the best Judges in that Case. *There have gone Home for Ordination from the Northern Colonies fifty-two; of those forty-two have returned safe, and ten have MISCARRIED.* Page 341. What a Melancholy Loss is here, little less than 20 per Cent, which is eight Times as great as our Loss on the several Kinds of Merchanize which we generally import. This plainly evinces the Necessity of having an American Bishop. The Winds and Seas forbid our continuing any longer on the present Footing.

But the Care of the Negroes, the Indians and the White People in general, furnishes us with so many distinct Arguments in Favour of an American Bishop.—We shall consider them apart.—The Cause of an American Episcopate derives a powerful Argument from the State of the Negroes, who constitute the Majority of those numerous Souls, that fill up and adorn our List as Members of the Church in America. *The Number of blacks in the Islands and Colonies is above EIGHT HUNDRED and FORTY THOUSAND. These Negroes may be said in an imperfect Sense to belong to the respective religious Classes of their Owners with whom they are connected, and by whom they are governed.* So that whatever is the Religion of the Master, that also may be called the Religion of the Slave. But *the Masters are chiefly known to be Church-Men*; consequently above half a Million of Negroes *belong to the Church of England.* Such have been the fruitful Labours of our Missionaries, such the rapid Increase of our Church in this Part of the World. Now though it is generally known that *these Slaves are brought up in Ignorance without any Ray of religious Hope to cheer them, and to the eternal Disgrace of Teachers and Masters, are no Christians at all, yet as the Sense of Religion will* certainly *increase in their masters by the* Presence of a Bishop, *so it will also increase in the*

Slaves, and the good Work which we have so happily begun, will then be carried on to the desired Perfection. Page 57. To illustrate this, let us suppose a Bishop settled in Philadelphia, his pious Influence would soon diffuse a Spirit of Religion, as well through all the neighbouring Provinces as this City. Then we might expect in a short Time to equal that Purity of Morals, and that religious Disposition, which is generally observed in London and other great Cities, that have providentially become the Residence of a Bishop. Suppose then a Bishop were settled in Philadelphia, the Planters in Jamaica and the other West-Indian Islands, being under his lordship's immediate Observation, would soon become very sober and religious, and consequently their Negroes, who are general a discreet, intelligent Sort of People, would in Imitation of their Masters, become religious and good Christians. Whoever is well acquainted with the Condition of Slaves in our Southern Provinces and the West-India Islands, and has observed the compassionate Manner in which their Masters express their Desire of seeing those Outcasts of humanity instructed in the Christian Religion, must readily see the Force of this Argument, and tho' illiterate Americans in general may not be able to comprehend it, yet we are persuaded that our Superiors in England, for whom, by the Way, Dr. Chandler's Address was chiefly designed, will easily perceive its Weight and will see that so glorious a Prospect of adding half a Million of Church Men to the Christian Church, proves beyond all Doubt, the Necessity of an American Bishop. D.

NOTES: "ANTI-CENTINEL" I

1. Apparently, a deliberately incorrect version of "Tecum havita & novis quam sit tibi curta supellex." "I live by myself and know how little wherewithal I have." Persius *Satires* IV. 1. 52

Anti-Centinel Number II

September 29, 1768

At length after many a promise and many a threat, portending great events, the ecclesiastical Anatomist stands forth brandishing his knife. Long had our Church complained that a person of such profound erudition and mighty in words; long distinguished as the hopes and pillar of episcopacy in this new world, should like another Achilles, have lain by in his camp, while our enemies were carrying all before them with fire and faggot; but he so saw and marked the critical season, when the Centinel being asleep, he might fall upon him, cut him limb from limb, and give his flesh for food to the fowls of the air and the beasts of the field. Long had I desired to contribute towards the desirable work of demolishing that doughty Centinel; but while the first rate advocates of our Church stood by in silent gaze, I thought it would be prudent to forbear.—Encouraged now by the Anatomist, who kindly invites all *the enemies of faction and friends of religion, liberty and toleration*, to communicate their thoughts to the Public, I have ventured, tho' not so fortunate, as he is in leisure and ABILITIES, to bespeak the attention of the Public, while I offer a few arguments in favour of an American Episcopate; in opposition to the Centinel, and all his *scribling, factious friends.* I have said, I shall offer some arguments, the reader is not to suppose they are such trifling ones as Bacon or Locke would have offered; but such as are usually advanced by the advocates of our Church in this more enlightened age:—Yet conscious how unfit I am to produce any new arguments that will bear this test, I shall generally take the liberty of borrowing from the Anatomist,—

Hanc veniam petimus: damus que vicissim[1]

I shall borrow from him in particular

1. Because I am persuaded that for certain reasons we are both acquainted with, he cannot in conscience complain of my using the freedom.

2. I am persuaded he will say, all that need be said on the subject, and so render it needless for me to attempt investigating new arguments.

3. I take this to be the most effectual method of convincing our antagonists; for *one* good argument well seconded, that is, as lawyers understand it, advanced a second time with a little abbreviation or paraphrase, as may seem best, has always been found to do more execution than twenty arguments simply advanced without any friend to support them.

By this time the reader understands that I do hardly assume the character of an author, being content with the more humble rank of an editor or translator, and yet considering the greatness of my original, this same is no inconsiderable station.—Even as the secretary of a powerful Monarch is dignified above the clerk of some little pedling store-keeper. I have taken the liberty to call this paper the Anti-Centinel, and would have it considered as a supplement to a paper that was published some months ago, of which, as the author seems to have discontinued it, I have ventured to borrow the title, since my plan too is very similar to his, *mutatis mutandis.*[2]—In prosecuting this work, tho' I don't preclude the liberty of saying any clever thing that may occur on the subject, yet I shall generally continue myself to seconding, inforcing, abreviating and explaining the arguments of the Anatomist; and that he may have the credit to which he has a title. When I use his arguments, they shall be marked with inverted coma's—when I use his very words, they shall be marked in Italick. Such, reader, is to be the plan of the following papers, proceed we now to demolish the Centinel.

EXORDIUM

"A *sett of shameless scribblers—an overbearing party, in three of the capital provinces in America, who* certainly *are actuated by some base and wicked design,* have had the insolence and temerity to speak and *write against the* CHURCH—against our CHURCH, against that *Church which is the bull-work of protestanism and true English liberty.* A Church, which *unawed by* Presbyterian *persecution,* fire and faggot *stood firm in defence of the Reformation,* and is now *the brightest example of moderation to all who differ from her*—and more moderate still to those who agree with her.—*We should have answered* those shameless scribblers and the Centinel among the rest much sooner, but we refrained, *least we should interrupt a union in councils* among the inhabitants of this province, *at this dangerous crisis,* and yet for all this was the reason we are determined not to have any union or communion with them, for they certainly have some dark wicked design lurking under such open (which is more dangerous than secret) abuse, and so we will not unite with them in councils, for we believe in our hearts that *they intend to make tools of us at the ensuing election,* to serve their purpose."—We imagine they intend to put a certain Republican Writer into the Assembly at next election—but we are resolved he shall not go there, for he is an enemy to the colonies, at least, he is an enemy to the prerogative of parliament and the ministers of state, from whose favour we hope for an Episcopal establishment; and whom, for that reason, we are determined to serve, come what will of the more trifling Liberties of our fellow subjects.[3]

"The Centinel *has painted the Church in the most odious character.* He calls her—*A Church that has long encroached on the rights of conscience and oppressed her fellow Christians*—which is not true, for she has no test act—A number of other falsehoods he has advanced about her *corrupting the pure word of God by human inventions—squandering away large sums of money in support of missionaries,* and such groundless aspersions.—Wherefore is our Church loaded with all this calumny? For no other reason than that *Dr. Chandler* in the spirit of MEEKNESS wrote a small book, in hopes of recommending an American Bishop—But why should Presbyterians be angry with Dr. Chandler for such an innocent milky performance, surely he said no harm of them." He only said, or rather hinted, that they are all rebels in America, and have no *natural right* to any place of profit or trust under the government—that their teachers are no ministers, and that they are no christians.— "Now surely, it is not fair to abuse the Dr. for this meek sort of writing, much less is it fair to abuse the church on the account of its advocate Dr. Chandler, any more than it would be fair to traduce the Synod of Philadelphia, on account of their advocate John Carmichael, for the cases are perfectly similiar," with this trifling difference, that the Dr. wrote by the approbation, order and assistance of a general convention of our clergy, and John only wrote for and by himself dis-connected with any soul living.[4] "Yet, notwithstanding that the cases are so perfectly similar, we have the good nature and modesty not to insist much on it." That the Synod are accountable for John's blunders, as when he says or swears that he is the learned member of a *learned body,* while the very performance proves that he is quite as illiterate as any son of our Church in that part of the country, which is saying a great deal for him. Ah John! John! It's a pity you had ever thought of printing your lucubrations since *you had no time to write for the Press.* If you should ever think of appearing again in print be persuaded to pursue a different plan—Take example from your brother Thomas up the way—Since you are ignorant, don't be ashamed to steal, 'tis a common and a thriving traffick; whether you preach or publish, don't trouble the world with any more of your slap-dash sermons; borrow or steal, tho' it were from another Church—Some good Christians hold all things in common—By such shifty means, as these, *unanimity and public spirit* not long since elevated a Missionary in our Church, to the highest pitch of eminence and litterary fame.—But of this on some future occasion. in the mean time I insist on it, that unless we traduce the Synod on John's Account, it will be very indecent of the Presbyterians to speak hard of any other person living, on Account of Dr. Chandler, who, as I proved just now, *has not uttered a single word reflecting on the principles of any protestant denomination. But the design of the following papers is not the defence of Dr. Chandler*—which by the way brings me in compliance with the prevailing custom to present the reader with a bill of fare. In the first place, negatively, tho' we are going to answer the Anatomist, who has attempted a formal refutation of Dr. Chandler's argument, yet we shall not so much as Attempt to support the Dr. and of course, we shall not interfere with the Centinel, except to call him a factious scribbler, &c.—I know better things than to defend the Doctor or his appeal, we have observed what advantage the adversary has gained over him, and have therefore resolved to surrender him and his appeal to be devoured by Whigs and Centinels, knowing, that it has ever been accounted better policy to desert a weak fortress, than attempt its defence.[5]—Secondly, by answering the Centinel, we humbly presume no man can be so absurd as to think we have any thing to do with the truth and validity of his arguments upon the danger of Episcopal establishments in this new world, &c. such arguments are below our notice. But thirdly we are determined to carry the war into the enemies country, and give them a Rowland for their Oliver—We shall prove that the Presbyterians and Independents are and have been enemies to our Church, and that for this and several other reasons they are a sett of factious, seditious, restless, ambitious, hypocritical, enthusiastic, fanatical, rebellious, impudent fellows. These things, with sundry others, being fairly proved or being frequently asserted, it must follow of natural consequences that a bishop is a very harmless person. That introducing him here by act of parliament, vesting him with proper powers, and maintaining him by a small public tax, &c. is not, and cannot be injurious to the civil or religious liberties of any denomination of christians on the continent. Perhaps the reader does not see how such consequences can follow from the premises; but they must and shall follow—for to speak our mind plainly, we have a bad opinion of the vulgar method of handling a debate.—Nothing is so stubborn as plain direct argument; We are determined to shun it—But we shall deal pretty freely with the characters of the dead, and if the Centinel or his ghost should ever think proper to answer us, we shall lead him such a wild-goose chace [sic] from one piece of scandal to another, that no person shall be able to guess, in a little time, what was the original subject of debate.—As to the question whether a bishop should be sent over to America, how he should be established, & how the liberties of other denominations of christians would be safe within his reach. These are articles we resolve not to meddle with. They are thorny questions.—We hope to keep them out of sight. Such is our present plan, which, for the prudence discovered therein, we hope will obtain the reader's approbation.

P.S. If any person has any objections to make against the Anatomist, let him send them to the Printers hereof, and they, with the proper answers to them, shall obtain a place in the Anti-Centinel, for we are determined to rescue his labours from all kind of darkness or ambiguity.

NOTES: "ANTI-CENTINEL" II

1. "The indulgence which we ask we do in turn vouchsafe." Horace *Ars Poetica* 1. 11

2. This is not an ancient expression but an original creation meaning, "allowing for differences in the particulars."

3. The "certain Republican Writer" was John Dickinson, whose recently published "Letters from a Pennsylvania Farmer" incited efforts by conservatives to block his re-election to the Assembly. "No Farmer in the Assembly" was their cry. See William Goddard, *The Partnership: or the History of the Rise and Progress of the Pennsylvania Chronicle* (Philadelphia, 1770), p. 18.

4. See "Remonstrant" I, note 2.

5. See the "Anatomist" I, *Pennsylvania Journal*, September 8, 1768, for the description of its endeavor which the "Anti-Centinel" is satirizing.

Remonstrant Number I

October 6, 1768

Qui perigit, qua vult, dicere, qua non vult, audiet. TER.[1]

Dr. Chandler's appeal is a noted performance, in which he represents the episcopal church in America as oppressed, persecuted and groaning under unparallelled hardships for want of an episcopate in these colonies. He with great confidence proposes a new plan of episcopacy, agreed on, as he asserts, by the episcopal church in England and America, which unlike the episcopate established in England, shall have no concern with the probate of wills or affairs matrimonial or relating to scandal, nor hurt the civil or religious rights of any other denomination; and he challenges every man in the colonies or else where to make objections to this new plan, if they have any, or if they be silent, it will be taken for granted that all parties acquiesce and are satisfied.

He has likewise strongly asserted the divine right of diocesan episcopacy, and the necessity of an uninterrupted succession of bishops for the ordination of ministers, nay he makes this unbroken line as necessary, as to believe in Jesus Christ, and thereby excludes all the ministers of the protestant churches from the number of Christ's ministers, who derive not their pedigree from St. Peter, disregarding this ridiculous pretension.

He represents the prelates that are to be sent on this new plan, as persons to be invested with great power and dignity, to protect both the clergy and laity; for whose support great funds are provided; who may possibly be entrusted with great power in our civil affairs, and for whose support he tells us, it is reasonable that we should all be taxed, and that we deserve not the name of good subjects if we should complain if taxed for this purpose; nay, he tells us, that the episcopal church is established in America as well as in England, for it is a part of that church and all that belong not to that church by law established, have no natural rights to any degree of civil or military power.

When such a challenge was given to all the American colonies, is it a crime, to make objections when thus called on by the Doctor? Were his high pretensions to be passed without notice? or how can this universal appeal be called a continuation of a dispute between the episcopal and other New England ministers? Was the appeal made to them only, or was it to every denomination in the English colonies? or did Dr. Chauncy who wrote a methodical answer to the appeal ever understand or suspect, that this was a continuation of an old controversy? The Centinel does not think that he had any concern with the New England controversies, the rejectors of diocesan episcopacy in those four provinces are able to manage their own affairs, and in the judgment of most men are more than a match for their adversaries in America even with the assistance of their friends beyond the Atlantic, though we are told that a high dignitary of the church of England refreshed their drooping spirits by his seasonable interposition, nay Dr. Chandler, sets this controversy in a different light and tells us, "that having addressed the public on the expediency of an American episcopate, he and his brethren judged it a matter of necessity and duty fairly to explain this plan on which bishops had been requested, to offer to the public the reasons of this request, and to obviate objections: For this reason he was ordered to publish the appeal, that all might either be satisfied or that such as were not might publish their objections," yet our modest *Anatomist* declares he was not the aggressor, and thus all these objects that he dislikes or cannot answer, are called unmerited abuse.

It has been often objected to Dr. Chandler, that he has given the world no assurance that his proposed plan of Episcopacy so favourable to civil and religious liberty is approved by all the Episcopal Churches in England and America; that if it gave all the colonies the universal satisfaction that he expected, yet it was proposed by himself only or by a few of his friends, and would be denied or opposed by all the narrow biggots in that church, it would probably be rejected by the powers that could confirm it for some political reasons, as it would weaken the dependency of the colonies on the mother country; and it would be rejected by all sober men, because these bishops were only to inspect the morals of the clergy, whilst the laity were totally to be neglected. And it was alledged that prelates, if once sent among us, would erect their ecclesiastical courts, as in former times, and possibly vex every religious denomination, that they were pleased to call dissenters, as in the days of

Archbishop Laud, and some of his successors, whose tyranny drove many to seek habitations in this wilderness. These fears aroused and alarmed great numbers who paid little regard to Dr. Chandler's fair words, whilst they saw the dangerous snare laid for their liberties by his specious proposals. And we find already by the *Anatomist*, that our fears were just, that most of the episcopalians paid no regard to his pretences, for he now asks "had Dr. Chandler any general commission from that church or even from his brethren belonging to it in America? This is not, says he, pretended. It is certain that not more than half a dozen of them ever had an opportunity of seeing his pamphlet till in print."

The Centinel's debate is only with Dr. Chandler, and he with his friends are loudly called on to answer the Centinel and to shew his mistakes; if he bears hard on the church of England as by law established, with respect to her ecclesiastical courts, or any other part of her conduct, he or they are to vindicate her as far as it can be done with truth and candour, and her vindication will be heard with pleasure and fairly acknowledged, where the defence is just; but this *doughty champion* declines this task. Yet to say something like argument, he cries the national church is abused, he will defend the national church—the religion of his Sovereign, and of the far greater and most respectable part of his subjects, and Dr. Chandler is, by him, set on a level with Mr. Carmichael, whom no man ever employed nor thanked for meddling with public affairs, both we hope are good men; but our respect for Doctor Chandler, makes us resent the comparison.[2]

How noble is the purpose of the Anatomist and how secure of a victory? He is in the same situation with the champion at a coronation, who armed *cap a pie* challenges all pretenders to the crown in the presence of the king and his guards—But the Anatomist with the bloody knife in his hand must be put in mind, that his argument had equal force in the mouth of all the heathen powers who persecuted the primitive church. It would have equal force in Turkey in defence of the Alcoran, against the religion of Jesus; and in France, against all the protestants, who have been inhumanly persecuted since the revocation of the edict of Nantes. They all plead for the national religion; the religion of their sovereign and of the most respectable part of his subjects.

We respect the church of England as by law established, and she is deservedly respected by all christian churches. She has had martyrs that sealed the truths of the gospel with their blood, and many bishops, ministers, and common christians eminent for learning, piety and charity, that have been esteemed bright ornaments of our holy religion: And with pleasure we acknowledge that her complexion is greatly mended by the Act of Toleration.

But she never pretended to infallibility. She daily confesses to Almighty God that she has erred and strayed like a lost sheep, and done many things which she ought not to have done, during the long and severe execution of the acts of uniformity, the act against conventicles and others, that distressed the followers of the same Redeemer and the children of the same heavenly Father, her looks were savage and severe, and bore a near resemblance to her who was drunk with the blood of saints; there were always in her a moderate and a high flying party, & the last were for severe measures to all that did not come into their measures. And had the corporation and test acts never existed she had been more lovely and the spouse of him who was meek and lowly in spirit. We revere her merit, but are not blind to her imperfection; in her there is great room for a reformation, this the best of her own sons do allow; nay they loudly call for it: The Lutheran and Calvinist churches were and are still more truly the bulwark of the reformation than the church of England. They bore the burden and heat of the day, when old Harry was pleading the cause of popery, and acquired from Rome the glorious title of defender of the Faith. The church of Scotland and the Dissenters in England and Ireland, and the Presbyterian states of Holland, deserve their share in these praises, for this boasted *bulwark* had on some occasions proved but a *tottering defence*.

The Anatomist tells us "the treatment this church has met with for many months past, from certain shameless scribblers, in three of the capital provinces in America, has been matter of astonishment and grief to good men of very different religious persuasions, who cannot but suspect some dark and wicked designs lurking under such unmeritted abuse." Men of dark signs are not so apt to give abuse, they strike in silence, and had not these three capital provinces been alarmed with the dark designs of a turbulent discontented party which began to appear in Dr. Chandler's Appeal, and been thereby aroused from their security, to examine how far an American episcopate was consistent with our civil and religious liberties, these shameless scribblers, as he politely calls them, had not set pen to paper on this subject. And if the danger from ecclesiastical courts, if they should take place among us, must not be mentioned, if it be unmerited abuse to set before the world, the tyranny and severity of these courts as they have been managed in England; all other religious denominations, from the days of Elizabeth have constantly abused that church, and the fears of being subjected to this yoke of bondage and nothing else has given occasion for what is here called unmerited abuse.

NOTES: "REMONSTRANT" I

1. An adaptation of "Si mihi perget quae vult dicere ea quae non unlt audiet." "The man who persists in saying whatever he likes, must count on hearing things he doesn't like." Terence *Andria* 920.

2. John Carmichael, a Scottish-born, colonial-educated Presbyterian minister in Chester, Pennsylvania, had recently defended in public a synodical decision to support a Professor of Divinity at the College of New Jersey. The trustees had ruled that students must complete all four years of study at that institution. This decision was viewed as discriminating against students of poor or moderate means who, unable to afford more than two years in Princeton, often had completed their early studies under a local schoolmaster before entering the college. Other issues were involved in this controversy which was carried on in the *Pennsylvania Chronicle* from June until September 1768. Many Presbyterians did not like such exposure and public discussion of their internal antagonisms. In his defense of the synod, Carmichael suggested that synod decisions were infallible, thus allowing the "Anatomist" to liken the colonial Presbyterian church to the Church of Scotland which was established.

Remonstrant Number II

October 13, 1768

The Quakers we are told are for introducing episcopacy; and a severe stroke is given to the disadvantages of the Presbyterians, because some of those people were persecuted in New England. We condemn persecution in New England, and every other church and nation; we plead for no national establishments, that bear hard on the civil or religious rights of mankind. But were not the Quakers persecuted in Jamaica, Antigua, Barbados, Nevis and Maryland, where Presbyterians had no authority? Were they not persecuted in Ireland? Were they not vexed, plundered, excommunicated, imprisoned, and dreadfully persecuted in every Shire of England? Read Neales history of the sufferings of that religious society.[1] Here I shall present the reader with abstracts of a petition of this persecuted people in the reign of James the second from another writer.

To the King and both houses of Parliament, the suffering condition of the people called Quakers, only for tender conscience towards almighty God humbly presented, shewing that of late above a *thousand five hundred* of the said people both men and women, having been detained prisoners in *England*, and part of them in *Wales*; some of which being since discharged by the judges, and others, freed by death through their long and tedious imprisonment—there are now remaining by late accounts, *one thousand three hundred eighty and three*; above *two hundred* women—many under sentence of *premunire*—many on *writs of excommunication* and fines for the King, & on the act for banishment, besides above *three hundred have died in prison*, and prisoners since the year 1660 (when all power was in the hands of the church of England)—Sewels history of the Quakers, page 563, 564.[2] As this petition is too long to transcribe, we shall give the reader one at length from the same Historian presented to *James* the second which is shorter and is as follows.

To The King

The distressed case and request of the suffering people commonly called Quakers, humbly presented shewing.

That according to accounts lately given above *fourteen hundred* of the said people both men and women are continued prisoners in England and Wales, only for tender conscience toward almighty God that made them; many under sentence of premunire, and many near it; not for refusing the duty or substance of allegiance itself, but only because they dare not swear. Besides some *hundreds have died prisoners*, many by means of this long imprisonment since the year 1680 (as it's judged) thereby making widows and fatherless, and leaving poor innocent families in distress and sorrow. These two hard winters confinement tending also to the destruction of many in cold holes and jails, their healths being greatly impaired thereby; besides violence and woeful spoil made by merciless informers on the conventicle act, upon many convicted, unsummoned and unheard in their own defence, both in city and country as also on *qui tam* writs and other process, on twenty pounds a month, and two thirds of estates seized for the King, all tending to the ruin of trade, husbandry and industrious families, to some not a bed left, to others no cattle to till their ground or give them milk, nor corn for bread or seed, nor tools to work withall? and all these and other *severities* done under pretence of serving the King and *church*, and thereby to force us to violate our consciences and consequently to destroy our souls, which we are very tender of, as we are of our peace with God and our own conscience, tho' accounted as sheep to the slaughter. And notwithstanding all these long sustained extremities, we the said people do solemnly profess & declare in the sight of the heart searcher, that we have nothing but good will and true affection to the King, praying for his safety and the kingdom's peace. We have never been found in any seditious or treasonable designs as being wholly contrary to our christian principles and holy profession.

And knowing where the word of the King is there is power, we in christian humility and for Christ's sake intreat, that the King will please to find out some expedient for our relief in these cases, from prison, spoil and ruin; and we shall (as in christian duty bound) pray God for the King's welfare, in this world, and his eternal happiness in that which is to come. Delivered to the King the 3d of the

1st month called, March, 1684–5, with the number of the prisoners in every Suite, and the name of the Shire; in all 1460.

This petition induced King James to write from his court at Whitehall, April the 18th., 1685, to all "*Archbishops and Bishops, and to their Chancellors* and Commissioners, and to all Archdeacons and other officials, and to all other ordinaries executing ecclesiastical jurisdiction to cause process against these persons to be stayed," And if they were in prison on the writ de excommunicatio capiendo to absolve, discharge and set them at liberty. See Sewel's history of the Quakers, page 566.[3]

Would the Quakers or any other men wish to be under the power of such instruments of cruelty? or is it unmerited abuse to the church of England, to say that her courts acted after this manner? But the old Puritans, comprehending under that name, Presbyterians, Independents, and Baptists, &c. felt these severe persecutions for nonconformity to the established church of England, thro' the long reign of Elizabeth & of James, before the Quaker became a religious society in England. And they were as severely handled, as these Quaker sufferers from the restoration, till the glorious revolution. And if the Anatomist's abusive pen thus continues to bespatter men called forth to plead for their liberties, we shall be obliged to revive the memory of those severe persecutions that are now almost forgotten; and well it is, if all gratitude due to God for our glorious deliverances from such cruelty, be not also forgotten.

We are not to be intimidated, though threatened with bloodshed by this writer; we pray God, that there may never be a religious establishment in America, to deprive any man or any religious denomination of their just rights, we desire none. But he adopts the glorious method, prescribed lately in our Chronicle by an episcopal clergyman, of clearing himself by recrimination. When he cannot vindicate himself and his friends, he boldly charges his accusers with the same crime, of erecting an establishment for themselves in this new world. The episcopal church, it is well known already, claims an establishment in all the colonies, and a superiority over all other religious persuasions; they claim it as a kind of birth right, to have their clergy every where supported by all other societies which they reproachfully call Dissenters. They have struggled hard for an establishment in North Carolina, and are oppressing that poor colony with new taxes from time to time, for purchasing glebes, building churches and parsonage houses for the support of their clergy, through the number of that church be small in comparison of other societies, and this unwearied industry we may expect in all the colonies to bring North America every where to pay tribute to hungry ambitious missionaries.[4] The Presbyterians in these provinces desire no establishments, they rather think them hurtful to religion, but, they that claim them and pant for them are willing to move Heaven and Earth for them, charge this as crimes on their innocent neighbors; but this abusive writer cares not what he affirms, nor on what foundation, and if persecution *to blood striving* must be our lot, if we strive to prevent such oppression, we hope we shall be armed with Christian patience and fortitude to do, or suffer according to the will of God. We desire no union with him, or any other society to do mischief, nay we abhor it. We neither desire nor expect the *attachment of churchmen* nor any of the human race, unless for good purpose, for the defence of our country in their just rights and privileges and the common good of all men.

But we would ask this blustering writer, have all churchmen as he calls them, given him a commission to abuse and threaten their neighbours? Or is he superior to Dr. Chandler, who is blamed by him for speaking for them without authority. When Presbyterians are slighted in general, and we hear great encomiums given to Episcopacy, as a national church, we must remind this writer that neither of these names can warrant men to do mischief; and that either, or both derive their honor from obeying the Gospel, and following the example of Christ, and not from worldly pomp or grandeur: Christ's Kingdom is not of this world. But if establishments and national churches make Christians more venerable; the Presbyterians or Reformed are one of the three religious persausions established by law in the German empire. It is one of the two religious persuasions established in Switzerland; it is the national religion of Holland and Geneva; and the national church of Scotland is Presbyterian; but all the ministers of these churches with all the Lutheran ministers of Sweden, Denmark and the German empires are rejected as unworthy of the name of Gospel ministers by this bulwark of the reformation, this mirror of charity, which is itself confined to the narrow bounds of Ireland and England. And let it be for ever remembered for the honor of Presbyterians, here called a *sour intollerant party*, that universal liberty of conscience was first proclaimed and established among protestants, in the national Presbyterian church of Holland, where men and women persecuted by both protestants and paptists, found a sure asylum and a city of refuge.

The Centinel equally pleaded the common cause of all other denominations, and the Presbyterians here abused, own no more thanks than are due to him by all that dread a yoke of bondage, that neither we nor our fathers could bear, and if he be cut up while asleep, and even devoured by this second Polypheme, we hope there will be men found to vindicate Presbyterians, and to defend the common cause of civil and religious liberty; but as champions and strong men are said to be merciful, we have hopes that the Centinel may yet escape his bloody knife and perform his duty.

NOTES: "REMONSTRANT" II

1. Daniel Neal, *The History of the Puritans, or, Protestant Non-Conformists, from the Reformation to the Death of Queen Elizabeth*, (4 vols., Dublin, 1759).

2. William Sewel, *The History of the Rise, Increase, and Progress of the Christian People called Quakers*, 3rd. ed. (Philadelphia, 1728), pp. 563–64, 566.

3. Ibid., p. 566.

4. North Carolina, a colony with many denominations and sects, had had Anglican missionaries since 1703. When Arthur Dobbs became governor in 1762, he attempted to advance the cause of the Anglican church. He reported to the SPG in 1764 that he had transferred to the governor the power of nominating clergymen for particular churches and obtained legislation ruling that each county must support an Episcopal miister. He also obligated the colonial government to spend ten shillings annually to purchase glebes and to build glebe houses for these ministers.

Remonstrant Number III

October 20, 1768

That there is a project on foot to establish Bishops in America, is publickly avowed and contended for by many of the episcopal Church; and they as confidently contend that they are part of the English established Church, and that all others are Dissenters. But as an episcopate with its ecclesiastical courts and other appendages has in former times been found hurtful to other religious societies, the plan now proposed is represented in such a favourable view, as, in their judgment, no reasonable man can object to it. For these Bishops are to have no powers but what are purely spiritual. They are only to ordain, confirm and inspect the morals of the clergy of their own denomination. Had twenty such Bishops been sent to America, provided they had no connexion with our *civil affairs*, nor a *prospect* of being able to *claim* or *exercise* the powers that made them terrible in England, no man had been uneasy about them. But for many reasons already offered on this subject, all the colonies have just grounds to fear that the episcopate really desired, and which will be established, if ever any be established among us, will not be so harmless and innocent as they pretend, nor so like those that were in the primitive Church. Even Doctor Chandler, who so strongly asserts that they desire no power that can be hurtful to the civil or religious rights and privileges of other denominations, paints his intended Bishops in such colours as must strike all considerate persons with terror, and convince them that if Bishops be once established, they will oblige thousands once more to seek shelter among the savage Indians.

But for want of arguments to refute Doctor Chauncy, the Centinel, Whig and others who have pointed out our danger; and with a view to turn the public attention from this avowed design of an establishment so dreadful in its consequences, the Anatomist cries aloud that the colonies are in danger from a Presbyterian establishment, which, as he alledges, is projected and carrying into execution.

"This sour turbulent party, says he, have justly alarmed the fear of every other religious persuasion in America, and created a jealousy that the sole view of this party is to erect an empire and establishment for themselves in this new world, on the ruin of every other religious denomination. But before they can succeed in their designs, they will meet with a resistance far different from what is to be expected in this paper; a resistance perhaps even unto *blood.*" That the episcopal Churches have an establishment in Maryland and Virginia, and the Independents (as he calls them) have a sort of establishment in some of the New-England provinces is well known. But a Presbyterian establishment in the colonies is neither projected nor desired, nor can it ever be attempted with any rational prospect of success. No denominations of christians in any of the other colonies, the episcopalians only excepted, have the least ground to expect it. They, and they only have power and interest in England, to get such a bill passed in their favour by the King and his Grandees, who are all of that persuasion; but no act passed in the colonies to establish Presbytery, or any religious persuasion, (*episcopacy* excepted) on the ruins of other societies, would obtain a sanction in England. It would be madness to attempt it. Nay the Lutheran and Presbyterian societies in New-York could not procure even a charter in England for securing their churches and burying grounds. Letters of incorporation, such as are granted to almost every company of mechanicks, were denied them by the interposition of gentlemen of the episcopal establishment, and in particular by one of their Bishops, as we are informed.[1] With what face then can the Anatomist alarm the world with the notion of a Presbyterian establishment, a thing in itself not only improbable, but even impossible; we utterly deny this charge; it is a groundless calumny, without the least foundation; and we call on this abusive writer either to make good his assertion, or to take to himself the shame of publishing notorious falsehoods, for want of better arguments; but this he did to amuse other religious societies, and to turn their attention from the common danger.

But suppose, for argument sake, that this establishment was projected, is this a good reason why the Anatomist should shake his bloody knife, and puff and abuse the Presbyterians? Is it a sufficient reason to threaten them with a resistance far different from what is in his paper, possibly he intends prosecutions, and fines, and imprisonments, and banishment, and confiscation of goods, as in old times. Is every attempt to have an establishment sufficient provocation to *resist even unto blood.* Let us then turn his arguments against himself, and ask what should other societies do to prevent an episcopal establishment, that dreadful evil, so ruinous to every other religious denomination, when it comes to be determined that it shall take place among us. Are we abused, are we accused and threatened for writing against it, and pointing out the direful consequences of a well-known establishment which had already by its courts persecuted and oppressed thousands of loyal subjects, and sincere christians, and driven many to seek habitations in a howling wilderness. He and his party threaten to *strive* even to blood to prevent a Presbyterian establishment, which is impossible to accomplish; and yet he will not allow others even to lament their danger from his projected, and almost executed establishment, nor to complain that they are in danger. All denominations are loudly or humbly to petition those that are in power and authority to prevent this evil. But how must the world detest a persecuting Church, or a Churchman threatening blood and slaughter to any that would aim at an establishment, though it be a thing that he, and almost all episcopalians contend for, as for a blessing to a religious society. This is not the christian spirit; this is not to obey his commands, who enjoins us to do to others as we would be done by.

The Centinel was as much an advocate for every society in the colonies as the Presbyterians, yet they and the New England Independents only must bear the lash of this writer. What has the New-England Independents to do with this controversy? If they dealt harshly by the missionaries or the people of their persuasion, we would by no means vindicate them, but will this pretended abuse warrant Episcopalians to unite in England and America once more to harrass the world with their ecclesiastical courts? If the first settlers in New-England were unfriendly to the Episcopalians and other denominations, they imported the bitter root of persecution and intolerance, and a love of religious establishments from England to Boston, and under these unhappy prejudices enacted, that other denominations should contribute to the support of the established or town minister: This crying iniquity was done, and still is done in England before the face of all Israel, and in the face of the sun. For there all other denominations must, and do maintain the established clergy. But when the Episcopalians had their own measures returned, what clamours did they raise? What cries of injustice and oppression? The bishops and zealous high fliers interposed for their relief, and the New-England Independents were told, that not withstanding their acts of assembly, every denomination must maintain their own clergy. And this just and equitable determination, beyond the Atlantic, we, and the Independents themselves highly approve; but is this equity and justice observed in Old England, where near a million of Dissenters must maintain the established clergy? Is this equity and justice regarded in the episcopal colonies, as in Maryland or Virginia? Or is this equity and justice observed in North-Carolina, where Governor Dobbs obtained severe and oppressive laws to maintain the episcopal clergy?[2] In these cases there are no cries of injustice, no advocates to plead the cause of other societies, that are burdened and oppressed. And all such acts, when once confirmed in England, are not likely ever to be repealed. The Independents in New England were led by the practices and laws of Old England to treat Dissenters from their establishment such as it was, in the same manner the episcopalians did, and still do treat Dissenters from their religious establishments. Of all men in the world they should be the last to condemn others, for what they justify in themselves. We condemn all persecution, severity and injustice in all establishments, whether Roman Catholic, Episcopal, Independent or Presbyterian. But what have we to do with these affairs in New-England, or with their present debate with the missionaries? Is it an attack on the Church of England, to dispute with a few of her missionaries; or is it unlawful to write against her bigotted sons, who contend for an unbroken succession, a divine right of episcopacy, and other chimeras that are depised by the best and most moderate part of that Church. And her missionaries so sacred that all Presbyterians in America must be abused, because Mr. Smith, a Presbyterian historian, has omitted to give one of them a full compliment of praises?[3] What have all these trifles to do with the present dispute? They solve none of our objections; they are only designed to draw our attention from a gathering storm, ready to burst on us and destroy us.

Ecclesiastical courts like a furious wild beast are at present under restraints, but are not tamed. They have in some degree maintained their influence, even under the milder administrations, since the glorious revolution; and if an episcopate be here established, we fear they will rage with sevenfold fury. One great reason of our fear, arises from the nature and constitution of these colonies. In England, the nobility in general hate oppression, and have on many occasions checked the exorbitant power of ecclesiasticks, and delivered their friends, tenants and religious societies, from persecution. The judges in England, are men of great reputation and influence; they are raised above the frowns of the proudest ecclesiasticks, nay they are set above the pride or malice even of the

King's ministers, that they may without danger, adhere to the laws, and defend the rights of the people. They are enpowered to grant, and do frequently grant prohibitions to check the tyranny, and to stop the rigour of the bishops courts. But should episcopacy with its courts be here established, (and that they certainly will be established is what we fear) we have no powerful nobility to check their rage, no independent judges established for life to interpose and deliver us. A judge, or even a governor in the colonies, would be treated with insolence and abuse, that would appear against the oppression of any of our proud unmerciful prelates, most bitter complaints of his conduct would be made to the Archbishops and Bishops and the King's ministers. He would be traduced as a republican, an enemy to the church of England, and to his Majesty's government in the colonies, and to Monarchy itself. The old cry would be raised again, no Bishops, no King, and possibly the offender whether Judge or Governor, would be tumbled down with disgrace from his station and made an example to all who would not bow down their necks to our American Bishops. Let me on this occasion, use the words of the Anatomist, "O my children, on the prospect of this change, how I tremble and lament for you."[4]

How carefully has the Anatomist raked up every thing to blacken the Independents in New England; even the Boston Almanack, is pressed into his service. But do these shifts and evasions satisfy any reasonable man, that the intended episcopate will not be hurtful to other religious societies: or that it will not introduce confusion, into our civil courts, and overturn many of our laws? Does a story of Independent Reflectors, and Watch-Towers, or of a Historian, that did not extoll one of their Missionaries as much as he deserved and expected, prove that the Presbyterians are labouring for an establishment? Our granting that they were, which is a notorious falsehood, would that convince us that our civil and religious liberties were in no danger from the intended episcopate and its ecclesiastical courts? If he thinks it any advantage to his cause, to mention the faults of Presbyterians and Independents, who were ever as moderate in the exercise of power, as the church of England; we are ready to ballance accounts with him, and our accounts of the severities of the Highfliers in the church of England, and their severe acts of Parliament to distress all non conformists, shall not be taken from almanacks, pamphlets, or unprinted histories, but from Historians of undoubted authority and good reputation. We intend to give the world an abstract of the acts of parliamant, which distressed the British churches from the memorable act of Elizabeth, which condemned "all persons refusing premptorily to come to church, after conviction, to banishment and in case of return to death without benefit of clergy," down to the severe act called the Schism Bill, in the reign of Queen Ann, and shall at the same time, mention some of the grievous sufferings of many thousands, by the cruel execution of those laws.

NOTES: "REMONSTRANT" III

1. See "Centinel" I, note 5.
2. See "Remonstrant" II, note 4.
3. The "Anatomist" V, *Pennsylvania Journal* (October 6, 1768), accused New York historian, William Smith, Jr., of lacking "impartiality and candor" when reviewing the accomplishments of the Anglican church in his *History of the Province of New York*, published in 1757. See also the "Anatomist" VI, *Pennsylvania Journal* (October 13, 1768).
4. The "Anatomist" II, *Pennsylvania Journal* (September 15, 1768).

Remonstrant Number IV

November 3, 1768

The Anatomist and his Friend Horatio have raked together abstracts of pamphlets, written in the New England provinces, from which they have picked an expression here and there, which they dislike, and having pressed it in *Italicks* and double commas, cry out, that the whole performances are written in a bitter intollerant spirit. If in their controversies with any of the missionaries, the independent ministers have set the vain pretensions of these gentlemen, to an uninterrupted succession, and power which the church claims to ordain or decree rites and ceremonies &c., in a true light, there is loud outcry raised, that they attack the whole body of the church, her doctrine and discipline and the principles of the clergy and members. It is so rotten a fabrick that it cannot bear to be touched; a church that's so very tender should give no provocations. But does any of the quotations prove that the independents would have harmed the church of England, or that they were the first aggressor in any of these debates. No, it is well known, that Episcopal missionaries or their friends, first proclaimed the war and when they were soundly drubbed they would make the world believe that the whole church of England has been roughly handled, but what has these squabbles to do with Chandler's appeal? every colonist and religious denomination are equally called forth by that Champion for an American Episcopate; they are to make their objections if they have any, or all parties are supposed to acquiesce in his plan.

[a]The first Episcopal church set up among the independents in New-England, was about the year 1680. They were poor and few in number and were allowed the use of the town house by the independents, as he calls the congregational churches. Was not this an instance of brotherly love? It was an evidence of no malignity of spirit or a desire to crush them. But how did they requite this kindness? Under the administration of Sir Edmund Andros, they declared that they were of the church of England and by law established; they would no longer assemble into the town house,

but demanded the keys of the South meeting house; and when some gentlemen, proprietors of that house refused to deliver them Governor Andros told them, "he would presently seize on that house, and all dissenting bodies in the country, and hinder them from contributing the value of two pence towards the maintenance of any Nonconformist minister." And when this threatening could not prevail they thrust themselves into the meeting house, and there continued until by interrupting the people of the South Congregation, often in the times and sometimes in the very *parts* of their worship, the whole town cried shame upon them. Here was a sample of the same persecuting spirit from which the independents fled to this wilderness. At the funeral of one Mr. Liley, their minister came with his *Gown and Book* to read the service, and to sett this laudable custom in that barbarous country. One Mr. Flayray a relation of the deceased, in the name of the rest, only with fit words, desired him to forebear, but Mr. Flayray was bound over to the court for this offence, where they intended to have ruined him, had not the *unlucky revolution* prevented these designs.[2]

And that the ministers might have their share Mr. Cotton Mather was prosecuted upon the act of Uniformity, and illegally condemned, but the revolution prevented the execution of the sentence against him. For on that very day on which he was to be committed, to *half a year's imprisonment*, those that would have wronged him were justly taken into custody. This beloved act of uniformity, and the penal laws in support of it, tore the established Church of England to pieces, and brought unnumbered mischiefs on many of its own ministers, and people which it drove from their communion. And this same act of uniformity which the Episcopal church is determined to establish in New-England, began all those controversies, that the Anatomist complains of, and it had been more for his honour; and for the benefit of his cause, rather, to have let them sleep in silence, than to have so spitefully revived them.

It is urged that since the act of tolleration an exemplary spirit of moderation and christian charity, has prevailed among the Episcopalians, for this we thank God and for this we cheerfully praise and give them their own commendations. But are things really so.[b] Let us remind the Episcopalians of their conduct in New-York since the toleration act. Under the administer of Lord Cornbury, Mr. Makamie a worthy Presbyterian minister, preached a sermon in New-York, at a desire of a number of inhabitants who were Presbyterians, and tho he produced a certificate of his having qualified according to the act of tolleration, he was committed to prison and prosecuted upon an indictment that says, "that he unlawfully used other rites, ceremonies, forms and manner of divine worship, than what are contained in a certain book of Common Prayer and administration of the Sacraments, &c. and against the form of the Statute, &c." Here the attack was vigorously begun by the church of England against the Presbyterians in open defiance of the act of tolleration, and in a city that was originally settled with Dutch Presbyterians, &c. where the Episcopal church in its infant state had been kindly cherished & had received many favours. Was not the unmerciful and scandalous Schism Bill, enacted in the last year of Queen Anne, and enacted in open defiance to the tolleration act, by which the friends of this beloved *Act of Uniformity*, deprived all parents that were not of the established church, of the great trust committed to them by God & nature, to train up their own children, according to their own sentiments in religion, and the fear of God.[4] No catechism was to be taught to children but that of the Church of England; and no man under severe penalties was allowed to teach even an English school, who did not in all things conform to that church. Let our Anatomist call this unmerited abuse; it is the truth and was done when High Church rode triumphant. And had not God in mercy placed the Hanover family on the Throne of Great-Britain, all the severities that distressed England for near one hundred years, and ruined many thousands of families, had been felt once more, with sevenfold rigour.

In Connecticut the Episcopal Party carried their pretensions to an establishment in the plantations, by the *act of* uniformity, to a very high pitch. This was urged by Caner and Wetmore from a principle established, as Wetmore said, by skillful Lawyers, *that Colonies transplanting themselves carry the laws of their Mother Country with them.*[5] And from these struggles and attempts to establish themselves by the *act of uniformity*, the world may judge who have been the aggressors in these disputes, who strive to defend their liberties and privileges, are most to be blamed? But this aspiring restless, ambitious spirit of the Missionaries never was content to have equal privileges, but strove always for something superior to all other religious societies and to introduce the *act of uniformity* with its penal laws. These struggles have given just ground to fear them as a common enemy, and to believe, that if an Episcopate be established amongst us, it will not be so innocent and harmless as some pretend, but that it will bring with it the usual appendages, its tyrannical ecclesiastical Courts, and with them vexations, lawsuits, expensive appeals, and distress and confusion.

As the old story of the New England persecutions is again repeated by the Anatomist, to the disadvantage of the Presbyterians, though he himself allows it was done by the Independents, we will once more give it due attention. We declare in the most solemn manner, that we detest and abhor persecution for conscience sake in Presbyterians, Independents, Episcopalians, and Roman Catholicks, as inhuman and anti-christian. We observed already, that the people of New England were led into those severities by an act of Parliament, made in the 35th. year of Elizabeth, which condemns all non conformists, after they are convicted, to *banishment*, and in case of return, without licence, to *death* without benefit of Clergy. This severe law, was again renewed Anno 1664, in the act against Conventicles, with some additional severities in the reign of King Charles, by which the Quakers, with all other Protestant Dissenters suffered most severely. The persecution in New England was in a time of troubles both in Church and State. The persecution in Old England was in a time of peace and tranquility, when the Church of England sat at the Helm and carried all before her. The Quakers could not with any colour or pretence be protected by the Government, for any plots or conspiracies, or any disturbance given to the peace of the State, yet a law was enacted against *them in particular*, Anno 1662 entitled, an act for preventing mischiefs and dangers that might arise from certain people called Quakers, by which they were made liable to severe fines and imprisonment, and after the third offence to transportation for *refusing to swear*. I shall here transcribe a passage from Sewel's history (page 335).[6] "Having now left America and returned to England, let us go and see the state of persecution at London where desperate fury now raged; though it was not in that chief city alone the Quakers so called, were most grievously persecuted. For a little before this time, there were published in print, a short relation of their persecution through all England, signed by twelve persons, shewing that more than *four thousand two hundred* of those Quakers both *men and women* were in prison in England, and denoting the number of them that were imprisoned in each county, either for frequenting Meetings, or for *denying to swear*, &c. Many of these had been grievously beaten or their cloaths torn or taken away from them, and some were put into such stinking dungeons, that some great men said they would not put their hunting dogs there. Some prisons were crowded full both of men and women, so that there was not sufficient room for all to sit down at once, and in Chessin sixty eight persons, were in this manner locked up in a small room, an evident sign that they were a harmless people that would not make any resistance nor use force. By such ill treatment, many grew sick and *not a few died* in such gaols, for no age nor sex was regarded. Even ancient people of sixty, seventy or more years of age were not spared. And most of these being tradesmen, shopkeepers and husbandmen, were thus reduced to poverty. For their goods were also seized for not going to church (so called) or for not *paying tithes*. Many times they were fain to lie in prison on cold, nasty ground, without being suffered to have any straw, and often they have been kept several days without any victuals. No wonder therefore many died by such hard imprisonments as these. At London & in the suburbs were about this time no less than five hundred of those people called Quakers imprisoned, and some in such narrow holes, that every person had scarcely convenience to lie down, and the felons were suffered to rob them of their cloaths and money."—This author proceeds to relate many instances of cruelty and severity to these people during the administration of the two brothers, Charles and James. He informs us (page 517) that since the restoration of King Charles, till the year 1676, above *two hundred* of the people called Quakers had *died in prisons* in England, because of their religion. But they were not the only sufferers. It is well known that De Laune, who wrote the plea for non-conformity, was one of near eight thousand, who had perished in prison in the reign of King Charles the IId. meerly for dissenting from the church in some points for which they were able to give reasons; and that one Jeremiah White, had carefully collected a list of the dissenting sufferers and of their sufferings, and had the names of sixty thousand persons who had suffered on a religious account, between the restoring of King Charles the IId. and the revolution by King William, five thousand of whom died in prison, (Neal, Vol. 4,—450).[7] The Anatomist threatens us with *unfolding a tale* to our disadvantage, if we speak of these severities: We assure him, we never intended to have mentioned the severe acts that bore down dissenters for near one hundred years, had he not proclaimed presbyterians sour and intolerant, and tried to blacken *them* as a body, who are so respectable a part of the protestant churches; it is well known that they were the first people in Europe that gave universal toleration to all religious denominations; but we fear no tales, if they be but true, let them be farely told to the dishonor of all persecutors. We have neither the inclination nor the power to impose an establishment to harrass and disturb other religious societies in America. But that the episcopal missionaries and others of their party, were they encouraged and protected by bishops, have both the power and the inclination, is what we greatly fear; we are prepared to hand out the persecutions of a Parker, a Whitegift, a Laud and Bancroft, &c. to the world, to excite the hatred of mankind against religious tyranny, and to raise their horror & abhorence of these severe acts that cloath oppressors with power to do mischief.[8] Yet if the Anatomist instead of abusing his neighbors, proceeds with sober arguments to answer the charges as raised by the Centinel against Dr. Chandler's appeal, we shall leave him and his adversary to dispute the point; only we desire that he may do it with the calmness which does honour both to the Centinel and the Doctor. We shall be upon our oars, and if relieved of our fears, shall say no more of penal laws and persecutions; but if instead of arguments and sound reasons, we have nothing but shifts and evasions, we must reason by analogy; and by what has happened from an English episcopate, shall argue what we must fear from an episcopate, if it be established in America.

INTERNAL NOTES: "REMONSTRANT" IV

[a]See Vindication of New-England, pages 12, 13, 14. A Life of Cotton Mather, page 43 &c. Hobart's Second Address, pages 24, 25, 26, 27.[1]

[b]See Mr. Makamie's Tryal, page 17. And Mr. Hobart's Second Address, pages 28, 29.[3]

NOTES: "REMONSTRANT" IV

1. [Increase Mather], *A Vindication of New England* (Boston, 1690), pp. 12–14; Samuel Mather, *The Life of the Very Reverend and Learned Cotton Mather* (Boston, 1729); Noah Hobart, *A Second Address* (Boston, 1751), pp. 24–27.

2. Sir Edmund Andros was appointed by James II in 1686 to serve as royal governor to the Dominion of New England, a newly created merger of the colonies of New Jersey, New York, Connecticut, Rhode Island, Plymouth, Massachusetts, New Hampshire and Maine. Andros met continual opposition from the colonists, who finally imprisoned him and restored their old governments when they heard that William and Mary had replaced James II on the British throne in the Glorious Revolution of 1688.

3. Francis Makamie, *A Narration of a New and Unusual American Imprisonment* (New York, 1707), p. 17; Hobart, *A Second Address*, pp. 28–29.

4. The Schism Bill, passed in 1714, forbade any nonconformist to keep a school. The intent of the bill was to wipe out nonconformity in the professional classes and was extended to Ireland.

5. Henry Caner and James Wetmore, Anglican ministers in Connecticut, joined others of their denomination in petitioning for a colonial bishopric in 1746. In answer to Noah Hobart's attack on the Anglican churches in New England, Wetmore argued that episcopacy came to the colonies in 1630 along with the common law and statutes of the realm. The pamphlet controversy continued into the 1750s.

6. William Sewel, *The History of the Rise, Increase, and Progress of the Christian People called Quakers*, 3rd. ed. (Philadelphia, 1728). Page numbers in the text are correct.

7. Daniel Neal, *The History of the Puritans, or, Protestant Non-Conformists, from the Reformation to the Death of Queen Elizabeth*, (4 vols., Dublin, 1759), 4: 450.

8. Matthew Parker, John Whitgift, Richard Bancroft, and William Laud held the office of archbishop of Canterbury from the mid-sixteenth until the mid-seventeenth century. They were known for their opposition to dissenters.

Index